A SURVEY OF MANUSCRIPTS
ILLUMINATED IN THE BRITISH ISLES
VOLUME ONE
INSULAR MANUSCRIPTS
6TH TO THE 9TH CENTURY

BY J·J·G· ALEXANDER

Frontispiece: Canon Table, Leningrad, State Public Library, Cod. F.v.I.8, f. 12 (cat. 39)

A SURVEY OF MANUSCRIPTS ILLUMINATED IN THE
BRITISH ISLES~GENERAL EDITOR: J·J·G· ALEXANDER

INSULAR MANUSCRIPTS

6TH TO THE 9TH CENTURY

BY J·J·G· ALEXANDER

WITH 380 ILLUSTRATIONS

HARVEY MILLER~LONDON

A SURVEY OF MANUSCRIPTS
ILLUMINATED IN THE BRITISH ISLES

General Editor J. J. G. Alexander

Volume One: INSULAR MANUSCRIPTS FROM THE 6TH TO THE 9TH CENTURY

Volume Two: ANGLO-SAXON MANUSCRIPTS 900-1066

Volume Three: ROMANESQUE MANUSCRIPTS 1066-1190

Volume Four: EARLY GOTHIC MANUSCRIPTS 1190-1285

Volume Five: GOTHIC MANUSCRIPTS 1285-1385

Volume Six: LATER GOTHIC MANUSCRIPTS

© 1978 Harvey Miller · 20 Marryat Road · London SW19 5BD · England

ISBN 0-905203-01-1

Designed by Elly Miller

Printed in Great Britain at the University Press, Oxford
by Vivian Ridler, Printer to the University

CONTENTS

Fig. 1. Frontispiece to Four Gospels. Utrecht, Universiteitsbibl. 32, f. 101ᵛ (cat. 8)

FOREWORD

THIS FIRST VOLUME of the *Survey of Manuscripts Illuminated in the British Isles* includes two of the most famous of all illuminated manuscripts, the Book of Lindisfarne and the Book of Kells. They can be seen here in the context of the manuscripts which lead up to and succeed them and in company with a number of other manuscripts only slightly less splendid. The most original achievement of artists in Ireland and England in the 7th and 8th centuries was to introduce abstract ornament to enrich the pages of the book on an unprecedented scale, thus creating the great initial and carpet pages which are the chief marvel of these books. It is a period of close cultural co-operation between the two countries accurately reflected in the works of art. Then in the train of Irish and English settlers and missionaries abroad the results of that co-operation soon became known on the Continent, so that a number of the manuscripts included here were either made by Insular artists in Europe or taken there at an early date. Their artistic influence is profound and continues to be felt for two centuries at least. For just as Bede was the greatest scholar of his age and read everywhere, so the great Insular manuscripts have no rivals in Europe at the time; and many, like the Book of Kells, have been the objects of admiration ever since.

As with other volumes of the *Survey*, the material presented is only a selection. Naturally since fewer illuminated manuscripts survive from the earlier periods a higher proportion of these can be included than in the later volumes on the 12th to 15th centuries. But still even here this volume cannot be, and does not pretend to be, a *Corpus* publication. Such a publication is certainly needed, but it will have to be on a quite different scale and to contain comprehensive descriptions as well as illustrations. As before the aim of the *Survey* is to present the most important material with essential guide-lines for further study.

This volume has had two difficult problems to face in the matter of selection. The first concerns the numerous manuscripts which were made on the Continent either by Anglo-Saxon or Irish scribes and artists, or by Continental scribes and artists either directly copying Insular models or working in a style strongly influenced by Insular forms. The second problem is one of chronological limits, since the Insular style in Ireland is extraordinarily tenacious and continues at least into the 12th century. It has seemed more logical to include examples of this later Irish art in this volume rather than in Volumes Two and Three of the *Survey* to which they belong chronologically; and for these manuscripts as for the Continental ones a selection of the material which seemed particularly important or characteristic has been included. The bibliography of these entries will give guidance for further study.

The literature, especially on the most famous Insular manuscripts, has become immense, and the bibliography given here is necessarily selective. It concentrates on art-historical literature and on more recent publications. Some earlier publications are sometimes included even if now outdated, for example those of Westwood, to give some idea of the history of studies and the progress of knowledge in this area. A fuller bibliography, particularly for textual and paleographical matters, can be found in the volumes of *Codices Latini Antiquiores*.

The compiler of a book on Insular illumination must be well aware of the perilous and controversial seas on which he sails and of how many navigational aids he lacks. For my first introduction to Insular art as a student I am grateful to Professor Otto Pächt, and I have also benefited from hearing lectures at various times on aspects of Insular art and paleography by Professor Julian Brown, Professor Carl Nordenfalk, and Professor David Wright. On specific points I should like to acknowledge the help of Dr. B. Barker Benfield who read an ownership inscription in the Rawlinson Gospel Book (no. 43); Dr. John Plummer who lent me his detailed description of the Lothian Psalter (no. 31); Mr. William O'Sullivan who told me of the offsets of the miniatures on the text pages of the Book of Mulling (no. 45); Mr. B. Rhodes who is working on an M.A. thesis on the Barberini Gospel Book (no. 36); and Mr. C. D. Verey for allowing me to read his unpublished M.A. thesis on the Durham Gospel Books. I owe a particular debt to all those librarians who have allowed me to see manuscripts in their care, and also to those who have answered questions by letter, since the way in which Insular manuscripts are so widely scattered, has meant that unfortunately I have not been able to see for myself all the manuscripts included here. I am also extremely grateful to the publishers of this series and especially to Mrs. Elly Miller and Mrs. Isabel Hariades for their help in improving my text and in particular for the imaginative arrangement of the illustrations so that they, as it were, tell their own story. For all errors and omissions, and for the opinions expressed, I am of course alone responsible.

Finally in dedicating this book to Carl Nordenfalk I not only acknowledge a debt which I, like all students of the early Middle Ages, owe to the author of so many seminal works on the art of the period, but also express my special gratitude for the generosity in matters of scholarship and the personal kindness from which all who know him, benefit.

Fig. 2. Carpet page. London, B.L., Cotton Nero D. IV, f. 210ᵛ (cat. 9)

INTRODUCTION

IN 597 ST. AUGUSTINE, Apostle of the English, sent from Rome by Pope Gregory the Great, arrived in Kent on his mission to convert the pagan King Egbert and his people to Christianity. Some years before St. Colmcille (Columba) coming from Ireland, which had been Christian for more than a century, had in 563 founded a monastery on the island of Iona off the west coast of Scotland. This was followed in 635 by the foundation, from Iona, of the monastery of Lindisfarne in Northumbria by St. Aidan.[1]

The conversion of the British Isles to Christianity is the essential background to the creation of the manuscripts discussed in this volume, because Christianity is a religion where revelation is enshrined in written texts, the Old and New Testaments. Both Celtic and Benedictine monasticism emphasized the necessity of studying and also copying those texts. The manuscripts listed here in this first volume of the *Survey of Manuscripts Illuminated in the British Isles* are almost all Christian in content and are probably all the products of Christian monastic *scriptoria*. More than half of them including the earliest (*Codex Usserianus Primus*, no. 1) and the most famous, the Books of Durrow (no. 6), Lindisfarne (no. 9), and Kells (no. 52) are Gospel Books, thus reflecting the evangelical role of the early church in Ireland, Scotland, Wales, and England, and later, as the missions spread, on the Continent.

The complex task of evaluating the relative contributions of Celts and Anglo-Saxons to the art of book illumination has been the theme of scholarly study for more than a hundred years now, a study which has not always been free from partisanship. The term 'Insular' to describe the art of this period has been adopted here deliberately as a neutral description as opposed to a term like 'Hiberno-Saxon'. Even after the synod of Whitby in 664 had resulted in a victory of the pro-Roman Anglo-Saxon party on the matters at issue between the two churches and a partial withdrawal of the Celtic bishops, the Irish influence remained strong in England with continuing contacts and is as strongly documented in the works of art.[2] As Sir Frank Stenton has written: 'The strands of Irish and Continental influence were interwoven in every kingdom, and at every stage of the process by which England became Christian.'[3] Concerning the art Professor Schapiro has written: '. . . the polarity of the Celtic and Roman within Insular art, like that of Lindisfarne and Jarrow—the differences corresponding to the larger opposition of Celtic and Roman Christianity in the islands—does not exclude the rich interplay of the opposed traditions in the same works, as in the church itself—although one or other may dominate in the most individual achievements.'[4]

As so often in the history of art the masterpieces are the result of a cross-fertilization of different traditions. The theme of this first volume of the *Survey* is not a conflicting struggle of opposed forces, Celtic and Anglo-Saxon, one supposedly more creative than the other, but the story of a varying reaction to an alien Mediterranean tradition by Celtic and Anglo-Saxon craftsmen to which both contributed much that was original in a process from which both also learnt much from each other.

Some of the Christian communities which certainly existed in Roman Britain, survived the pagan invasions in remote areas of Cornwall, Wales, and Scotland. It is quite possible, therefore, that some tradition of book production remained in those areas, which might have provided continuity. As regards book illumination we have no certain evidence of any continuity, however, and such fundamental changes in book production had taken place in the period of the Roman withdrawal and the Saxon invasions that totally new artistic solutions were necessary in any case.[5] In the 2nd to the 4th centuries the revolutionary change had occurred by which the roll, usually made of papyrus, was gradually replaced with the *codex* (bound book), usually made of animal skin. The studies of the last thirty years have resulted in a much better understanding of the effect of the adoption of the new format and the new material on the illumination and decoration of books.[6] The techniques and even more important the relationship of illustration to text inevitably changed, and this probably began to happen in the second half of the 4th and in the 5th century. Fully painted miniatures comparable to more monumental forms of painting are now introduced into the book. The author portrait, for example, now becomes a picture of a scholar meditating or teaching in an architectural or landscape setting (fig. 23) rather than a small introductory medallion at the beginning of the roll. These changes affected Christian as they did pagan book illumination; indeed Christian art in general changed radically as the result of the adoption of Christianity as the official religion. Also in the 4th century the text begins to be decorated by embellishments in the headings, the colophons, and the letters themselves, a change of attitude in part caused, as Professor Nordenfalk has pointed out, by the change of identity of scribes from the slaves of the ancient world to independent, often Christian, copyists.[7]

It is not until the early 7th century that we have the first signs of Insular artists reacting to the various possibilities for book decoration now open to them to copy, adapt, or develop. From then on the rapid transformation of the late antique book they affected was sensational. It can be argued that, untrammelled by any tradition or preconception of what the book should be, they, rather than the Mediterranean artists, were the first to realize the full potential of the codex format. As opposed to the continuous unfolding space of the roll, the finite two-dimensional surface of the codex page was ideally suited to form a containing boundary for the infinite interweaving patterns of Insular art, setting up the tension between static enclosure and dynamic movement which is an essential element in this art. In this way were created the carpet-pages and the initial-pages which are the most original of the Insular contributions to the history of medieval book illumination.

Insular artists were heirs to a very different tradition from that of the Mediterranean figural art with which they were now brought into contact. Their own artistic vocabulary was mainly an abstract decorative one used above all in the applied arts on small portable objects. It has survived to us mainly in metalwork. The rich vocabulary of a long tradition of ornamental design, varying amongst the two peoples, is transferred to the initials and the carpet pages and even to representational forms such as the architectural capitals, arches, and columns of the Canon Tables (ill. 32) or to the figures themselves which illustrate the text (ill. 14). Its main component is pattern which gives a sense of living movement, which is 'kinetic', to use Koehler's term.[8] Thus interlace pattern taken from Mediterranean art but varied and enriched, plays a major part. It can be of strapwork, of indeterminate zoomorphic forms, of birds, animals, or even humans (ill. 249). The animal interlace appears to be a Germanic inheritance, already found in objects from Sutton Hoo (fig. 9) and from some such source transferred to the pages of the Book of Durrow (ill. 22). The bird interlace may be a specific invention of the Lindisfarne scriptorium (ill. 32). The pelta and trumpet patterns inherited from the Celtic tradition also have this vital energy and the many different fret, key, diaper, and step patterns often resembling millefiori enamel, another Celtic speciality, are likewise used for variety and the intricate counterbalancings which from the first (no. 3, ill. 6) characterize Insular art.

The way in which such patterns were made has been reconstructed from the actual compass holes in the Book of Lindisfarne (no. 9) by Dr. Bruce-Mitford (fig. 3).[9] The variety of pattern is immense and the technical skill and patience with which it is deployed in its minute intricacy astonishing. The most fundamental principles, however, are constant, an alternation and counterpoint of forms which stresses always the ambiguity of relationships. Shapes can be read as patterns on a ground or as intervals seen through a pierced field.[10]

Fig. 3. Reconstruction of the design of the upper right-hand quarter of the central square of curvilinear geometrical ornament of f. 138ᵛ in the Lindisfarne Gospels, ill. 34

For Insular artists forms need not be definite or regular or separable as they need to be for classical artists. Thus the letter form which should, to perform its function, be always the same in order to be recognized, can be transformed now into a fish now into a piece of interlace, forms which distort its shape. This process of fragmentation had already begun in the late antique period as part of a general anti-classical trend and is taken up with enthusiasm by Irish artists in the Cathach of St. Columba (no. 4, ills. 2–5) and the Bobbio Jerome (no. 2, ill. 8). Once the principle of the dissolution of the letter form is accepted, as it never was wholly in late antique manuscripts, the letter can as it were swell and grow to be something magical and otherworldly until the great pages of the 'Xp' initials in the Books of Lindisfarne and Kells (ills. 44, 244) are talismanic signs to be revered, not letters to be recognized and read.[11]

The same attitude of reverence and awe may perhaps lie behind the Insular use of the carpet-page which is as it were laid out at the opening of each Gospel to introduce the Lord's entry via His Word. The idea of prefacing the Gospel texts with a representation of a cross already existed in the early Christian period as can be seen in the Coptic Gospel Book of c. 500, the Glazier Codex (fig. 12).[12] A number of later examples of such crosses in Gospel Books exist among them that in the 16th-century Persian copy of Tatian's Diatessaron which as Nordenfalk has shown bears such a striking resemblance to the first cross-carpet page in the Book of Durrow (ill. 11, fig. 13).[13] But whereas in the Glazier codex and to some extent in the Diatessaron the cross exists in a free space, the Insular crosses are imbedded in a field and once again they can be read either as object or interval.

Another example of Insular artists taking up a decorative idea already used in the late antique period is the use of coloured dots. These appear in the Greek Dioscorides manuscript made in Constantinople in 512 (Vienna, Nationalbibliothek, Cod. Gr. Med. 1) to emphasize the initials.[14] The same dot outline for the initials is used in some of the earliest Insular manuscripts, but by the time of the Book of Lindisfarne (ill. 46) dots are also woven into complex filling ornament, whether abstract or zoomorphic, on the initial pages, once again articulating the background interstices between the continuation lettering. Another use of the dots is to decorate holes or flaws in the parchment which by a typically Insular flight of fancy can be turned, for example in the Echternach Gospel Book (no. 11), into birds or fish!

Insular artists could respond to and enlarge on the decorative aspects of the late antique book, but it was more difficult for them to come to terms with the representational illusionistic aspects of Mediterranean art. In general their reaction was to convert natural forms, human, animal, or vegetative, into patterns, as they do in the earliest example of Insular figurative art, the Evangelist symbols of the Book of Durrow (ills. 14–17). The extent to which the stylization extended varied considerably from one end of the scale in the Echternach Gospel Book (no. 11) where the Matthew symbol becomes a series of ovoid shapes (ill. 54), or the Macregol Gospel Book where the Evangelists' drapery is converted into striped coloured bands (ills. 262–4) to the first Maeseyck Gospel Book (no. 22, ill. 87) or some of the Canterbury group of manuscripts (nos. 29, 30) in which the classical style of their models is still apparent.

The extent of the stylization may be taken as an index of the differences between Celtic and Anglo-Saxon artists inasmuch as the works generally agreed to be or documented as being Irish, such as the St. Gall Gospel Book (no. 44, ills. 203–8) or the Macregol Gospel Book (no. 54, ills. 262–4) appear more extreme in their reduction of naturalistic forms to pattern. This must be qualified in so far as a work like the Echternach Gospel Book (no. 11) has been argued on paleographical grounds to come from Northumbria, whilst the origin of the Book of St. Chad (no. 21, ills. 80, 82) and of the Book of Kells (no. 52, ill. 243) in both of which there is a notable reduction of form to pattern, remains in dispute. Celtic artists certainly remain astonishingly faithful to an art of stylization as can be seen in later works such as the Gospel Book of Macdurnan (no. 70, ills. 326–8) or the Southampton Psalter (no. 74, ills. 350–2).

It is not surprising, considering the historical situation, that Anglo-Saxon artists should have attempted to render more faithfully their Mediterranean models just as they regarded themselves as the true upholders of the tradition of the Roman church. This is especially true of the group of manuscripts produced at Canterbury, which even include in the Stockholm *Codex Aureus* (no. 30, ills. 158–9) adaptations of the script patterning (*carmina figurata*) invented by Constantine's court poet Porphyrius, and use purple parchment emulating the splendour of late antique imperial manuscripts. But it is also true of the miniatures of the Lindisfarne Gospels (no. 9, ills. 28–31) where the figure style is a phenomenon parallel to the carvings of the Ruthwell and Bewcastle crosses and the Coffin of St. Cuthbert (figs. 5, 6).

The origin of the most remarkably faithful rendering of late antique style found in Insular art, the Ezra miniature in the Codex Amiatinus (no. 7, ill. 27), is fortunately documented as Wearmouth/Jarrow, Benedict Biscop's foundation in which Bede was later to write with satisfaction of the final triumph of Roman Christianity. The Ezra miniature is so faithful a copy that it was once thought to be a 6th-century original, part of Cassiodorus' *Codex Grandior* incorporated in the Northumbrian Bible Pandect. Recently the theory that it is the work of a foreign craftsman has been revived, though Bruce-Mitford's arguments seem conclusive that it is indeed that very rare thing in medieval art as a whole, a facsimile copy reproducing the style as well as the iconography of the model.

That such a facsimile was possible only highlights the fact that the version of the same or a similar figure copied by Eadfrith, scribe and probably artist of the Lindisfarne Gospel Book (no. 9, ill. 28) for his St. Matthew, is put forward as an alternative solution consciously favouring the different aesthetic of Insular art. Eadfrith converts the illusionistic painterly style of his model into an abstract linear style in which forms are related not in a three-dimensional space but by the two-dimensional illogical overlappings which Professor Meyer has called 'false connections'.[15] The result is that even in a figural illustration the frame is a space to be

Fig. 4. Opening of St. Luke. Dublin, Trinity College Lib.,
A. 4. 5 (57), f. 126 (cat. 6)

filled with counterbalancing forms which can be distorted at will. In the St. Matthew page the lettering of the inscription in two dimensions is an essential part of the page, contributing to the filling of the space, which sets up the typically Insular tension between the static outer boundary and the contained forms within.

The same comparison between the Ezra and the St. Matthew makes clear the contrast between the naturalistic late antique use of colour in which forms are modelled in light and shade, for instance on the cupboard doors, and the new Insular non-naturalistic abstract colour used to contrast forms which do not merge or harmonize, but give the page variety, whilst at the same time unifying its elements in a balancing mosaic of juxtaposed shades (colour plates, ills. 147 and 354).[16]

One important consequence of the Insular artist's attitude to the letter form as something transmutable, and the illustration as something reducible to a two-dimensional pattern, was the possibility of uniting the two to create the historiated initial. The earliest examples of this genre which was to continue in use throughout the Middle Ages are Insular (nos. 19, 29, ills. 84, 143–4), and it seems probable that this was an Insular invention.[17] A number of more recent studies have also emphasized the importance of Insular aesthetic principles for the genesis of the Romanesque style.[18]

The problems of the Insular artists' sources are so complex that in many cases they are still unresolved and we are unable to see clearly whether and to what extent they were icono-graphical innovators. For example, Professor Schapiro has remarked on the diversity of types of Evangelists and their symbols in Insular art.[19] Were these various types all derived from various early Christian models or were some of them at least Insular creations? An example is the trumpeting symbols in the Book of Lindisfarne (no. 9). The same question needs to be asked concerning the iconography of the Beast Canon Tables found in three Insular Gospel Books, the Maeseyck and Barberini Gospel Books and the Book of Kells (nos. 22, 23, 36, 52). Like all iconographical problems of the early Middle Ages they are rendered so difficult because we have so little idea of what is lost and whether the chance survivals give us an accurate picture or not. The question comes up acutely in the discussion of the Book of Kells, of course. But to give another example it is not quite certain whether the Stockholm *Codex Aureus* (no. 30) copies the so-called Gospel Book of St. Augustine (fig. 23, ills. 147, 153), since the latter has only one Evangelist portrait surviving, St. Luke, and the former only two, St. Matthew and St. John, so that there is no overlap. Similarly, did the Insular artist avoid copying the figure scenes in the 6th-century Gospel Book altogether, or were they copied on pages of the *Codex Aureus* now lost, or in other Insular Gospel Books also lost?

More study is certainly needed on the nature of the models available in England and Ireland, but a general point of importance is that often both stylistic and iconographic comparisons seem to lead to the eastern Mediterranean. One reason for this, apart from the various historical links with Eastern monasticism which may be demonstrated, is that in that area some of the canons of classical art had already begun to break down in the 4th and 5th centuries, so that Insular artists found a kindred art of stylization which was sympathetic to them.[20]

One way in which it may prove possible to extend our knowledge on these matters is to work backwards from later copies of Insular books. Already in the 6th and 7th centuries Irish monks were travelling and settling on the Continent so that, for example, some of our earliest Irish manuscripts (nos. 2, 3) come from Bobbio in North Italy which was founded by St. Columbanus (*c.* 550–615) in 612. St. Gall, whose patron saint was one of Columbanus' companions on the journey from Bangor to Luxeuil in France *c.* 590, is another continental centre from which important Irish manuscripts survive (nos. 44, 50, 57, 58, 60, 68). In the late 7th century the Northumbrian St. Willibrord (658–739) began his mission to the Frisians which resulted in the foundation of Echternach in 698 (cf. nos. 11, 24, 25, 26, 27, 28) and a little later the missions of St. Boniface (680–754), the Apostle of Germany, resulted in an even greater spread of Insular influence so that centres such as Fulda, founded *c.* 743 (cf. no. 49), and many others in southern Germany become enclaves of Insular influence.[21] This influence lasts throughout the 8th century and into the Carolingian period and, as is well known, is felt even in the Gospel Books produced in the court school of Charlemagne, the so-called Ada Group of manuscripts (fig. 16), above all in the decorative vocabulary and the initial pages.

An example of the further investigation to be done is an unpublished Gospel Book (Amiens, Bibliothèque Municipale, MS. 225) of unknown origin, perhaps of the 10th century. It has

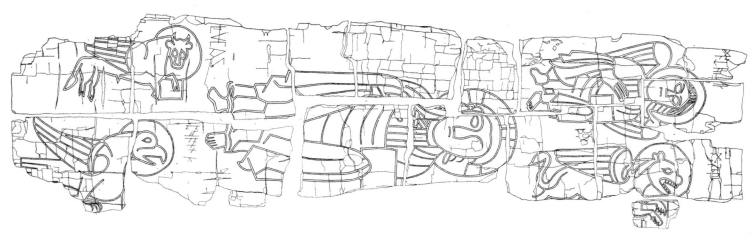

Fig. 5. Christ and Evangelist Symbols.
St. Cuthbert Coffin, lid (*drawn by D. McIntyre*). Durham Cathedral

Evangelist symbols which seem to derive from the rare type of terrestrial symbol as seen in the Books of Durrow and Echternach (nos. 6, 11, ills. 14–17, 54–6, 59), with no wings and the Matthew symbol is a frontal standing figure (figs. 19–22). The Calf accompanies a portrait of St. Luke writing, but the other three symbols are alone. They seem to be affected by a different type in that they all carry books and the Man and the Lion are haloed. Nevertheless, the standing frontal Man in particular is so unusual that the question must be asked as to whether they depend on an Insular source or an even earlier model. If the former, either it must have been in a more naturalistic style than Durrow or Echternach or the Carolingian artist has trans-formed the style of his Insular model. If the latter, does it have to be connected with the Per-sian Diatessaron set or could it have come from some such model as the Valerianus Gospel Book (Munich, Bayerische Staatsbibliothek, Clm. 6224, figs. 17, 18)?

It is for this reason that the inclusion here of certain manuscripts which were either produced by Insular scribes or artists on the Continent such as the Cutbercht Gospel Book (no. 37) or which are close copies of Insular works now lost, can be justified. Into this second class come the Antwerp Sedulius (no. 65) and the Valenciennes Apocalypse (no. 64). So little Insular figural art survives, as has been said already, that it seemed essential to include these two books at least. Other examples are the Würzburg St. Paul (no. 55) and the copy of an Insular Gospel Book probably from Brittany (no. 56). Nevertheless selection was obviously difficult. Whereas it would have unjustifiably extended the scope of the book to include for instance, works of the Charlemagne Court School, the line between 'close copy' and 'strongly influenced by' is harder to draw in the case of a work such as the Flavigny Gospel Book (Autun, Biblio-thèque Municipale, MS 3), which is certainly important for the question of the Insular Beast Canon Tables.[22] There are also very numerous manuscripts with Insular script and Insular style initials from Continental centres, for example Echternach or Würzburg, which could not be included here because of their numbers. For a full survey of Insular art on the Continent the reader must turn to the indispensable pioneer work of Mrs. Marsh-Micheli.[23]

As will be clear from certain remarks already made, Insular book illumination cannot be properly studied in isolation. The manuscript book is always, of course, a unity only to be understood by considering all its other aspects, the type of text, its later history, the binding, the script, and all the various features of its making subsumed by the term codicology. The study of the script of this period is particularly important for the art historian, however, first, because, as we have seen in the matter of the initials, the script and the decoration are intimately connected. This connection is further to be expected since in many cases scribes like Eadfrith (no. 9) or Macregol (no. 54) were also the illuminators and this is an important factor in the development of the decoration of the book in the early medieval period.[24] In the text pages of the Book of Kells, for example, script merges into illumination through pen arabesque, line fillers, and initial without a break (ills. 257–9), and the sense of design apparent on the cross-carpet pages of the Book of Lindisfarne is equally present on each page of text. Other examples of this intercon-nection between script and decoration are the sump-tuous pages with display capitals in the Royal Gospel Book (no. 32, ill. 160) and the script patterns in the pages of the Stockholm *Codex Aureus* (no. 30, ills. 158–9).

Secondly, since paleographers have a much larger mass of material surviving, including more dated or datable works, art historians must depend to a large extent for their chronology on the paleographical evidence. There may, of course, be cases where the two kinds of evidence seem to lead to different

Fig. 6. Virgin and Child. St. Cuthbert Coffin, side (*drawn by D. McIntyre*). Durham Cathedral

conclusions as to date or origin (the Book of Kells seems to be one). Where they do so, the art historian must state his case, but he will do so with the proper reservations and a due sense of disquiet.

A detailed continuous history of Insular script is still to be written, but for the early period up to 800 the masterly volumes of *Codices Latini Antiquiores* by E. A. Lowe act as guide. The reader will also find references in the bibliographies to the books and papers particularly of Professor David Wright and Professor Julian Brown as well as to E. A. Lowe's *English Uncial*, in which many of the problems of the origin and development of Insular script are treated.[25] Dr. Patrick McGurk's study of the early Gospel Books is also indispensable in showing the place of the Insular manuscripts within the development from the late antique to the early medieval period as far as codicological features and textual arrangement are concerned.

Textual evidence which is also difficult for the non-specialist to evaluate, has already and will certainly continue in the future to contribute important information as to the origins and relationships of Insular manuscripts. The biblical texts have already been the subject of much study, though, as C. D. Verey has shown, there is a need for caution in accepting certain past conclusions as well as for a great deal of further research.[26]

A third branch of study which is essential to the full understanding of Insular illumination concerns the other works of art produced at the same time, particularly of course the metal-work already mentioned, and the other notable feature of the art of the period, the numerous carved crosses, and other pieces of stone sculpture. The discovery of the burial hoard at Sutton Hoo made possible a completely new understanding of the illumination of the Book of Durrow, for example (figs. 9, 10). Here we can especially hope that new archaeological discoveries such as that of the St. Ninian's Isle treasure will bring new material to light.[27] Since the present volume is not a general history of Insular art, this material is only referred to occasionally in passing and again the reader must turn to the monographs particularly those of Professor Françoise Henry and Sir Thomas Kendrick to see the manuscripts in the wider context of Insular art.[28]

Many of the Insular manuscripts have been the subject of continuous study for over a century and in some cases longer, and the bibliography of the most famous of them is by now immense.[29] In looking back at what has been done it is clear that attention has focused above all on the earliest manuscripts. It is striking that the later 8th-century Gospel Boosk including such splendid examples as the Trier, Leningrad, and Barberini Gospel Books (nos. 26, 39, 36) have so far received rather little detailed examination. The great exhibition at Aachen in 1965 devoted to Charlemagne included some of the later Insular books, but though the influence of Insular art on the Continent has been stressed, we still need to understand this better and also to know if there was an influence in the reverse direction (the problem of the Book of Kells, once again). It is also striking that there has never been a great exhibition in which Insular art has been shown in all its variety on its own account. The material is so widely scattered that the benefits of seeing it brought together would be immense and it is not chauvinistic to say that such an exhibition would be a stupendous demonstration of the brilliance of one of the most artistically creative periods in the history of the British Isles.

Fig. 7. Initial S. London, B.L., Cotton Vespasian A. I, f. 64ᵛ (cat. 29)

NOTES

1. The essential source for the history of the early period is Bede' *Ecclesiastical History*. See also F. Stenton, *Anglo-Saxon England*, Oxford, 1947. L. Bieler, *Ireland, harbinger of the Middle Ages*, London, 1963. N. Chadwick, *The Celts*, Harmondsworth, 1970. Kathleen Hughes, *Early Christian Ireland: Introduction to the Sources*, London, 1972. *Eadem, The Church in early Irish Society*, London, 1966. *Eadem*, 'The distribution of Irish scriptoria and centres of learning from 730–1111', *Studies in the Early British Church*, Cambridge, 1958, 243 ff. J. F. Kenney, *Sources for the early history of Ireland*, New York, 1929. P. Hunter Blair, *Northumbria in the days of Bede*, London, 1977. I. Henderson, *The Picts*, London, 1967. D. Wilson, *The Anglo-Saxons*, Harmondsworth, 1971. C. Thomas, *Britain and Ireland in Early Christian Times, A.D. 400–800*, London, 1971.

2. K. Hughes, 'Evidence for contacts between the churches of the Irish and English from the Synod of Whitby to the Viking Age', *England before the Conquest. Studies in primary sources presented to Dorothy Whitelock*, ed. P. Clemoes, K. Hughes, Cambridge, 1971, 49 ff.

3. Stenton, *op. cit.*, p. 125.

4. M. Schapiro, 'The decoration of the Leningrad manuscript of Bede', *Scriptorium*, 12, 1958, 191–207.

5. There may be some continuity in learning and in script, however. See T. J. Brown, 'An historical introduction to the use of classical Latin authors in the British Isles from the fifth to the eleventh century', *Settimane di studio del Centro italiano di studi sull' alto medioevo*, 22, 1975, 241–2.

6. K. Weitzmann, *Illustrations in roll and codex*, Princeton, 1947. *Id.*, *Ancient Book Illumination*, Cambridge, Mass., 1959. And particularly the important paper 'Book illustration of the fourth century: Tradition and Innovation' reprinted in K. Weitzmann, *Studies in Classical and Byzantine Manuscript Illumination*, ed. H. L. Kessler, Chicago, 1971, 96 ff. Also C. Nordenfalk, 'The Beginning of Book Decoration', *Essays in honor of Georg Swarzenski*, ed. O. Goetz, Chicago, 1951, 9–20. For late antique art in general see the masterly short survey by E. Kitzinger, *Early Medieval Art in the British Museum*, London, 1940, second edn. 1955, and his *Byzantine Art in the Making*, London, 1977.

7. C. Nordenfalk, *Die spätantiken Zierbuchstaben*, Stockholm, 1970, 98 ff.

8. W. Koehler, *Buchmalerei des frühen Mittelalters*, ed. E. Kitzinger, F. Mütherich, Munich, 1972, esp. pp. 184-6.

9. *Codex Lindisfarnensis*, 221 ff., figs. 51-9. J. Romilly Allen, *Celtic Art in Pagan and Christian Times*, London, 1904. B. Salin, *Die altgermanische Thierornamentik*, Stockholm, 1935. Nordenfalk, *Celtic*, 13 ff. See also G. Bain, *Celtic Art. The Methods of Construction*, London, 1951.

10. For a fine analysis of Insular aesthetic in these matters see Schapiro, 'Leningrad Bede', *op. cit.* He describes the process as 'the articulation of the background spaces as contrasting ornament (p. 199)'. See also Kitzinger, 37-40.

11. See Nordenfalk, *Zierbuchstaben*, 181 ff. and his paper 'Before the Book of Durrow,' *Acta Archaeologica*, 18, 1947, 151 ff. Also H. Jantzen, 'Das Wort als Bild in der frühmittelalterlichen Buchmalerei', *Über den gotischen Kirchenraum und andere Aufsätze*, Berlin, 1951, 53 ff. Interesting suggestions as to symbolic meanings included in the designs of the initial- and carpet-pages have been made by V. H. Elbern and O.-K. Werckmeister (see LITERATURE for Books of Durrow and Kells, nos. 6, 52). As with many such interpretations of medieval art, since the suggested meanings are not documented by any contemporary source, there is no possibility of incontestable proof that they really were intended.

12. H. Bober, 'On the illumination of the Glazier Codex', *Homage to a Bookman. Essays on manuscripts, books and printing written for Hans P. Kraus*, New York, 1967.

13. C. Nordenfalk, 'An illustrated Diatessaron', *Art Bulletin*, 50, 1968, 119-40.

14. Nordenfalk, *Zierbuchstaben*, cit., 40-1, pl. 26-31.

15. J. Duft, P. Meyer, *The Irish miniatures in the Cathedral Library of St. Gall*, Berne, 1954, 129-30.

16. J. J. G. Alexander, 'Some aesthetic principles in the use of colour in Anglo-Saxon art', *Anglo-Saxon England*, 4, 1975, 145 ff.

17. Schapiro, 'Leningrad Bede', *op. cit.*

18. O. Pächt, 'The pre-Carolingian roots of early Romanesque art', *Romanesque and Gothic Art. Studies in Western Art. Acts of the 20th International Congress of the History of Art*, ed. M. Meiss *et al.*, Princeton, 1963, I, 67 ff.

19. M. Schapiro and seminar, 'The miniatures of the Florence Diatessaron', *Art Bulletin*, 55, 1973, 528.

20. The influence of Coptic art in particular has been both strongly argued and strongly denied. See against J. Raftery, '*Ex oriente . . .*', *Journal of the Royal Society of Antiquaries of Ireland*, 95, 1965, 193 ff. and the warnings of D. H. Wright in A. Dold, L. Eizenhöfer, *Das Irische Palimpsestsakramentar im Clm. 14429 der Staatsbibliothek München* (Texte und Arbeiten, Heft 53/4), 1964, 39. In support see M. Werner, 'The Madonna and Child miniature in the Book of Kells', *Art Bulletin*, 54, 1972, 1 ff.

21. W. Levison, *England and the Continent in the eighth century*, Oxford, 1946. S. J. Crawford, *Anglo-Saxon influence on Western Christendom 600-800*, Oxford, 1933.

22. *Manuscrits à peintures du VIIe au XIIe siecle*, Bibliothèque Nationale, Paris, exhibition catalogue by J. Porcher, no. 9, pl. 1. *C.L.A.*, VI, no. 717 a,b.

23. G. L. Micheli, *L'enluminure du haut Moyen Âge et les influences irlandaises*, Brussels, 1939.

24. J. J. G. Alexander, 'Scribes as artists', *Medieval Scribes, Manuscripts and Libraries: Essays presented to N. R. Ker*, ed. M. B. Parkes, A. G. Watson, forthcoming.

25. For a general survey see L. Bieler, 'Insular palaeography: present state and problems', *Scriptorium*, 3, 1949, 267 ff. See also T. J. Brown, 'Latin Palaeography since Traube', *Codicologica, I, Théories et principes*, ed. A. Gruys, J. P. Gumbert, 1976, 66-7.

26. C. D. Verey, *A collation of the Gospel texts contained in Durham Cathedral Mss. A. II. 10, A. II. 16 and A. II. 17*, unpublished M.A. thesis, Durham University, 1969.

27. D. M. Wilson, 'Reflections on the St. Ninian's Isle treasure', *Jarrow Lecture*, 1969, with earlier literature.

28. Also I. Finlay, *Celtic Art. An Introduction*, London, 1973; L. Laing, *The Archaeology of Late Celtic Britain and Ireland, c. 400-1200 A.D.*, London, 1975.

29. Cf. A. N. L. Munby, *Connoisseurs and Medieval Miniatures, 1750-1850*, London, Oxford, 1972 and *Color of the Middle Ages, A survey of book illumination based on color facsimiles of medieval manuscipts*, catalogue by C. Nordenfalk, Pittsburgh, 1976.

ABBREVIATIONS

Åberg, *Occident*

N. Åberg, *The Occident and the Orient in the art of the seventh century, I; the British Isles*, Stockholm, 1943

C.L.A. I–XI, *Supplement*

E. A. Lowe, *Codices Latini Antiquiores*, Oxford, I, 1934, II, 1935, 2nd corr. edn, 1972, III, 1938, IV, 1947, V, 1950, VI, 1953, VII, 1956, VIII, 1959, IX, 1959, X, 1963, XI, 1966, *Supplement*, 1971.

Duft, Meyer, *St. Gall*

J. Duft, P. Meyer, *The Irish Miniatures in the Cathedral Library of St. Gall*, Berne, 1954

Codex Durmachensis

A. A. Luce, G. O. Simms, P. Meyer, L. Bieler, *Evangeliorum Quattuor Codex Durmachensis*, 2 vols., complete facsimile, commentary, Olten and Lausanne, 1960

Codex Lindisfarnensis

T. D. Kendrick, T. J. Brown, R. L. S. Bruce-Mitford, H. Roosen-Runge, A. S. C. Ross, E. G. Stanley, A. E. A. Werner, *Evangeliorum Quattuor Codex Lindisfarnensis*, vol. I, complete facsimile, vol. II, commentary, Olten and Lausanne, 1956, 1960

Gilbert, *Facsimiles*, I, II

J. T. Gilbert, *Facsimiles of National Manuscripts of Ireland*, Part I, 1874, Part II, 1878

Henry, *Irish Art*, I, II, III,

F. Henry, *Irish Art in the Early Christian Period (to 800 A.D.)*, London, 1965; *Irish Art during the Viking Invasions 800–1020 A.D.*, London, 1967; *Irish Art in the Romanesque Period 1020–1170 A.D.*, London, 1970

Henry, *Kells*

F. Henry, *The Book of Kells*, London, 1974

Karl der Grosse, 1965

Karl der Grosse — Werk und Wirkung (Zehnte Ausstellung unter den Auspizien der Europarates), Aachen, 1965

Kendrick, *Anglo-Saxon*

T. D. Kendrick, *Anglo-Saxon Art to A.D. 900*, London, 1938, reprinted 1972

Kenney, *Sources*

J. F. Kenney, *The sources for the early history of Ireland*, New York, 1929

Ker, *Catalogue*

N. R. Ker, *Catalogue of manuscripts containing Anglo-Saxon*, Oxford, 1957

Koehler, *Buchmalerei*

W. Koehler, *Buchmalerei des frühen Mittelalters* (Fragmente und Entwürfe aus dem Nachlass herausgegeben von E. Kitzinger, F. Mütherich), Munich, 1972

Lowe, *English Uncial*

E. A. Lowe, *English Uncial*, Oxford, 1960

Masai, *Origines*

F. Masai, *Essai sur les origines de la miniature dite Irlandaise*, Brussels, 1947

McGurk, *Latin Gospel Books*

P. McGurk, *Latin Gospel Books from A.D. 400 to A.D. 800*, Paris, Brussels, 1961

Micheli, *L'enluminure*

G. L. Micheli, *L'enluminure du haut Moyen Âge et les influences irlandaises*, Brussels, 1939

Mynors, *Durham*

R. A. B. Mynors, *Durham Cathedral manuscripts to the end of the twelfth century*, Durham, 1939

New Pal. Soc., I and II

New Paleographical Society: Facsimiles of Ancient Manuscripts, etc., ed. E. M. Thompson, G. F. Warner *et al.*, 1st series, London, 1903–12, 2nd series, London, 1903–30

Nordenfalk, *Celtic*   C. Nordenfalk, *Celtic and Anglo-Saxon painting. Book Illumination in the British Isles 600–800*, New York, 1976

Nordenfalk, *Early Medieval*   A. Grabar, C. Nordenfalk, *Early Medieval Painting from the fourth to the eleventh century*, Skira, 1957

Pächt and Alexander, III   O. Pächt, J. J. G. Alexander, *Illuminated manuscripts in the Bodleian Library, Oxford, 3. British, Irish and Icelandic Schools*, Oxford, 1973

Pal. Soc., I and II   *Palaeographical Society: Facsimiles of Manuscripts and Inscriptions*, ed. E. A. Bond, E. M. Thompson, G. F. Warner, 1st series, London, 1873–83; 2nd series, London, 1884–94

Rickert, *Painting in Britain*   M. Rickert, *Painting in Britain: The Middle Ages*, 2nd revised edition, Harmondsworth, 1965

Saunders, *English Illumination*   O. E. Saunders, *English Illumination*, 2 vols., Paris, Florence, 1928

Temple, *Anglo-Saxon*   E. Temple, *Anglo-Saxon Manuscripts 900–1066* (A Survey of Manuscripts Illuminated in the British Isles, II), London, 1976

Werckmeister, *Irisch-northumbrische Buchmalerei*   O.-K. Werkmeister, *Irisch-northumbrische Buchmalerei des 8. Jahrhunderts und monastische Spiritualität*, Berlin, 1967

Westwood, *Facsimiles*   J. O. Westwood, *Facsimiles of the miniatures and ornaments of Anglo-Saxon and Irish manuscripts*, London, 1868

Westwood, *Palaeographia*   J. O. Westwood, *Palaeographia sacra pictoria*, London, 1843–5

Zimmermann, *Vorkarolingische Miniaturen*   E. H. Zimmermann, *Vorkarolingische Miniaturen*, Berlin, 1916

Fig. 8 Papil Stone, Burra (Shetland).
Edinburgh, National Museum of
Antiquities of Scotland

Fig. 9. Gold Buckle from Sutton Hoo.
London, British Museum

Fig. 10. Purse-lid from Sutton Hoo.
London, British Museum

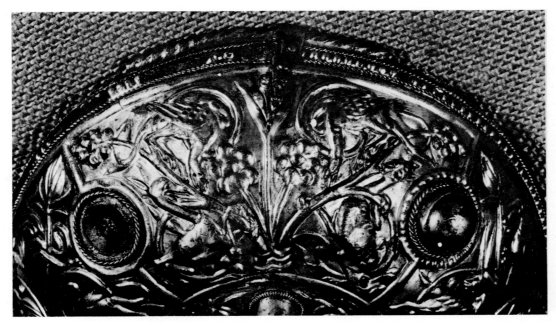

Fig. 11. Decorative detail from
the Ormside Bowl.
York, Yorkshire Museum

Fig. 12. Cross-page (Coptic). New York, Pierpont Morgan Lib.,
Glazier Codex 67, f. 215

Fig. 13–14. Carpet page and
Four-symbols page.
Florence, Bibl. Medicea-Laurenziana,
Orient 81, f. 127ᵛ and f. 128ᵛ

Fig. 15. Canon Table. Vatican, Bibl. Apostolica, Lat. 3806, f. 2ᵛ

Fig. 16. Canon Table. London, B.L., Harley 2788, f. 6ᵛ

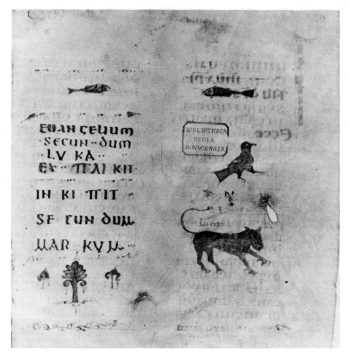

Figs. 17–18. Evangelist symbols of St. Mark. and St. Luke. Munich, Bayerische Staatsbibl.,
Cod. Lat. 6224, f. 12 and f. 82ᵛ

Figs. 19–20. St. Matthew symbol and Lion of St. Mark.
Amiens, Bibl. Mun., 225, f. 28ᵛ and f. 69

Figs. 21–22. St. Luke with symbol and Eagle of St. John.
Amiens, Bibl. Mun., 225, f. 98ᵛ and f. 150

Fig. 23. St. Luke. Cambridge, Corpus Christi College 286, f. 129ᵛ

Fig. 24. St. Matthew. Athens, National Library, 56, f. 4ᵛ

Fig. 25. St. Matthew. Copenhagen, Royal Library, G.K.S. 10, 2⁰, f. 17ᵛ

Fig. 26. St. Luke. Copenhagen, Royal Library, G.K.S. 10, 2⁰, f. 82ᵛ

GLOSSARY

Ammonian Sections
Divisions of the Gospel texts attributed to Ammonius of Alexandria. They were used by Eusebius of Caesarea in his Canon Tables (q.v.) and are now thought to have been composed by him.

Canon Tables
A concordance table of references to passages occurring in one or in two or more of the four Gospels compiled by Eusebius of Caesarea in the 4th century and usually arranged in columns under arches.

Colophon
Note at the end of a manuscript giving information such as the name of the scribe, the place where the manuscript was written, the date, details of the text copied, etc.

Continuation Lettering
Term used here for the letters of a word or words introduced in a text by an initial letter. They are in some way enlarged, coloured, decorated or set in panels so that they form a transition between the initial and the script (cf. fig. 4, ill. 33). Often they decrease in size gradually from the initial according to the Insular habit of diminution. The paleographical term 'display script' is used for headings, incipits, explicits, etc., where there is no initial.

Cumdach
Casket to enclose a manuscript made of leather or precious metals and ornamented.

Evangelist Symbols
The four symbols deriving from the visions of Ezekiel (I, 5–8) and St. John in the Apocalypse (IV, 6–8), whose normal equivalence, made canonical by St. Jerome, is Man or Angel—St. Matthew; Lion—St. Mark; Calf—St. Luke; and Eagle—St. John.

Explicit
Closing word of a text (in Latin, 'it ends').

Incipit
Opening words of a text (in Latin, 'it begins').

Ogam
Ancient British and Irish alphabet.

Palimpsest
Parchment used for a second time after the original writing has been erased.

Singleton
Single leaf added to a quire of conjoint folios.

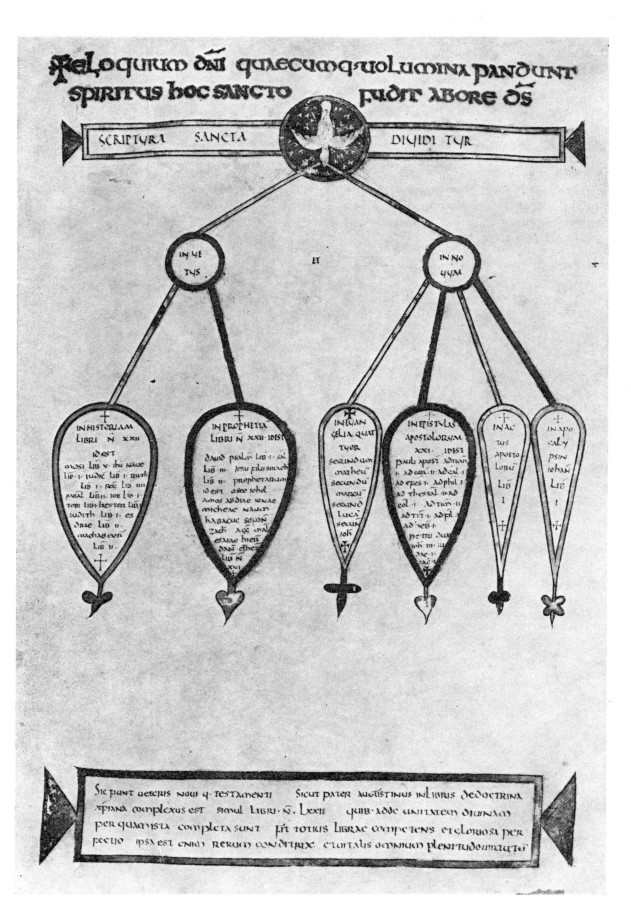

Fig. 27. Books of the Bible according to St. Augustine. Florence,
Bibl. Medicea-Laurenziana, Amiatinus I, f. 8 (cat. 7)

CATALOGUE

1. Dublin, Trinity College MS A. 4. 15 (55)

Gospel Book (Codex Usserianus Primus)
Writing space *c.* 175 × 120–30 mm., remains of
about ff. 180 remounted on paper
Early 7th century. (?) Ireland

Ill. 1

The leaves are damaged and discoloured. The book
was enclosed in a *cumdach* (shrine). The only remaining decoration is a cross ('Xp' monogram) in reddish
brown at the end of St. Luke (f. 149ᵛ) with the
explicit of Luke and the *incipit* of Mark written on
either side. The cross is accompanied by the Greek
letters 'α' and 'ω', is outlined with black dots, and
has a double frame of small 's' forms with corner
motifs. Initials in black (ff. 94, 101, and 107) also
have small red dots.
Nordenfalk (1947, 1972) has compared the cross
(staurogram) with those found in the Bologna
Lactantius, Univ. Bibl., 701, 5th century, the Paris
St. John, Bibl. Nat., lat. 10439, *c.* 500 and the
Valerianus Gospels, Munich, Clm. 6224, second
half of the 7th century. The concentration of decoration at the end rather than at the beginning of the
text is an early feature (cf. no. 5). Though there are
some paleographical similarities with the earliest
Bobbio manuscripts (cf. nos. 2, 3), the Gospel Book
is now thought to have been written in Ireland
(Lowe, Wright). It is thus probably the earliest
example of an Insular artist copying a Mediterranean
form of decoration, and stands at the beginning
of the development which will lead to the cross-
carpet pages.

PROVENANCE: In spite of its usual title it is unlikely to have belonged to James Ussher, archbishop
of Armagh (d. 1576).

LITERATURE: Westwood, *Palaeographia*, no. 19;
Gilbert, *Facsimiles*, I, vi, pl. II; T. K. Abbott,
*Evangeliorum versio antihieronymiana ex codice
Usseriano*, 2 vols., 1884; *Pal. Soc.*, II, pl. 33; T. K.
Abbott, *Catalogue of the manuscripts in the library of
Trinity College, Dublin*, 1900, 7; Kenney, *Sources*,
no. 453; Åberg, *Occident*, 89; C. Nordenfalk, 'Before
the Book of Durrow', *Acta Archaeologica*, 18, 1947,
147 ff., fig. 5; F. Henry, 'Les débuts de la miniature
Irlandaise', *Gazette des Beaux-Arts*, 6ᵉ pér., 37,
1950, 5–34, figs. 3, 11; McGurk, *Latin Gospel Books*,
no. 84; D. H. Wright in A. Dold, L. Eizenhöfer,
*Das Irische Palimpsestsakramentar im Clm. 14429
der Staatsbibliothek München* (Texte und Arbeiten,
Heft 53/4), 1964, 36; Henry, *Irish Art*, I, 62, 64,

187, pl. 58; B. Bischoff, 'Kreuz und Buch im Früh-
mittelalter', *Mittelalterliche Studien*, II, 1967, 288;
C. Nordenfalk, *Die spätantiken Zierbuchstaben*, 1970,
63 f., 141, fig. 16; *C.L.A.*, II, no. 271; Koehler,
Buchmalerei, 26; Nordenfalk, *Celtic*, 13, fig. I.

2. Milan, Biblioteca Ambrosiana MS S. 45. sup.

Jerome, Commentary on Isaiah
235 × 215 mm., pp. 156
Early 7th century. Bobbio, North Italy

Ill. 8

The illumination consists of an initial N in black
ink which is decorated with whorl and cross patterns
and pelta motifs with touches of green and orange,
The cross-bar is partly formed of two fishes. There
are other minor initials coloured in yellow and
orange (e.g. E, p. 121).
The manuscript is palimpsest reusing an earlier text
of Ulfilas written in Gothic uncial, 6th century.
Since Lowe accepts the evidence of the inscription
connecting the manuscript with Atalanus (p. 2) and
dates it before 622, this is one of the earliest Insular style initials, preceding, probably, the Cathach
(no. 4). It is comparable in design to the Durham
Gospels 'In' (no. 5, ill. 9). It seems likely, however, that the manuscript was written at Bobbio
rather than in Ireland.

PROVENANCE: *Lib' de arca domno Atalani*, p. 2.
Atalanus succeeded St. Columbanus, the founder of
Bobbio, as Abbot, in 615 and died in 622. 15th-
century Bobbio *ex libris* and no. 87, p. 3.

LITERATURE: É. Chatelain, *Uncialis scriptura
codicum latinorum novis exemplis illustrata*, 1901–2,
151 ff., pls. LXXXIV–LXXV; *C.L.A.*, III, no. 365;
P. Collura, *Studi paleografici. La Precarolina e la
Carolina a Bobbio* (Fontes Ambrosiani, XXII), 1943,
79–80, pls. 26–7; F. Henry, 'Les débuts de la
miniature Irlandaise', *Gazette des Beaux-Arts*, 6ᵉ
pér., 37, 1950, 5–34, figs. 1, 2, 10, 16, 18, 20; A. R.
Natale, *Studi paleografici. Arte e imitazione della
scrittura insulare in codici bobbiesi*, 1950, 77–90, pl.
XIII; H. Vanderhoven, F. Masai, *La règle du
Maître* (Publication de Scriptorium, III), 1953,
48–9; *Codex Lindisfarnensis*, 108, 113 n. 7, 115,
260, pls. 20 c, e, fig. 11b; Henry, *Irish Art*, I, 63–4,
165, pl. VI; E. A. Lowe, 'The Ambrosiana, Milan,
and the experiences of a palaeographer', *Folia
Ambrosiana*, I, 1965, 44, pl. XII (reprinted *Palaeo-*

graphical Papers, ed. L. Bieler, 1972, 586–7, pl. 142);
Henry, *Kells*, 226, fig. 1.

3. Milan, Biblioteca Ambrosiana MS D.23. sup.

Orosius, Chronicon
210 × 150 mm., ff. 48
(?) Early 7th century. (?) Bobbio, North Italy

Ills. 6, 7

The importance of the illumination in this manuscript lies in its early date. It is the earliest carpet
page of Insular art. On f. 1ᵛ a decorated frontispiece
contains a large central rosette with four smaller
corner rosettes contained in a nearly square frame
(155 × 125 mm.). The colours used are pink, yellow,
a little bluish green and perhaps orange. They have
faded, and it is not entirely clear how the page
looked originally.

The design, at first sight deceptively simple, is, in
fact, extremely complicated and already shows the
Insular subtlety of pattern and love of alternation
of colour. The outer (left) edge of the page is
emphasized by the motifs in the corner squares of
the frame, at the top a cross within a circle (cf. no.
6, ill. 22), and at the bottom a rosette. The frame
panels at top and bottom are composed of triangles
and chevrons. These alternate the filling colours of
pink and yellow so that at the side the triangles are
yellow then the chevrons pink, etc., and at the top
and bottom the triangles are pink and the chevrons
yellow, etc. The panels run to the inner margin but
the last square on the inner (right) margin is emphasized not this time by a change of pattern, but by
a slight change of colour. The upper chevron is
greenish blue instead of yellow. The vertical panels
contain cable motifs. The larger on the outer side in
white reserved on pink reflects the circular forms
in the corner squares. On the right, the triangular
pattern is reflected by two thinner cables reserved
white on pink and separated by a yellow bar.

The central rosette set on a blank ground has eight
petals. Originally, they were probably alternately
orange and white (the blank parchment). On two of the
latter, yellow dots around the perimeter are still visible.
The rosette is set on a pink ground and surrounded
by concentric circles from the outside—orange,
yellow, black, pink, yellow, and orange (or pink ?).
The four corner rosettes are also subtly balanced.
The outer at top and bottom read as pink petals on
a white ground in a pink circle, the inner as con-
cave triangles coloured pink and yellow on a white
ground. For a reconstruction in colour see *Codex
Lindisfarnensis* cited below.

On f. 2 the initial P and the opening words *Praeceptis
tuis pa(rui)* are hollow shafted capitals filled in pink
and orange. The stem of the P runs the whole
length of the page. The stem and the bowl have a
cable pattern reserved in white. There are rows of
dots filling the bowl and the space below it, and
triple dots in the bowl of the R. Other initials are
a D (f. 5) filled with orange and outlined in dots and
an N (f. 33) rather larger with a cable pattern reserved

in white on orange in the uprights. The crossing bar
and the finial to the left upright are green. Triplet
orange dots fill the ground. There is some suggestion
of diminution (cf. no. 4).

E. A. Lowe has said that 'the decoration is perhaps a later addition; it is not at all typically Insular'.
Though the motifs are unusual and the pink colour
of the frontispiece and f. 2 differs from the more usual
orange on f. 33, the use of pattern and colour is, as has
been shown, thoroughly Insular, as are the initials
with the use of dotted ornament. Wright argues for
a date early in the 7th century, though the initials
show considerable development (cf. Nordenfalk,
1970, expressing reservations on the date). The
question of the source of the carpet page is treated
in the Introduction (p. 11) and see also description
of the Book of Durrow (no. 6).

PROVENANCE: From Bobbio which was founded
by St. Columbanus in 612 and where he died in 615.
No. 52 in the inventory of 1461 and *ex libris* of
the 15th century, f. 1. Given to the Ambrosiana by
the monks on its foundation by Cardinal Federico
Borromeo in 1606 (note on a paper flyleaf by Antonio
Olgiato, first Prefect).

LITERATURE: *C.L.A.*, III, no. 328; Micheli,
L'enluminure, 104; P. Collura, *Studi paleografici. La
Precarolina e la Carolina a Bobbio* (Fontes Ambrosiani,
XXII), 1943, 90, 94, pl. 30; F. Henry, 'Les débuts
de la miniature Irlandaise', *Gazette des Beaux-Arts*,
6ᵉ pér., 37, 1950, 5–34, figs. 4, 8, 9, 10; A. R. Natale,
*Studi paleografici. Arte e imitazione della scrittura
insulare in codici bobbiesi*, 1950, 21 ff., pl. II; *Codex
Lindisfarnensis*, 113, 115, pl. 20 a, b, d; Henry, *Irish
Art*, I, 62, 64, 163, 165, 168–9, pl. 58; D. H. Wright
in A. Dold, L. Eizenhöfer, *Das Irische Palimpsestsakramentar im Clm. 14429 der Staatsbibliothek
München* (Texte und Arbeiten, Heft 53/4), 1964, 36
ff.; Werckmeister, *Irisch-northumbrische Buchmalerei*,
31, pl. 10a; R. Cipriani, *Codici miniati dell' Ambrosiana*
(Fontes Ambrosiani, XL), 1968, 23; M. L. Gengaro,
G. V. Guglielmetti, *Inventario dei codici decorati e
miniati della Biblioteca Ambrosiana*, 1968, 3–4, pls.
1, 2; C. Nordenfalk, *Die spätantiken Zierbuchstaben*,
1970, 131 n. 1, 141; Henry, *Kells*, 160, 182, 213, 225,
fig. 29.

4. Dublin, Royal Irish Academy MS S.n.

Psalter (Cathach of St. Columba)
200 × 130 mm. (maximum size with margins
all lost), ff. 58
(?) Early 7th century. Ireland

Ills. 2–5

The illumination consists of initials to each Psalm
in black ink with decoration in the form of trumpet,
spiral, and guilloche patterns. On f. 48 a Q has a fish
tail with a cross above it. The initials are often outlined with orange dots and the headings to the Psalms
are written in orange minium. The manuscript is
damaged and incomplete.

The initials establish two points cardinal to the future of Insular book illumination. The first is the decoration of the initial in ways which break up or distort its form. The patterns are not merely fillers or appendages but affect the shape of the letter (cf. no. 2). The second is the principle of diminution by which the first initial is larger in size and is followed by other letters gradually reduced until they reach the same size as the script (cf. no. 3).

Lowe dates the script in the first half of the 7th century, Wright argues for the 630's, and T. J. Brown (*Codex Lindisfarnensis*) for the 6th–7th century. Traditionally, the manuscript is connected with St. Columba (d. 597) and Lowe comments: 'the early date for the manuscript is palaeographically possible.' The manuscript could thus precede the Book of Durrow (no. 6) by some fifty to seventy years.

PROVENANCE: Traditionally identified as a copy made by St. Columba (d. 597) of a book lent him by St. Finnian, an event leading to disputes culminating in the Battle of Cul Dremhe (561). The story is now discredited. It was contained in a shrine (*cumdach*) made at Kells between 1062 and 1098. This was carried into battle to ensure victory, hence the name *Cathach* (battler). It was taken to France by Daniel O'Donnell after 1691 and was brought back in 1802. The shrine was opened in 1813 and the book discovered. It was deposited in the Royal Irish Academy in 1842 by Sir Richard O'Donnell, to whose family it still belongs. For the *cumdach* (now in the National Museum of Ireland, Dublin) see H. S. Crawford, 'A descriptive list of Irish Shrines and Reliquaries. Part II', *Journal of the Royal Society of Antiquaries of Ireland*, 53, 1923, 152–3, pls. VI–VII, and Henry, *Irish Art*, III, 77, 80–1, 83, 85, 88, 90–5, 99, 120–1, 138, 191, 198–9, fig. 7.

LITERATURE: Westwood, *Palaeographia*, no. 19; Westwood, *Facsimiles*, 82–3; Gilbert, *Facsimiles*, I, vii–viii, pls. III–IV; H. J. Lawlor, E. C. R. Armstrong, W. M. Lindsay, 'The Cathach of St. Columba', *Proceedings of the Royal Irish Academy*, 33, Section C, no. 11, 1916, 241–443, pls. XXXIII, XXXV–XXXVIII; Zimmermann, *Vorkarolingische Miniaturen*, 21; Kenney, *Sources*, no. 454; Åberg, *Occident*, 88, fig. 58; C. Nordenfalk, 'Before the Book of Durrow', *Acta Archaeologica*, 18, 1947, 151–9, figs. 7, 8, 12, 14, 15, 17; F. Henry, 'Les débuts de la miniature Irlandaise', *Gazette des Beaux-Arts*, 6ᵉ pér., 37, 1950, 5–34, figs. 10, 12, 13, 20; *Codex Lindisfarnensis*, 112–13, pl. 18 a–j; D. H. Wright in A. Dold, L. Eizenhöfer, *Das Irische Palimpsestsakramentar im Clm. 14429 der Staatsbibliothek München* (Texte und Arbeiten, Heft 53/4), 1964, 34 ff., pls. V, VI; Henry, *Irish Art*, I, 58–63, 66–7, 166–7, 172, pls. 9, 12; Rickert, *Painting in Britain*, 12–13; *C.L.A.*, II, no. 266; T. J. Brown, 'Northumbria and the Book of Kells', *Anglo-Saxon England*, 1, 1972, 221, 229, 233, 241; Koehler, *Buchmalerei*, 26, 185; Henry, *Kells*, 150–1, 205, 226, fig. 2. Nordenfalk, *Celtic*, 13, fig. II.

5. Durham, Cathedral Library MSS A. II. 10, ff. 2–5, 338–8*a*, C. III. 13, ff. 192–5, and C. III. 20, ff. 1, 2
Gospel Book (fragment)
385×250 mm., ff. 12
Mid 7th century. Northumbria

Ills. 9, 10

The illumination consists of an 'Ini' monogram for the beginning of St. Mark's Gospel (A. II. 10, f. 2) and a frame (A. II. 10, f. 3ᵛ) containing, above, the *explicit* of St. Matthew and the *incipit* of St. Mark and, below, the *Pater noster* written in Greek transliterated in Latin letters. The uprights of the initial are formed of plain coloured panels of blue, olive-green, yellow, and orange separated by a cable pattern in black and white. The panels are ornamented with dots in contrasting colours. There are beast head terminals of the cross bar and of the left upright at its base. The frame of the colophon, which fills the right-hand column of the page, is of yellow interlace with orange dots superimposed and shaped, as it were, into three D's. The spaces between the bows to the right are filled with interlace knots in yellow, orange, and green and blue. There are some smaller initials coloured with yellow and orange and outlined with orange dots which mark Matthew XXVII, 38 and XXVIII, 1.

While only a fragment this manuscript is of great importance as the earliest of the series of great Insular Gospel Books, though it has also been suggested it could originally have been a complete New Testament (Lowe, Dean, 1935). The two Insular principles of initial decoration, the one of breaking up the letter form, and the other of diminution linking the initial to the text, both already seen in the Cathach (no. 4), are taken a stage further, and colour is added. The colour also illustrates a fundamental principle of Insular decoration in the way it is applied in panels resembling enamel plaques. These emphasize the component shapes of the letter and also the fact that the colours alternate in a counterpoint of contrasting shades, for example in the upright of the initial N. The form of the initial can be compared to the N in the Bobbio Jerome (no. 2, ill. 8), but the combination of the uprights of the I, the N and the I into a monogram is a new feature which will be taken up in many of the later Insular manuscripts. The frame on f. 3ᵛ is also important as the first example of an Insular illuminator experimenting with interlace pattern which from now on will be used with increasing virtuosity in a wide variety of contexts to convey expressive movement on the two-dimensional surface of the page (see Bober).

Nordenfalk (1947) has drawn attention to the fact that the concentration of decoration at the end rather than the beginning of a text is a feature of late antique book production and is seen, for example, in the Valerianus Gospel Book, 7th century (Munich, Bayerische Staatsbibliothek, Clm. 6224), and the *Codex Usserianus Primus* (no. 1). The text is in part very close to that in the latter manuscript (Verey, 1969). Presumably the manuscript was written in

Northumbria, though by an Irish scribe (Wright) or at least one 'trained in the pure Irish Tradition' (Lowe).

PROVENANCE: The fragments in A. II. 10 are bound with a Peter Lombard, Commentary on the Psalter, third quarter of 13th century. This is included in the Durham library catalogue of 1391.

LITERATURE: E. A. Lowe, R. J. Dean, 'Nouvelle liste de membra disjecta', *Revue Bénédictine*, 47, 1935, 308–10; Mynors, *Durham*, 17–18, no. 6, pl. 4; C. Nordenfalk, 'Before the Book of Durrow', *Acta Archaeologica*, 18, 1947, 141–74, figs. 20, 21, 24; F. Henry, 'Les débuts de la miniature Irlandaise', *Gazette des Beaux-Arts*, 6e pér., 37, 1950, 5–34, figs. 15, 19, 20; *C.L.A.*, VI, x; Nordenfalk, *Early Medieval*, 113, 118; *Codex Lindisfarnensis*, 113–15, pl. 18 k, l; *Codex Durmachensis*, 163, figs. 91, 116; McGurk *Latin Gospel Books*, no. 9; D. H. Wright in A. Dold, L. Eizenhöfer, *Das Irische Palimpsest-sakramentar im Clm. 14429 der Staatsbibliothek München* (Texte und Arbeiten, Heft 53/4), 1964, 34–40, pls. VII, VIIIa; Henry, *Irish Art*, I, 127, 161–9, 174, pls. 53, 61; H. Bober, 'On the illumination of the Glazier Codex', *Homage to a Bookman. Essays on manuscripts, books and printing written for Hans P. Kraus*, 1967, 46 ff., fig. 16; C. D. Verey, *A collation of the Gospel Texts contained in Durham Cathedral MSS. A. II. 10, A. II. 16 and A. II. 17*, unpublished M.A. Thesis, Durham University, 1969; T. J. Brown, 'Northumbria and the Book of Kells', *Anglo-Saxon England*, 1, 1972, 229, 232–3; *C.L.A.*, II, no. 147; Koehler, *Buchmalerei*, 26–7, 35–6, 40–1; Henry, *Kells*, 214, 226; Nordenfalk, *Celtic*, 14, 15, 32, figs. IV, VI, pl. I.

6. Dublin, Trinity College MS A. 4. 5 (57)

Gospel Book (Book of Durrow)
245 × 145 mm., ff. 248
Second half of 7th century (? *c.* 675)

Ills. 11–22, fig. 4

The Gospel Book is illuminated with carpet pages, Evangelist symbol pages and initials. There are six carpet pages, the first (f. 1ᵛ) a double-armed cross, the second (f. 3ᵛ) with trumpet spirals, the third (f. 85ᵛ) with interlacing circles, the fourth (f. 125ᵛ) with interlace and panels of pattern, the fifth (f. 192ᵛ) with a circle of interlace with a cross in the middle and panels of biting beasts as a frame, and the sixth (f. 248, moved in the rebinding, formerly f. 13) of interlace with inset square crosses. The six pages thus come at the beginning and the end of the book, before the Prefaces (f. 3ᵛ) and before the openings of the Gospels of St. Mark, St. Luke, and St. John. Possibly a seventh carpet page before St. Matthew is lost, unless that on f. 3ᵛ originally preceded it. Opposite the first carpet page is a page with an interlace cross in the centre with the four Evangelist symbols in the corners and a broad outer frame of diamond pattern (f. 2). Framed pages with the single

Evangelist symbols precede each Gospel coming before the carpet pages (except St. Matthew where there is none), always on versos, the Man (f. 21ᵛ), the Eagle, preceding St. Mark (f. 84ᵛ), the Calf (f. 124ᵛ), and the Lion, preceding St. John (f. 191ᵛ). Lastly there are the initials, St. Matthew, 'Li', five lines (f. 22), 'Xp', five lines (f. 23), St. Mark, 'In', twenty-one lines (f. 86), St. Luke, Q, nine lines, and F, ten lines (f. 126) and St. John, 'In', whole page (f. 193). There are also small initials for the Prefaces and Lists of Chapters, N (f. 4), N (f. 11), M (f. 14), 'Et' (f. 15), M (f. 17), L (f. 18), H (f. 19ᵛ).

The Canons (ff. 8–10) are enclosed in rectangular frames ornamented with panels of interlace (cf. the Echternach Gospel Book, no. 11 and the Book of Kells, no. 52). The pages are divided by a grid of lines ornamented with small red dots and blobs of colour, and the numbers are written in groups, usually of five, in the squares or rectangles of the grid. Irregular spaces are left blank on ff. 8, 9, 9ᵛ, and 10 in some of which are written *incipits* and *explicits*.

The colours used in the manuscript are limited to yellow, orange, some green, white, and black.

Durrow is the earliest of the surviving fully illuminated Insular Gospel Books. It has been and remains, therefore, at the centre of controversy in discussions of the relative contributions of Ireland and Northumbria to 7th- and 8th-century Insular art. Neither its exact date, nor its place of manufacture, nor the models lying behind its decoration have been established beyond doubt.

A date falling between the Durham Gospel fragment (no. 5) and the Lindisfarne Gospels (no. 9) in the middle of the second half of the 7th century seems most probable, and, though in the past the book has been dated both earlier and later, this dating seems now to be generally accepted by both art historians and paleographers. The later provenance and the colophon give some reasons for thinking that the book was produced in a Columban monastery, and are used as supporting evidence by those who consider the manuscript to have been written in Ireland or Iona (Henry, Nordenfalk). Textual and paleographical evidence is adduced by those who, favouring an origin in Northumbria (Lowe, Bruce-Mitford, Brown), also tend to a slightly later date *c.* 680.

As for the decoration two main sources can be distinguished. The first is a barbarian vocabulary of pattern which was probably developed mainly in metalwork. The spiral and trumpet patterns can be found in many pieces of Celtic metalwork and also in the escutcheons of the hanging bowls. The millefiori patterns are also thought to be a sign of Celtic influence. On the other hand, the animal motifs (f. 192ᵛ especially) are thought to be Germanic and excellent parallels are found on objects from the Sutton Hoo burial, now tending to be dated before the mid 7th century and certainly earlier than Durrow. Even at this early stage, therefore, there is evidence of the mixing of the two cultures.

The second main source would appear to be Mediterranean and very probably eastern Mediterranean.

Both Syrian and Coptic parallels exist for prefatory pages with crosses, for carpet pages, and for the use of interlace in connection with the crosses. The cross in the Coptic Glazier *codex* of *c.* 500 (fig. 12) is of particular significance (see Bober). Kendrick made the suggestion that Roman mosaic pavements with similar designs might still have been visible in north Britain and acted as sources (cf. Lindisfarne, no. 9). It seems more likely that the similarities are explicable in that the Eastern Mediterranean illuminators would have been familiar with such pavements and the principles of their design. Bindings whether of leather or in the form of metal shrines might also have influenced the designs, and even have given the idea of the carpet pages.

A distinction should be made between the source of the idea of including these carpet pages and the sources of the patterns used to embellish them once decided upon. Since two of the pages incorporate a cross it seems likely that the idea came from some form of prefatory frontispiece making use of a cross and therefore specifically designed for a Gospel Book. At the same time it must be remembered that the Milan Orosius (no. 3, ill. 6) already includes an abstract frontispiece. And it should be noted that the Glazier cross is in a free space, not combined with a carpet page.

Nordenfalk (1968) has suggested a specific Mediterranean source, a manuscript of Tatian's *Diatessaron* with decoration similar to that found in a 16th-century copy now in Florence. The Florence manuscript has a carpet page with a cross on a stepped base strikingly similar to that of the double-armed cross of Durrow (fig. 13). The comparison seems too close to be dismissed as only the result of a parallel development in East and West as Schapiro (1973) proposes. When this particular form of cross first occurred, when it was first combined with a carpet page, whether it first occurred in the context of a Tatian text, and if so whether it was transmitted to the Durrow artist in a Tatian or through some other text, are still questions open to debate (cf. Schapiro, Nordenfalk, 1973).

The symbol pages are also puzzling. Discussion has focused on two anomalies. First, the order of equivalence is not the usual one made canonical by St. Jerome in the late 4th century, in that the Eagle precedes St. Mark not St. John, and the Lion St. John not St. Mark. The most likely of the various explanations proposed is that the artist follows the order of equivalence proposed by St. Irenaeus (*c.* 130–200).

Secondly the symbols are neither winged nor haloed and do not carry books as in the majority of known examples. Unfortunately, there is no inscription to interpret them for us but it seems possible that we have here not an identifying symbol as in so many Evangelist portraits, but rather a personification of the Evangelist (cf. Cerne, no. 66). If this is so, then this is a separate tradition of portrayal from the identifying type seen, for example, in the Lindisfarne and Stockholm Gospels (nos. 9, 30).

Nordenfalk has named this type of symbol 'terrestrial'. It is found in the mid 6th century at San Vitale, Ravenna, and in the 7th-century Valerianus Gospels in Munich (Clm. 6224, figs. 17, 18). Similar symbols also occur in a table of equivalences of the Four Rivers of Paradise and the Four Paradisiacal Foodstuffs in the Florence Diatessaron manuscript just mentioned (fig. 14). Nordenfalk has proposed that the Durrow artist adapted a similar composition of the four symbols on one page and that this explains the awkward spacing of the single symbols on their pages, a problem overcome in the later Echternach Gospels (no. 11, ills. 54–56, 59) where the Lion and the Eagle are closer to the Diatessaron Symbols than those in Durrow. On the other hand, if the Durrow artist only knew some such example as the Valerianus Gospels (figs. 17, 18) and decided to place the terrestrial symbols in a full-page frame he would have had the same problem to overcome.

In form the symbols are strikingly similar to animals found on a series of Pictish carved stones (fig. 8), particularly in the way the outline of the legs of the Lion and the Calf become spirals. All the symbols are treated as flat silhouettes which are then filled with pattern like a piece of enamel work. The effect is heraldic in its two-dimensional outline.

The four symbols on f. 2 are different in form—they are all frontal views, the Man perhaps three-quarter length, the others full-length (*not* busts). The Calf and the Lion in particular are unusual and suggest an ultimate foreshortened frontal model which would therefore be of considerable antiquity. The Eagle which is of the Imperial type, resembles that on f. 84ᵛ which may in fact have copied it or its model in preference to the profile type found in the Echternach and Cambridge Gospels (nos. 11, 12). Werner connects the page with Coptic examples showing zooanthropomorphic symbols (combining human bodies with animal heads) arranged round a cross or Majesty figure, though none of the Durrow figures are zooanthropomorphic. The idea of Evangelist symbols surrounding a Cross is found in various earlier and later examples, e.g. Mausoleum of Galla Placidia, 4th century, Orosius in Laon, 8th century, Essen Gospels, 8th century (cf. also nos. 21, 26, 52, 53, 70). Nordenfalk (1973, p. 536) suggests the four-symbols page derives from a frontispiece to a Juvencus, *Historia Evangelica*, a versified Life of Christ composed in the time of Constantine, of which, however, no example with such a Cross is known.

The initials in Durrow take up the two principles already seen in the Cathach (no. 4) and the Durham Gospel Book (no. 5), the fragmentation of the letter, and the diminution. The smaller Preface initials in particular find close parallels. The larger Gospel initials develop the monograms of 'In' for St. Mark and St. John and the 'Xp' for St. Matthew which are followed in most Insular Gospels (cf. Kendrick, *Anglo-Saxon*, figure on p. 96 tracing the development of the 'Xp' initials to the later Gospels).

Whatever its sources and wherever it was made Durrow shows many signs of being at an experimental stage and whether or not it was the first Gospel Book to incorporate the carpet page and the symbol pages or is only the first surviving example, many of the lines of development of the later Insular Gospels can be traced back to it.

PROVENANCE: On f. 247ᵛ an inscription written by the scribe of the manuscript asks for prayers for the scribe Columba. It has been altered and rewritten. Perhaps the volume was copied from an exemplar written by St. Columba (d. 597), or perhaps this is merely a pious forgery. An inscription was copied in 1677 from the *cumdach* which was presented by King Flan (d. 916) but which disappeared after 1688. It included a dedication to St. Columba. In the late 11th to 12th century the Gospel Book was presumably at Durrow, a Columban foundation, when a document concerning the monastery was entered on the last leaf (f. 248ᵛ). Henry Jones, scoutmaster of Cromwell's army, vice-chancellor of Dublin University, Bishop of Meath, acquired it in 1661 and gave it to Trinity College.

LITERATURE: Westwood, *Palaeographia*, no. 19; Westwood, *Facsimiles*, 20 ff., pls. IV–VII; Gilbert, *Facsimiles*, viii f., pls. V–VI; T. K. Abbott, *Catalogue of the manuscripts in the library of Trinity College, Dublin*, 1900, 7; Zimmermann, *Vorkarolingische Miniaturen*, 22, 25–8, 32–3, 35, 92–6, 125, 231–4, pls. 160–5; K. Pfister, *Irische Buchmalerei*, 1927, pls. 20–3; R. I. Best, 'An early monastic grant in the Book of Durrow', *Ériu*, 10, 1926–8, 135–42, pl.; W. R. Hovey, 'Sources of the Irish illuminative art', *Art Studies*, 6, 1928, 105–20, figs. 12, 13, 19; Saunders, *English illumination*, 9, 11; Kenney, *Sources*, no. 455; A. W. Clapham, 'Notes on the origins of Hiberno-Saxon Art', *Antiquity*, 8, 1934, 43–57, fig. 16; Kendrick, *Anglo-Saxon*, 94 ff., pls. XXXVII–XXXVIII. 1; Micheli, *L'enluminure*, 8, 11–12, 14–16, 44, 64, pls. 2, 3, 23, 45, 97; Åberg, *Occident, passim*, figs. 10, 67–8, 73, 75, 76.3, 83; Masai, *Origines*, 29 ff., 41 ff., 52 ff., 77 ff., 95–110, 126 ff., etc., pls. III, IV, VI. 4, VII; C. Nordenfalk, 'Before the Book of Durrow', *Acta Archaeologica*, 18, 1947, 141–74, figs. 2–4; F. Henry, 'Les débuts de la miniature Irlandaise', *Gazette des Beaux-Arts*, 6ᵉ pér., 37, 1950, 5–34, figs. 5, 17–18, 20, 23; *C.L.A.*, VI, x; Duft, Meyer, *St. Gall*, figs. 86–7; V. H. Elbern, 'Die Dreifaltigkeitsminiatur im Book of Durrow', *Wallraf-Richartz Jahrbuch*, 17, 1955, 7–42, figs. 9, 10; E. Kitzinger, 'The Coffin Reliquary', *The Relics of St. Cuthbert*, ed. C. F. Battiscombe, 1956, 224–6, 229, 233 and n. 1, 234–5, 237–8, 240, 245 n. 1, 296, 300; R. Powell, 'The Book of Kells. The Book of Durrow. Comments on the vellum, the make-up and other aspects', *Scriptorium*, 10, 1956, 3–21; Nordenfalk, *Early Medieval*, 62, 109 ff., 113 f., 118, 126, 2 pls. (pp. 110–11); W. Oakeshott, *Classical Inspiration in Medieval Art*, 1959, 26–7, 123, pls. 44b, 45a; A. A. Luce, G. O. Simmons, P. Meyer, L. Bieler, *Evangeliorum quattuor Codex Durmachensis*, 2 vols., text and complete facsimile, 1960; *Codex Lindisfarnensis*, 57, 90, 118, 255–7, etc., pls. 26 a–d, m–p, 33c, 53 a, b, c; McGurk, *Latin Gospel Books*, no. 86; C. Thomas, 'The Animal Art of the Scottish Iron Age and its origins', *Archaeological Journal*, 118, 1961, 43–4; V. H. Elbern, *Das erste Jahrtausend,*

Tafelband, 1962, pl. 180; F. Henry, 'The Lindisfarne Gospels', *Antiquity*, 37, 1963, 109 n. 27; D. H. Wright in A. Dold, L. Eizenhöfer, *Das Irische Palimpsestsakramentar im Clm. 14429 der Staatsbibliothek München* (Texte und Arbeiten, Heft 53/4), 1964, 34 ff., pls. VIII b–c; D. H. Wright, 'The Italian stimulus on English Art around 700', *Stil und Überlieferung in der Kunst des Abendlandes. Akten des 21. Internat. Kongress für Kunstgeschichte, Bonn, 1964*, I, 1967, 84 ff., pls. 4/5, 5/5; Henry, *Irish Art*, I, 105, 161–3, 166–76, 181, 184, 202, 212, pls. 31, 55, 57, 60–1, E; Rickert, *Painting in Britain*, 11–13, pls. 1, 2, 3d; Werckmeister, *Irisch-northumbrische Buchmalerei*, 3, 8, 11 f., 25, 41–2, 51, 63 f., 65 f., 69, 82–3, 85–7, pls. 6c, 19b, 22a, 40a; H. Bober, 'On the illumination of the Glazier *Codex*', *Homage to a Bookman. Essays on manuscripts, books and printing written for Hans P. Kraus*, 1967, 41, 46 ff., figs. 17, 18; R. L. S. Bruce-Mitford, 'The reception by the Anglo-Saxons of Mediterranean Art following their conversion from Ireland and Rome', *Settimane di studio del Centro italiano di studi sull'alto medioevo, Spoleto*, 14, 1967, 799, 807–8, pls. XII–XIV, XVa, XVI; L. de Paor, 'The Book of Durrow', *Great Books of Ireland (Thomas Davis Lectures)*, 1967, 1–13, pl. 1; C. Nordenfalk, 'An illustrated Diatessaron', *Art Bulletin*, 50, 1968, 119–40, pls. 2, 23 a–d; M. Werner, 'The four Evangelist Symbols page in the Book of Durrow', *Gesta*, 8, 1969, 3–17, figs. 1–5; *C.L.A.*, II, no. 273; Koehler, *Buchmalerei*, 10 f., 18–23, 25 ff., 29, 32–8, 40–1, 46 ff., 53 f., 69, 76, 90, 184–5, 187–91; T. J. Brown, 'Northumbria and the Book of Kells', *Anglo-Saxon England*, 1, 1972, 219–46; M. Schapiro and seminar, 'The miniatures of the Florence Diatessaron', *Art Bulletin*, 55, 1973, 494–531, pls. 15, 33; C. Nordenfalk, 'The Diatessaron miniatures once more', *Art Bulletin*, 55, 1973, 532–46, fig. 6; C. Nordenfalk, 'Corbie and Cassiodorus', *Pantheon*, 32, 1974, 225, fig. 1; Henry, *Kells*, 150–1, 153, 160, 163, 167, 172, 180, 182, 198, 205, 207, 213–14, figs. 24, 33b. Nordenfalk, *Celtic*, 19–47, pls. 2–8, fig. VI.

EXHIBITED: *Treasures from Trinity College, Dublin*, London, Burlington House, 1961, no. 79, pls.

7. Florence, Biblioteca Medicea Laurenziana MS Amiatinus 1

Bible (Vulgate, Codex Amiatinus)
c. 505 × 340 mm., ff. 1030
Before 716 (? late 7th century). Wearmouth or Jarrow

Ills. 23–27, fig. 27

The illumination is concentrated at the beginning of the Old and New Testaments respectively. The Bible is at present foliated in Roman numerals in ink from ff. I–VII and then in arabic in pencil, ff. 8–1030. We shall use this foliation as it stands (see under FOLIATION). The first gathering is now bound out of order, however. On f. Iᵛ is the dedication inscription (partly erased and rewritten, see under PROVENANCE) recording the gift of the Bible by

Ceolfrid, Abbot of Monkwearmouth/Jarrow, to Pope Gregory II. It is framed by a thin plain arch. Originally the portrait of Ezra (now f. V, originally f. 2) came next on the recto opposite. Ezra is seated writing; behind him is a cupboard containing a Bible in nine volumes, the spines labelled with their contents. He wears the tallith and the jewelled breast-plate of the Hebrew priest. Above a couplet identifies him:

Codicibus sacris hostili clade perustis
Esdra deo fervens hoc reparavit opus.

The verso was blank and then came the prologue and list of contents (now. f. IV and IV^v, originally f. 3, 3^v) under a double arch on a purple-stained leaf. The succeeding recto was blank, followed by the opening with a representation of the Tabernacle in the Temple at Jerusalem, (now ff. II^v–III, originally ff. 4^v–5). The next verso was again blank and this was followed by diagrams showing the order of the books of the Old and New Testaments according to SS. Hilary (now f. VII, originally f. 6), Jerome (now f. VI, originally f. 7), and Augustine (f. 8, *sic* arabic, originally f. 8). At the top of the three diagrams are roundels showing God the Father—a bearded bust figure—for St. Hilary; God the Son—a Lamb—for St. Jerome; and God the Holy Spirit—a Dove—for St. Augustine. There is a further diagram on f. VII^v, the verso of the St. Hilary diagram, concerning the books of the Pentateuch. This leaf is stained purple, as is f. IV, and was originally conjoint with it. Folio 8^v is blank and the Preface 'Desiderii mei' follows on f. 9 with the chapter lists on ff. 9^v–10^v and the beginning of Genesis on f. 11.

After the end of Maccabees (f. 796) there is a full-page miniature preceding the New Testament (f. 796^v) of Christ in Majesty. He is flanked by Angels and surrounded by circular bands of which the innermost is ornamented by ribbon patterns. A rectangular frame encloses the miniature touching the circle at the sides. In the four corners are standing haloed figures holding books in their veiled hands. They are presumably Evangelists since they are accompanied by winged whole-length symbols: (reading clockwise from the upper left), the Angel, the Eagle, the Calf and the Lion. The St. John is clean-shaven, the others wear short beards.

The Canon Tables follow after the Preface 'Novum Opus' (f. 797–797^v) on seven pages (ff. 798–801^v). The initial L of St. Matthew (f. 802) is a relatively small letter ornamented with orange and yellow interlace. There are flourishes on the initial P of Ephesians (f. 972^v) but otherwise no other decorated initials.

The *Codex Amiatinus* is one of the few securely dated and placed manuscripts of Insular art. Moreover it is of the greatest interest as showing the artist's desire and ability to assimilate his Mediterranean models. Its great size and the splendour of its script make it one of the most outstandingly impressive of all medieval manuscripts.

We are exceptionally well informed both about the origin of the manuscript and about its model. De Rossi first restored the inscription of the gift of the manuscript by Ceolfrid (f. I) which was subsequently found to be quoted *in ipsissimis verbis* in the anonymous Life of Ceolfrid. Ceolfrid became Abbot of the twin monasteries of Monkwearmouth/Jarrow in 689. The Life records the making of three Bibles (Pandects) under Ceolfrid (detached leaves of one of the other copies survive, B.L. Add. 37777 and the so-called Middleton leaves, Add. 45025, *C.L.A.*, II, nos. 150, 177) and the fact that whilst taking one of these to Rome he died at Langres in Burgundy in 716. Bruce-Mitford (1969, p. 7) argues on various grounds that the *Amiatinus* was not written specially for presentation to the Pope, but was made some years earlier (cf. Corssen, 1888). The donation inscription (f. I^v) is thus a slightly later addition to the manuscript.

Bede in his Lives of the Abbots adds the information that Ceolfrid brought back a Pandect of the Old Translation (this was in 678) from Rome and that this was the only Pandect at the monastery prior to the making of the three new Pandects containing the Vulgate version of St. Jerome (for the Amiatinus text see Fischer, 1962). The Bible of the Old Translation described by Bede is identifiable. In his *Institutiones* Cassiodorus (d. 598) states that he had had made a Pandect of the Old Translation in one volume (*Codex Grandior*) and that he had had inserted in it a plan of the Temple of Solomon at Jerusalem and also diagrams of the different ways in which SS. Hilary, Jerome, and Augustine arrange the various books of the Bible; in other words precisely the pictures in the prefatory gathering of the *Amiatinus*. Bede, moreover, refers elsewhere to a picture of the Temple which he and his readers had seen, as 'Cassiodorus' picture'. The Pandect brought from Rome in 678 by Ceolfrid must have been, therefore, the *Codex Grandior* of Cassiodorus.

Cassiodorus also mentions in the *Institutiones* a second Bible he had had made, which was divided into nine volumes. Since the titles on the spines of the volumes in Ezra's book cupboard correspond in their contents, this must be a representation of the *Novem Codices*, the nine-volume Bible. The inscription above the miniature also suggests that Cassiodorus was intending to compare his work in preparing copies of the Holy Scriptures with that of Ezra as scribe and preserver of the Law. It seems certain, therefore, that the portrait is a copy of a Cassiodoran model, the frontispiece either of the *Codex Grandior* or as Bruce-Mitford argues (*Codex Lindisfarnensis*) of the first of the *Novem Codices*.

Both the Ezra portrait and the Majesty page are painted in a late antique illusionistic style with forms modelled in light and shade and a relatively naturalistic use of colour. The painting does not always follow the drawing (for example, St. Luke's foot, and see also under no. 9, Lindisfarne Gospels). The frame of the Ezra portrait is illusionistic, simulating marble and acting as a window through which the scene is viewed. Nordenfalk points out (1968) that the cast shadow of the ink pot is shown. The way in which the scribal tools are scattered about on the floor is also very typical of late antique art (mosaics, miniatures in the *Notitia Dignitatum*). Gold is used, however, particularly in the background of the Ezra miniature, perhaps suggesting Eastern influence. The portrait resembles closely in iconography a portrait of St. Matthew in a 10th-century Byzantine Gospel (Athens, National Library MS 56, fig. 24), which certainly copies an earlier pre-iconoclastic model. Possibly a similar model was available in Cassiodorus *scriptorium*. The similarity of the book cupboard to that in the St. Lawrence lunette mosaic of the Mausoleum of Galla Placidia, Ravenna, mid 4th century, has also been noted.

There can be no doubt that the Insular artist aimed to reproduce exactly his 6th-century Cassiodoran model. In this his work can be strikingly contrasted with Eadfrith's copy in the Lindisfarne Gospels (no. 9). He was so successful in fact that earlier scholars considered that the first gathering of the *Amiatinus* was actually part of the *Codex Grandior* reused, and more recently Nordhagen (1976) has again suggested that the Ezra is the work of a Byzantine or Italo-Byzantine craftsman. However, it has been shown conclusively by Wright (1961, see also Lowe, 1960) that the first gathering was written by Insular scribes of whom seven altogether worked on the Bible. Nordenfalk (1937) already pointed to misunderstandings by the northern artist of his southern model and more recently Bruce-Mitford has demonstrated that the technique and pigments used in the Ezra and the Majesty pictures are identical. He considers both to be by the same artist using, however, different models in a different style.

The Majesty page is admittedly less classical in style and the figures in particular less articulated. But the colour banding of the sky, for instance, is late antique. Whether the *Codex Grandior* contained a *Majestas* page or not is doubtful. Evidence that such a composition was known in Italy by the 6th century is provided by two 9th-century Tours Bibles which have Majesty frontispieces for the New Testament, for which Koehler has posited an early 5th-century Roman model (cf. W. Koehler, *Die Karolingischen Miniaturen, I. Die Schule von Tours*, 1930, reprinted 1963). The *Majestas* composition on the lid of the Coffin of St. Cuthbert (fig. 5) shows similar symbols, however, and it is also possible that the miniature is an Insular pastiche from a variety of models (cf. Kitzinger, 1956).

The diagram pages are important as early examples of teaching schemata, though this aspect of them does not appear to have received detailed attention. Schapiro (1958) remarks that their formal patterns may be an example of the forms that underlie the complex frames of certain pictorial pages of the Book of Kells (no. 52). The name 'Serbandus' ('O KYRIC CEPBANΔOS AΠIΠOIHCEN', f. 86^v) is likely to have been taken over from the exemplar.

PROVENANCE: The inscription on f. I originally read:

> Corpus [Cenobium] ad eximii merito
> venerabile Petri [Salvatoris]
> Quem caput ecclesiae dedicat alta fides
> Ceolfridus Anglorum [Petrus Langobar-
> dorum] extremis de finibus abbas

> *Devoti affectus pignora mitto mei*
> *Meque meos optans tanti inter gaudia patris*
> *In caelis memorem semper habere locum*

This inscription was altered (words in square brackets inserted over erasure) after the manuscript reached the monastery of Monte Amiato in central Italy, perhaps under the abbacy of Peter the Lombard, 9th to 10th century, whose name was inserted over Ceolfrid's. The manuscript came to the Laurenziana after the suppression of the monastery at the instance of Peter Leopold, Duke of Etruria, 1765–90, Emperor, 1790–2.

FOLIATION: There are two ink foliations, one in Arabic which is superseded, one in Roman. They can both be seen on Bruce-Mitford's pl. IX (where, however, the folio is given as f. VII *vice* VI). The Arabic ink foliation appears to be that of the leaves as bound when Bandini described the manuscript. It runs 1, 12, 7, 3–6, 8–11 and then stops, though it reappears later in the volume, e.g. f. 802. There is no f. 2 in this foliation. Various stains and offprints are still visible as a result both of this ordering of the leaves and of the original ordering. The first gathering was rearranged in the mid-19th century (present foliation in Roman), but still not in the original order (see Corrsen *Academy*, 831). For a clear discussion of the problems of the original order of the leaves see White, 1890. The original order as suggested by Bruce-Mitford is followed here.

LITERATURE: A. M. Bandini, *Dissertazione sull'antichissima Bibbia creduta dei tempi di S. Gregorio P.P.*, 1786; *id.*, *Bibliotheca Leopoldina Laurentiana*, I, 1791, 701 ff.; P. Corrsen, 'Die Bibeln des Cassiodorius und der Codex Amiatinus', *Jahrbücher für protestantische Theologie*, 9, 1883, 619–33; G. B. de Rossi, *De Origine, Historia, Indicibus Scrinii et Bibliotecae Sedis Apostolicae commentatio*, (Biblioteca Apostolica Vaticana, Codices Palatini, I) 1886, LXXV ff.; J. Wordsworth (Bishop of Salisbury), *The Academy*, no. 771, 12 Feb. 1887, 111–13, and no. 773, 26 Feb. 1887, 149–50; F. J. A. Hort, *ib.*, no. 773, 26 Feb. 1887, 148–9, and no. 788, 11 June 1887, 414–15, and no. 872, 19 Jan. 1889, 41–3; G. F. Browne, *ib.*, no. 782, 30 April 1887, 309–10, and no. 835, 5 May 1888, 307–8; P. Corrsen, *ib.*, no. 831, 7 April 1888, 239–41, and no. 838, 26 May 1888, 361; G. B. de Rossi, *La Bibbia offerta da Ceolfrido Abbate al Sepolchro di S. Pietro. Al Sommo Pontefice Leone XIII omaggio giubilare della Biblioteca Vaticana*, 1888, 1–22, pl.; H. J. White, 'The *Codex Amiatinus* and its birthplace', *Studia Biblica et Ecclesiastica*, 2, 1890, 273–308; *Pal. Soc.* II, pls. 65–6; G. Biagi, *Reproductions from illuminated manuscripts. Fifty plates from manuscripts in the R. Medicean Laurentian Library*, 1914, pls. IV–VII; Zimmermann, *Vorkarolingische Miniaturen*, 31–2, 38, 95, 111–13, 127, 131–2, 260–2, fig. 24, pls. 222*, 222**; H. Quentin, *Mémoire sur l'établissement du texte de la Vulgate. Ière partie. Octateuque* (Coll. Bibl. Lat. VI), 1922, 438–52, figs. 74–80; E. G. Millar, *The Lindisfarne Gospels*, 1923, 25 f., 35, pl. 37; C. Nordenfalk, 'Vier Kanonestafeln eines spätantiken Evangelienbuches', *Göteborgs Kungl. Vetenskaps- och Vitterhets-Samhälles handlingar. Femte följden*, Ser. A, Bd. 6, Nr. 5, 1937, 8, 15 n. 1, 26, 40–2; Kendrick, *Anglo-Saxon*, 106, 113, 127, pl. XLII; *C.L.A.*, III, no. 299; Micheli, *L'enluminure*, 15, 18, 29, 114; C. Nordenfalk, 'Eastern style elements in the Book of Lindisfarne', *Acta Archaeologica*, 13, 1942, 159–60, fig. 1; P. Courcelle, *Les lettres Grecques en occident de Macrobe à Cassiodore*, 1943, Eng. trans. H. E. Wedeck, *Late Latin writers and their Greek sources*, 1969, 376–82, 394, 401; F. Saxl, 'The Ruthwell Cross', *Journal of the Warburg and Courtauld Institutes*, 6, 1943, 15–19, pls. 5 a, b; Masai, *Origines*, 44 f., 79 ff., 106 ff., 127 ff., etc., pls. I, II; E. A. Lowe, 'The uncial Gospel leaves attached to the Utrecht Psalter', *Art Bulletin*, 34, 1952, 237–8, fig. 4; E. Kitzinger, 'The Coffin Reliquary', *The Relics of St. Cuthbert*, ed. C. F. Battiscombe, 1956, 223, 235, 240, 245, 248 n. 2, 278 n. 1, 295, 297, 301–2, pl. XIII. 1; Nordenfalk, *Early Medieval*, 121, pl. p. 119; M. Schapiro, 'The decoration of the Leningrad manuscript of Bede', *Scriptorium*, 12, 1958, 207; W. Oakeshott, *Classical Inspiration in Medieval Art*, 1959, 34–6, 123, pl. 47a; Lowe, *English Uncial*, 8–15, 18 ff., 23 f., pls. VIII, IX; *Codex Lindisfarnensis*, *passim* and 145–6, 155–6, 187–8, 286–7, pls. 21, 24, 25 l–o, 34, 35 a, b, 38a, 50i; D. H. Wright, 'Some notes on English Uncial', *Traditio*, 17, 1961, 441–56, pls. I–III, V d, e; B. Fischer, 'Codex Amiatinus und Cassiodor', *Biblische Zeitschrift*, NF, 6, 1962, 57–79; O.-K. Werckmeister, 'Three problems of tradition in pre-Carolingian figure style', *Proceedings of the Royal Irish Academy*, 63c, no. 5, 1963, 183, pl. XXXIIb; Rickert, *Painting in Britain*, 10, 15, 17, 217 nn. 30–2, pl. 7b; D. H. Wright, 'The Italian stimulus on English Art around 700', *Stil und Überlieferung in der Kunst des Abendlandes. Akten des 21. Internat. Kongress für Kunstgeschichte, Bonn, 1964*, 1, 1967, 84 ff., pls. 5/1, 6/7; R. L. S. Bruce-Mitford, 'The reception by the Anglo-Saxons of Mediterranean Art following their conversion from Ireland and Rome', *Settimane di studio del Centro italiano di studi sull'alto medioevo, Spoleto*, 14, 1967, 813–17, pls. XVIII–XXIII, fig. 2; Werckmeister, *Irisch-northumbrische Buchmalerei*, 45, 85, pl. 13b.; R. L. S. Bruce-Mitford, 'The art of the *Codex Amiatinus*', *Journal of the Royal Archaeological Association*, 32, 1969, 1–25, pls. A–D, I–XX; C. Nordenfalk, *Codex Caesareus Upsaliensis*, 1971, 105, fig. 52; Koehler, *Buchmalerei*, 13, 71, 187; Henry, *Kells*, 151, 153, 163, 183, 186, 214; P. J. Nordhagen, 'An Italo-Byzantine painter at the scriptorium of Coelfrith', *Studia Romana in honorem P. Krarup*, 1976, 138–45, figs. 1–6. Nordenfalk, *Celtic*, 10, 24, fig. X; K. Weitzmann, *Late Antique and Early Christian Book Illumination*, 1977, 24, 126, fig. XVII, pl. 48.

EXHIBITED: *Mostra storica nazionale della miniatura*, Palazzo di Venezia, Rome, 1954, no. 31, pl. XI.

8. Utrecht, Universiteitsbibliotheek MS 32 (Script. eccl. 484), ff. 94–105
Gospel Book (fragment)

330×255 mm., ff. 12
Late 7th to early 8th century. Wearmouth or Jarrow

Fig. 1

The fragment contains prologues and chapter lists for St. Matthew, St. Matthew I, 1–III, 4 and St. John I, 1–I, 21. On f. 101ᵛ is a frontispiece to the four Gospels inscribed in a circle: *Incip. in nomine dni ni Ihu Xpi evangelia numero IIII sec. mattheum sec. marcum sec. lucan sec. johannem*. The broad outer band of the circle is composed of two rows of concentric interlacing half-circles coloured in pale green, blue, and yellow. There are plain initials in gold for the *incipits* of Matthew and John, 'Liber' (f. 102) and I (f. 105ᵛ).
The uncial script connects the fragment with the scriptorium of Monkwearmouth / Jarrow and in particular the *Codex Amiatinus* (no. 7), by one of whose scribes it was probably written. The decorated frontispiece would appear to copy a late antique model. The Insular artist may have taken the interlacing circles from his model or he may have transformed a more naturalistic frontispiece such as is found in the Livinus Gospels (Ghent, St. Bavo, cf. C. Nordenfalk, *Die spätantiken Kanontafeln*, 1938, 159, figs. 19–22).

PROVENANCE: The fragment was probably bound up with the famous 9th-century Rheims Psalter by Sir Robert Cotton (d. 1631) in whose library it was catalogued as Claudius C. VII. See E. T. Dewald, *The illustrations of the Utrecht Psalter*, 1933. Bequeathed to the Utrecht City Library by William de Ridder in 1716.

LITERATURE: Westwood, *Facsimiles*, 7; *Latin Psalter in the University Library of Utrecht, formerly Cotton Claudius C. VII*, 1874 (complete facsimile); C. Nordenfalk, 'A note on the Stockholm *Codex Aureus*', *Nordisk Tidskrift för Bok- och Biblioteksväsen*, 38, 1951, 151; E. A. Lowe, 'The uncial Gospel leaves attached to the Utrecht Psalter', *Art Bulletin*, 34, 1952, 237–8, figs. 1–3; Lowe, *English Uncial*, 11, 19, pls. XI, XII; D. H. Wright, 'Some notes on English Uncial', *Traditio*, 17, 1961, 441–56, pls. IV, Va; McGurk, *Latin Gospel Books*, no. 81; *C.L.A.*, X, no. 1587; R. L. S. Bruce-Mitford, 'The art of the *Codex Amiatinus*', *Journal of the Archaeological Association*, 32, 1969, 16, pl. VIII. 2; T. J. Brown, *The Stonyhurst Gospel of St. John*, 1969, 7–8.

9. London, British Library Cotton MS Nero D. IV
Gospel Book (Lindisfarne Gospels)
340×240 mm., ff. 258
Late 7th to early 8th century (? c. 698). Lindisfarne
Ills. 28–46, fig. 2

The illumination consists of Canon Tables, Evangelist portraits, carpet pages, and initials. The Canon Tables are on sixteen pages, ff. 10–17ᵛ. The structure of the columns and arches is emphasized by the outlining band of plain colour, orange, blue, yellow or purple, which contains dynamic filling patterns of zoomorphic and plain interlace. The capitals and bases of the columns are stepped.

Each Gospel is prefaced by an Evangelist portrait, a carpet page and an initial page. St. Matthew (f. 25ᵛ), labelled *O Agios Mattheus*, sits writing in a codex on his knee facing to the right. He is bearded and dressed in a *tunica* and *pallium*. Above his halo is his symbol, labelled *Imago hominis*, a half-length, winged, haloed angel blowing a trumpet held in his right hand and holding a book with his veiled left hand. To the right is a curtain from behind which peers a bearded, haloed figure holding a book in veiled hands. A plain thin band encloses the miniature with interlace knots at the four corners.

St. Mark (f. 93ᵛ), labelled *O Agius Marcus*, also sits in three-quarter view, facing to the left and holding a book in his left hand. He is clean shaven and dressed in a *tunica* and *chlamys* (cloak fastened at the neck). He writes at a round-topped lectern. His symbol, the Lion, labelled *Imago leonis*, is shown above, full-length, haloed, winged, and holding a closed book in its paws. From its mouth comes a trumpet similar to that of the angel. The frame is as before.

St. Luke (f. 137ᵛ), labelled *O Agios Lucas*, sits in three-quarter view to the right and writes on a scroll held in his left hand across his lap. He is bearded and wears *tunica* and *pallium*. His symbol, the Calf labelled *Imago vituli*, is inserted above his halo, full-length, haloed, winged, its head turned frontally, and holding a closed book. The frame is as before. St. John (f. 209ᵛ), labelled *O Agios Johannes*, is the only frontal portrait. With his left hand he holds a scroll across his knees. His right hand is held flat across his chest. His symbol, the Eagle, labelled *Imago aequilae*, emerges as it were three-quarter length from behind his halo. It is haloed and carries a closed book. The frame is as before.

There are five carpet pages, the first with a square-armed cross on an interlace ground with four step-pattern panels, acting as a frontispiece to the manuscript (f. 2ᵛ). Some of the interlace at the top is uncoloured and thus enables the underdrawing to be seen. The other carpet pages are on versos facing the initial pages on rectos: f. 26ᵛ, cross filled with zoomorphic ornament on a field of zoomorphic ornament; f. 94ᵛ, cross with interlace, step and fret patterns, pelta and trumpet spirals, and zoomorphic ornament; f. 138ᵛ, a form of cross moline with patterns; f. 210ᵛ, interlace panel cross with a field of bird interlace and panels of key pattern. It is possible that one other carpet page would have closed the book, balancing that on f. 2ᵛ, but there is no evidence that a page is missing.

The great initial pages are 'Lib', St. Matthew, (f. 27); 'Xpi', St. Matthew (f. 29); 'Ini', St. Mark (f. 95); 'Quo', St. Luke (f. 139); 'Inp', St. John (f. 211). The text continues on each page in black continuation lettering with colour filling and ornament, and with striking filling patterns of red dots. One capital C (f. 211) ends in a profile human head. There are

more or less regular framing panels on three or four sides of the pages. The initial to Jerome's preface *Novum opus* is also large with continuation lettering and dot patterns (f. 3), and there are smaller decorated initials for the other prefaces and lists of chapters, lists of festivals and for certain text passages: f. 5ᵛ, *Plures*; f. 8, *Eusebius*; f. 18ᵛ, *Mattheus*; f. 19, *Generationum*; f. 24, *Pridu*; f. 90, *Marcus*; f. 91, *Esaiae*; f. 93, *Sabbato*; f. 95ᵛ, *Fuit*, f. 130, *Secundum*; f. 131, *Lucas*; f. 131ᵛ, *Praefatione*; f. 136ᵛ, *Judas*; f. 137, *Haec*; f. 139ᵛ, *Fuit in diebus*; f. 203ᵛ, *Johannes*; f. 204, *In principio*; f. 208, *Dicit*, and 'In'; f. 211ᵛ, *Fuit*. There are also slightly enlarged initials at certain Gospel passages (ff. 34 recto and verso, 80ᵛ, 88, 89, 148, 179, 185ᵛ, 193ᵛ, 255ᵛ, see *Codex Lindisfarnensis*, 119–20). Small initials with orange dots mark the Ammonian sections and *capitula*. On f. 137 the Calf of St. Luke has been traced through from the verso (cf. the Macregol Gospels, no. 54). On a few pages the decoration is incomplete, letters being uncoloured or their outline not being inked in (ff. 2ᵛ, 27, 29, 131ᵛ, 139).

The Book of Lindisfarne and the Book of Kells (no. 52) are the two summits of Insular artistic achievement in book illumination. All problems concerned with the Lindisfarne Gospels are treated in the magisterial commentary volume (1960) to the full facsimile (1956), probably the most comprehensive, detailed, and scholarly treatment so far accorded to a medieval manuscript.

The 10th-century colophon (see under PROVENANCE) is generally accepted as reliable, based, it is presumed, on an original inscription, either on a leaf now lost or on the original metal binding. It has been pointed out that a forger would have attributed the writing to St. Cuthbert, not the relatively obscure Eadfrith. The Gospel Book must therefore have been made at Lindisfarne though, as we shall see, the Matthew portrait suggests a knowledge of a Cassiodoran exemplar also used in the *Codex Amiatinus* (no. 7), so presumably housed at Monkwearmouth/Jarrow. The dates must lie between the death of St. Cuthbert in 687 and the death of Eadfrith in 721. T. J. Brown and R. L. S. Bruce-Mitford have argued convincingly that Eadfrith not only wrote (a separate scribe, 'the rubricator', executed certain of the headings), but also illuminated the Gospels. They argue for an early date for the manuscript close to the Translation of St. Cuthbert's relics in 698. Aethelwald, who succeeded Eadfrith as Bishop, became successively Prior and Abbot of Melrose, sometime between 699 and 705. Bilfrith appears to have made his contribution to the binding later in the 8th century. Henry (1963) favours a later date and argues that Eadfrith could still have worked on the manuscript after becoming Bishop in 698. The Gospel text belongs, like that of the Gospels in the *Codex Amiatinus* (no. 7), to the so-called 'Italo-Northumbrian' family. The Gospel Book also contains what has been called a 'quasi-capitulary' preceding each Gospel, that is a list of rubrics for liturgical feasts; and these include the feast of St. Januarius of Naples. The Gospel text may depend, therefore, either on the Gospel volume, volume 7 of the Cassiodoran Vulgate Bible in nine volumes, the *Novem Codices* (cf. no. 7), or, as Brown argues is more likely, on a separate Neapolitan Gospel Book of the 6th century, which contained the lists of liturgical feasts.

The decorative programme of the Gospel Book shows a development of the pattern set by the Book of Durrow (no. 6). New models have become available, however, particularly for the Canon Tables and Evangelist portraits, and these are incorporated into the programme. The Canon Tables are arranged on sixteen pages with the openings matching (except ff. 13ᵛ–14), and the span of the arch being the same whether there are three or four columns. They correspond to what Nordenfalk (1938) has called 'the first larger Latin series' (as opposed to the 'shorter Latin series' arranged on twelve pages), and are the earliest complete and one of the best witnesses to the series. It was probably a 6th–century creation, and was certainly in use then, since McGurk (1955) has shown that the same arrangement occurs in the Canons of the Diatessaron of Victor of Capua of before 546 (*Codex Fuldensis*). The design of larger over smaller arches (Nordenfalk's 'm n' form) can be compared to that of the Canons in the fragment of a 6th-century Latin Gospel Book in the Vatican (Vat. Lat. 3806, fig. 15), and of the Canons in the Livinus Gospel Book (Ghent, St. Bavo) of *c.* 800, in which the illusionistic style suggests a close copy of an earlier model. The design of the arches, contrasting with the grid frames of Durrow (no. 6) and Echternach (no. 11), also resembles that of the Canons on seven pages in the *Codex Amiatinus* (no. 7). Bruce-Mitford argues that Eadfrith's model was not the 6th-century Neapolitan Gospel Book used for the text, which probably had no Canon Tables, since the Canons in the manuscripts which appear to derive their Gospel text from it differ among themselves (cf. no. 20), nor the *Amiatinus*, but volume seven of the *Novem Codices*.

In the Vatican Canon Tables birds perch on the outside of the arch and they are also found in procession on the outer arches of the Syrian Rabbula Gospel Book of 586 (Florence, Biblioteca Laurenziana, Plut. I, 56) and the Etschmiadin Gospel Book of 989. In Lindisfarne the interlacing bird and dog patterns are strictly confined within the arches and columns, thus being denied the free space of classical art. Whether this was so in the model or not is unclear. In the Maeseyck Gospel Book (no. 22) a frieze of birds is placed inside the main arch (ff. A, Dᵛ), and they are in a more naturalistic style than here. They may copy directly a late antique model, therefore; and so the Canon Tables of the presumed 6th-century Cassiodoran model may also have already been filled with similarly contained ornament as Bruce-Mitford argues. The dogs probably derive from antique textiles (Wright, 1967).

The problem of the origin of the carpet pages has been discussed with reference to the Book of Durrow (no. 6). They show a progression in size and splendour from the earlier book, and also in richness of decorative vocabulary. All five pages are complex in design using the Insular principle of ambiguity and alternation of colour, so that field and object interchange, it being possible to read the crosses as laid on or overlaid by the field. There is a similar development in the initial pages (cf. line drawings showing the increased size and complexity of initial and carpet pages in Insular manuscripts, *Codex Lindisfarnensis*, figs. 11, 60, 65). Bruce-Mitford (chaps. VII and VIII) gives a thorough analysis of the ornament used, and a particularly interesting reconstruction of the technical methods of designing the patterns, based on the actual surviving holes of the compass points in the pages (fig. 3). The pigments used have also been analysed by Werner and Roosen-Runge.

Lastly comes the very difficult question of the origin of the Evangelist portraits. The series is not found in any other surviving Insular Gospel Book. In general terms the three-quarter face, writing Evangelists belong to a type exemplified in numerous later Greek Gospel Books (fig. 24), as opposed to the frontal types found in one main Western recension (cf. the Stockholm Gospel Book, no. 30). The presence of the Greek inscriptions is further confirmation of an ultimate Eastern source.

The similarity of the Matthew portrait to the portrait of Ezra at the beginning of the Bible Pandect, the *Codex Amiatinus*, was first noted by G. F. Browne in 1887 (no. 7, ill. 27). Though the costume is altered from *chlamys* to *pallium* Bruce-Mitford has argued (see *contra* Saxl, 1943) that the two portraits are related. He has shown that the Matthew cannot copy the Ezra, since certain mistakes made by the painter of the Ezra miniature are corrected by Eadfrith, in particular that part of the cushion below the thigh of Matthew, incorrectly painted green as if part of Ezra's tunic, and the placing of the broader behind the shorter band of the upright front right leg of the stool. The underdrawing of the Ezra is still faintly visible, however, partly due to paint flaking, and in these particular features agrees with the correct version of the Lindisfarne Matthew. From this Bruce-Mitford concludes that Eadfrith was copying not the *Amiatinus*, but had the common exemplar in front of him, that is the 6th-century Cassiodoran miniature of Ezra.

If this is so, the next question concerns the source for the features not found in the Ezra miniature, that is the figure behind the curtain and the Evangelist symbol. The mysterious third figure seems to belong to the classical iconography of an author inspired by his Muse. This is seen in a Christian context in the only surviving portrait, that of St. Mark, in the 6th-century Greek Gospel Book at Rossano. There are various other later instances of 'accompanied' portraits, including those of SS. Matthew and John in the Livinus Gospel Book (Ghent, St. Bavo) of *c.* 800, who stand beside a seated figure of Christ. Bruce-Mitford considers the third figure here is probably intended to represent Christ, as the gold inscription on the initial page (f. 27) also suggests: *Ihs Xps Mattheus homo*. Baldwin-Brown argued that this identification is also supported by the sentence written on f. 259 by the glossator Aldred: *Matheus ex ore Christi scripsit*. On the other hand, the iconography would appear to be unprecedented if Matthew is seated in the presence of a standing Christ.

As for the immediate source of the inspiring figure, an 11th-century Anglo-Saxon Gospel Book, now in Copenhagen, whose portraits may have been executed at Canterbury (see Temple, *Anglo-Saxon*, no. 47), contains a similar Matthew portrait (fig. 25) with the same figure behind a curtain; but with the differences that the Angel flies down from a cloud, that the Evangelist rests his book on a circular-topped lectern, and that his chair is not the same. Bruce-Mitford has argued that this 11th-century miniature derives not from the Lindisfarne Matthew, but from another but different Cassiodoran model, the Matthew portrait in volume seven, the Gospel volume of Cassiodorus' nine volume Bible, the *Novem Codices*. Moreover, he thinks it preserves features of this model more accurately than does Eadfrith's copy, particularly the symbol, and the relationship between the Evangelist and the accompanying figure to whom the Matthew in Copenhagen looks up. Eadfrith would have copied his Matthew from the Ezra, probably in volume one of the *Novem Codices*, and taken the other features from the Matthew portrait in volume seven.

Bruce-Mitford further argues that the Luke portrait, which unfortunately is the only other portrait surviving in Copenhagen, is also a more accurate copy of the supposed Cassiodoran model, in that the Calf, unlike the Lindisfarne Calf, is half-length, has no book, and is blowing a trumpet (fig. 26), and that the Evangelist writes at a lectern not on his knee. Finally, since Eadfrith used the portraits from volume seven for his Matthew and Luke, though he altered them, it is argued that he probably had the same source for his profile Mark and his frontal John.

It is, of course, possible that Eadfrith used different models for his text and his illustrations, and in fact it seems likely that the Neapolitan Gospel Book which was the exemplar of the text, had no Canon Tables or Evangelist portraits. If some or all of the *Novem Codices* were in Northumbria, volume seven with the Four Gospels may well have been among them and have been illustrated with Greek profile-type Evangelists or a mixture of frontal and profile types (cf. the portraits at San Vitale, Ravenna). Cassiodorus' connections with Ravenna are sufficient explanation as to how he might have had knowledge of Eastern or mixed Evangelist types.

The problem that remains unanswered, however, is why Eadfrith should have used the Cassiodoran Ezra miniature as model for one of his portraits, the Matthew, and volume seven for the additional features and for the other three portraits. If volume seven was available and had a Matthew portrait as is assumed, why copy the Ezra at all? Two other possibilities will have to be canvassed. One is that the Matthew portrait of the *Novem Codices* was more or less identical in its Greek profile type Evangelist figure to the Ezra figure (cf. Saxl, 1943). After all the figure of Ezra is quite likely originally to have been

adapted from an Evangelist portrait in Cassiodorus' scriptorium. The other is that Eadfrith did not have a full set of writing portraits available at all, or at least not all together in one place. If volume seven was not available or did not include any portraits, he might himself have had to create a set from diverse models, not necessarily all book paintings (cf. Wright, 1967). The silver portable altar of St. Cuthbert had a seated figure of St. Peter on it, for example, which is the kind of object he might have used. In either case the inspiring figure might have come from some source, Cassiodoran or otherwise, where its meaning was different, and would only have been reinterpreted as the Christ in Northumbria. For example, a Greek 11th-century Gospel Book in the Morgan Library (M. 748) has portraits of Matthew and John seated and accompanied by standing figures without haloes, who are probably intended as secretaries.

Of the other three portraits only the John is frontal. The emphasis on St. John's Gospel in Northumbria has been noted in various contexts, and the gesture of the hand is identical to that of the John alone of the twelve Apostles on the Coffin of St. Cuthbert. Here again it is possible that the figure is a creation of Eadfrith's own by analogy with a frontal Majesty type figure as seen in the *Codex Amiatinus* (cf. Wright, 1967).

Bruce-Mitford has also argued that the Evangelist symbols were probably taken from volume seven of the *Novem Codices*. The trumpet, however, is an otherwise unknown attribute of an Evangelist symbol at this date or earlier, and Wright (1967) has made a striking comparison between the trumpeting Angel and the profile trumpeting Angels found in Apocalypse illustrations where, of course, the trumpets are required by the text. Since we know from Bede that Benedict Biscop introduced a cycle of Apocalypse pictures to his twin monasteries (cf. the Valenciennes Apocalypse, no. 64, ill. 306), this strongly suggests that Eadfrith went to a different source for his Matthew symbol.

The other symbols are equally unusual at this date or before, in that they are full-length, winged, and hold books (Kitzinger, 1956). The two main early Christian types are either half-length, as if emerging from the clouds, with wings, books, and haloes (e.g. Mausoleum of Galla Placidia, Ravenna, mid 4th century) or, much less commonly, full-length terrestrial animals without wings, books, or haloes (cf. Durrow, no. 6). The winged full-length Lindisfarne symbols, on the other hand, are very similar to those surrounding the standing Majestas Christ on the coffin of St. Cuthbert made for the translation in 698 (fig. 5), and those on the Majesty page of the *Codex Amiatinus* (no. 7), which, however, have no books. These full-length, winged symbols may nevertheless go back to early Christian times, since, significantly, they occur in the same Carolingian Apocalypse manuscripts, presumably copying faithfully the earlier models in this respect. Alternatively, they may be a fusion by Insular artists of the terrestrial type seen in Durrow and the winged half-length type. The turned head of the Calf suggests a flattening of a classical spatial pose and perhaps supports the former alternative. In either case, contrary to Bruce-Mitford, it seems more likely that these symbols as well as the Angel are additions by Eadfrith to portraits which had none. The trumpeting Lion in particular is a medieval rather than a late antique conception, perhaps created by Eadfrith by analogy with the Angel and bearing in mind either the Sedulius verses: *Marcus ut alta fremit*, or a similar titulus to that found on the Tours school Majesty pages: *Rex micat aethereus condigne sive prophetae | Hic, evangelicae quattuor atque tubae* (see W. Koehler, *Die Karolingischen Miniaturen, I. Die Schule von Tours*, I, 2, 1933, reprinted 1963, 132).

As for the Copenhagen Gospel Book, it seems unlikely that it is a direct copy of a late antique model. The position of St. Luke writing on his knee is more likely to be preserved by Eadfrith from an early model (cf. the Barberini Gospel Book, no. 36) and then altered by the later Anglo-Saxon artist by the addition of a lectern which by the 11th century was standard, rather than the other way round. The round-topped lectern seems rare, if not unknown, so at some stage in the transmission it would have had to be copied from St. Mark's lectern. The drapery on the lecterns must in any case be a later addition, as Nordenfalk has shown that this particular feature is a speciality of later Anglo-Saxon art ('The draped lectern. A motif in Anglo-Saxon Evangelist portraits', *Intuition und Kunstwissenschaft. Festschrift für Hanns Swarzenski*, 1973).

There is no reason to think that Lindisfarne was ever in southern England, and Bruce-Mitford therefore suggested that perhaps volume seven of the *Novem Codices* could have been given as a present, say, to Athelstan on one of his visits to the north, and the iconography thus transmitted to the south. The stages of transmission could have been more complicated, however, with more intermediaries. There is no reason why the Lindisfarne set of portraits should not have been copied in the 8th century in one or more Gospel Books now lost. A few examples of the trumpeting symbols occur in later Anglo-Saxon Gospels, and in the Benedictional of St. Ethelwold (B.L. Add. 49598), even the Eagle of St. John blows a trumpet! There is no Gospel Book with a full set of trumpeting symbols, however, and this suggests that the trumpets were only being extended to the other animals in the later period.

In addition to his detailed comments Bruce-Mitford argued in general terms that the homogeneity of the Evangelist portrait pages suggests that Eadfrith copied them unaltered from a Cassiodoran model. The view taken here is on the contrary that Eadfrith was capable himself of altering, combining, and assimilating different models. A final argument against his having copied a late antique set of Evangelist portraits with symbols unaltered is worth mentioning, and that is that there is apparently no confirmation for the existence of such a set in Carolingian or later Continental copies. Admittedly, this is only an argument *ex silentio* and, furthermore, it must be admitted that a more extensive study of the Western tradition of Evangelist portraits might prove the contrary.

Comparison of the Matthew portrait with the Ezra miniature in the *Codex Amiatinus* shows the transformation of a late antique illusionistic space and modelled colour to a medieval system in which forms are related by a system of overlapping ('false connections', Duft, Meyer, *St. Gall*) and colours are non-naturalistic (see Alexander, 1975). There is a tension between the enclosing frames and the objects arranged inside, which form a two-dimensional pattern. Even the inscriptions are part of that pattern and contribute to the dynamic tension. In the Ezra miniature, on the other hand, we look, as it were, into a room through a window and see objects scattered about in an illusionistic space. The same tension between filling patterns and containing frames is found on the Canon Table pages and on the initial and carpet pages.

The problem is whether this transformation of late antique style is achieved as part of a native aesthetic developing its own response to illusionistic Mediterranean art, or with the help of models in which the classical ingredients were already diluted. The answer to this question, of course, partly depends on the answer given as to the nature of Eadfrith's models for his Evangelist portraits.

Nordenfalk (1942) drew attention to stylistic similarities with a group of ivories (the St. Mark ivories) of disputed date and origin but perhaps of 7th- or 8th-century Eastern origin (cf. Weizmann, 1972). Saxl, on the other hand, suggested the influence of Romano-British sculpture of which much was no doubt still visible on Hadrian's wall. In either case the resemblances are with models from the remoter parts of the classical world, in which the transformation of classical style is already beginning, and the Insular artist is seeking out the models most consonant with his own aims.

The Book of Lindisfarne is an exceptionally coherent masterpiece by a scribe/artist from whose hand we have nothing else surviving. There is a tendency to think of it as a single work of art, but we must remember that every great illuminated page, not to speak of the text pages, is a fresh solution to a different problem. In this sense it is not one masterpiece, but many.

PROVENANCE: On f. 259 is a colophon written in Anglo-Saxon by Aldred, provost of Chester-le-Street in 970, who also wrote the interlinear Anglo-Saxon gloss (translation taken from *Codex Lindisfarnensis*): 'Eadfrith, Bishop of Lindisfarne Church, originally wrote this book, for God and for St. Cuthbert and—jointly—for all the saints whose relics are in the Island. And Ethilvald, Bishop of the Lindisfarne islanders, impressed it on the outside and covered it as he well knew how to do. And Bilfrith, the anchorite, forged the ornaments which are on it on the outside and adorned it with gold and with gems and with gilded-over silver—pure metal. And Aldred, unworthy and most miserable priest, glossed it in English between the lines with the help of God and St. Cuthbert. . . .' Eadfrith died in 721 and was succeeded by Aethelwald as Bishop from 721 to 740. Another shorter passage with the same four names is on f. 89ᵛ. Symeon of Durham records the same four names in connection with the making of the book and also says that Eadfrith wrote it himself. The Gospels together with the Relics of St. Cuthbert accompanied the community on their wanderings from Lindisfarne during the period of the Danish invasions to their establishment at Chester-le-Street from 883 to 995 and at Durham in 995. Robert Bowyer, early 17th century (possibly from his father). Sir Robert Cotton (1571–1631) whose library passed to the British Museum in 1753.

LITERATURE: Westwood, *Facsimiles*, 33–9, pls. XII–XIII; Westwood, *Palaeographia*, no. 45; *Pal. Soc.*, I, pls. 3–6, 22; *Catalogue of ancient manuscripts in the British Museum*, II. *Latin manuscripts*, 1884, 15–18, pls. 8–11; F. G. Kenyon, *Facsimiles of Biblical manuscripts in the British Museum*, 1900, pl. XI; G. F. Warner, *Illuminated manuscripts in the British Museum*, 1903, pls. I–II; *British Museum. Reproductions from Illuminated Manuscripts. Series III*, 1908, 9, pls. I–II; *Schools of illumination. Reproductions from manuscripts in the British Museum*, I, 1914, 8–9, pls. 1–5; Zimmermann, *Vorkarolingische Miniaturen*, 22–3, 25, 31–2, 34, 112–16, 139, 262–9, pls. 223–44; G. Baldwin-Brown, *The Arts in Early England*, V, 1921, 329 ff., pls. XXXII–XXXIX, XLI; E. G. Millar, *The Lindisfarne Gospels*, 1923, pls. I–XXXVI; K. Pfister, *Irische Buchmalerei*, 1927, pls. 33–4; Saunders, *English Illumination*, 3, 5, 6, 8–10, 120, pls. 1–3; Kenney, *Sources*, no. 490; C. Nordenfalk, *Die spätantiken Kanontafeln*, 1938, 208 ff., 218 n. 2, 283; Kendrick, *Anglo-Saxon*, 34, 95, 103, 105 ff., pls. XXXVIII. 2, 3, 4, XXXIX–XLI, LIX. 1; A. Schardt, *Das Initial*, 1938, 34, pls. pp. 35–7; Micheli, *L'enluminure*, 8–9, 15–18, 28–9, 62, 85, pls. 12, 42; Mynors, *Durham*, 17 (no. 5); C. Nordenfalk, 'Eastern style elements in the Book of Lindisfarne', *Acta Archaeologia*, 13, 1942, 157–69, figs. 2, 3, 5, 7, 11, 13; F. Saxl, 'The Ruthwell Cross', *Journal of the Warburg and Courtauld Institutes*, 6, 1943, 17–9, pls. 6b, 7 b, e; Masai, *Origines*, 49 ff., 52 ff., 71, 97 ff., 126 ff., etc., pls. XI–XVIII; P. McGurk, 'The Canon Tables in the Book of Lindisfarne and in the *Codex Fuldensis* of Victor of Capua', *Journal of Theological Studies*, 6, 1955, 192–8; T. D. Kendrick, T. J. Brown, R. L. S. Bruce-Mitford, H. Roosen-Runge, A. S. C. Ross, E. G. Stanley, A. E. A. Werner, *Evangeliorum Quattuor Codex Lindisfarnensis*, 2 vols., full facsimile, 1956, and commentary, 1960; E. Kitzinger, 'The Coffin Reliquary', *The Relics of St. Cuthbert*, ed. C. F. Battiscombe, 1956, 224–6, 233–5, 238–9, 240–1, 248 n. 2, 264, 281–2, 296–8, 300–2, pl. XII; Ker, *Catalogue*, 215–16 (no. 165); Nordenfalk, *Early Medieval*, 109 f., 121–2, 126, pls. pp. 116–17; W. Oakeshott, *Classical Inspiration in Medieval Art*, 1959, 31, 35–6, 123, pl. 48; *Codex Durmachensis*, *passim*, figs. 4, 5, 15, 26, 31, 61, 75, 97–8, 109–10, 139; McGurk, *Latin Gospel Books*, no. 22; F. Henry, 'The Lindisfarne Gospels', *Antiquity*, 37, 1963, 100–10; Henry, *Irish Art*, I, 106, 162, 171, 173–4, 176, 190–7, 214, 216, 218, 220–4, pls. 102, 104, figs. 32, 34; Rickert, *Painting in Britain*, 10, 13–16, 24, pls. 4, 5, 6a, 7a; D. H.

Wright, 'The Italian stimulus on English Art around 700', *Stil und Überlieferung in der Kunst des Abendlandes. Akten des 21. Internat. Kongress für Kunstgeschichte, Bonn, 1964*, I, 1967, 84 ff., pls. 4/1, 4, 5/4, 6, 6/2, 4, 5, 8; R. L. S. Bruce-Mitford, 'The reception by the Anglo-Saxons of Mediterranean Art following their conversion from Ireland and Rome', *Settimane di studio del Centro italiano di studi sull'alto medioevo, Spoleto*, 14, 1967, 799, 816–18, pls. XVa, XXIV–XXVIII; R. L. S. Bruce-Mitford, 'The Lindisfarne Gospels', *Great Books of Ireland* (*Thomas Davis lectures*), 1967, 26–37, pl. 2; Werckmeister, *Irisch-northumbrische Buchmalerei*, 12, 32, 51, 85 f., 106 f., pls. 11, 40b; R. L. S. Bruce-Mitford, 'The art of the *Codex Amiatinus*', *Journal of the Archaeological Association*, 32, 1969, 1–25, pls. XV, XVII, XVIII, fig. 3; *C.L.A.*, II, no. 187; Koehler, *Buchmalerei*, 5, 11, 13–14, 16–19, 21–3, 28 ff., 32–9, 41–5, 50, 56, 60 ff., 66–9, 71, 73, 76, 84, 86–7, 99, 103–4, 123, 185–91; T. J. Brown, 'Northumbria and the Book of Kells', *Anglo-Saxon England*, I, 1972, 219–46, pls. IIIb, VI a, b; K. Weitzmann, 'The ivories of the so-called Grado Chair', *Dumbarton Oaks Papers*, 26, 1972, 50–1, 77–8, figs. 50–2; Henry, *Kells*, 151–3, 155, 160, 180, 182–3, 187, 204–5, 207–8, 213, 214 n., 215, 226, figs. 4, 13; J. J. G. Alexander, 'Some aesthetic principles in the use of colour in Anglo-Saxon art', *Anglo-Saxon England*, 4, 1975, 145–7; W. Horn, E. Born, 'On the selective use of sacred numbers', *Viator*, 6, 1975, 82–3, figs. 44–50; Nordenfalk, *Celtic*, 10, 16, 24, 26, 60–73, fig. VI, pls. 15–22.

EXHIBITED: *Treasures from Trinity College, Dublin*, London, Burlington House, 1961, no. 84, pl.

10. Durham, Cathedral Library MS A. II. 17, ff. 2–102 and Cambridge, Magdalene College Pepysian MS 2981 (19)
Gospel Book
344×265 mm., ff. 108
Late 7th or early 8th century. Northumbria (? Lindisfarne)

Ills. 47, 202

Only the major group of initials to St. John's Gospel survives, *In principio* (f. 2). The initials are outlined in black with a green inner band which encloses a complicated interlace of lacertine animals reserved white on a black ground with some touches of rose. The terminals are of interlace, trumpet, and spiral patterns in black and yellow. The spirals are extremely fine.
The remaining three Gospels are now bound after St. John's Gospel. The prefatory matter is lost and all three Gospels begin incomplete. The end of St. Matthew is framed (f. 38₃) by a broad panel with projecting squares at the centre of each side in a cross shape cf. nos. 21, 52, 54). The frame is filled with dotted interlace. On the verso, preceding the chapters to St. Mark, is a full-page miniature of the

Crucifixion (f. 38₃ᵛ). The Christ is bearded and swathed in a long robe (*colobium*). To left and right below the cross are Longinus and Stephaton, the former piercing Christ's side with the lance, the latter holding the sponge to His lips. Above the cross on either side are six-winged Seraphim.

There are inscriptions above, below, to the sides, and inside the picture. Above the cross is Pilate's *titulus*: *Hic est Jesus Rex Judeorum*, and below this on either side A and ω and *initium et finis*. On either side of the Angels is: *utrumque sibi*, and over the left figure is: *Longinus*. In the upper margin is: *Scito quis et qualis est qui talia cujus titulus cui / nulla est inventa passus pro nobis propter hoc culpa* (copying and falsifying an earlier inscription, see Mynors). On the right side is: *Auctorem mortis deiiciens vitam nostram restituens si tamen compatiamur*. On the left side (badly faded) is: *Surrexit a mortuis* (pattern) [*sedet ad* (?)] *dexteram* (pattern) *patris*. In the lower margin is: *ut nos cum resuscitatos simul et regnare* [*faciat* (?)].

The page is very damaged and discoloured since it was used as a pastedown (offprint in MS A. II. 22, cf. Verey, 1969). The colours used are mauve, yellow, purple, orange, green, and blue-green. The cross is outlined with green and filled with orange. The outer frame is also green.

There then follow the list of chapters to St. Mark with initials 'de' (Iohanne Baptista, f. 38₄) and a glossary of Hebrew names with the Preface to Mark with initials *Abba* and *Marcus* (f. 39). These have beast heads, interlace, orange dot and other ornament, and there are continuation capitals with colour fillings. There are other initials or groups of initials emphasizing the following passages: Matthew XXVI, 1, *Et factum est* (f. 38ₓᵛ); Matthew XXVI, 31, '*Tunc*' (f. 38₂ᵛ); Mark XIV, 27, *Et ait* (f. 66); Mark XVI, 2, *Et valde* (f. 69); Luke I, 26, *In mense* (f. 70ₓᵛ); Luke I, 68, *Benedictus* (f. 72); Luke II, 1, *Factum est* (f. 72ᵛ); Luke II, 21, *Et postquam* (f. 73ᵛ); Luke XXII, 1, *Adpropinquabat* (f. 102ᵛ); John I, 6, *Fuit homo* (f. 2ᵛ); John II, 1, *Et die tertia* (f. 4ᵛ).

Pages missing suggest there were Evangelist portraits or carpet pages and large initial pages at the beginning, as well as a miniature at the end of each Gospel. For the concentration of decoration at the end rather than the beginning of a text see nos. 1 and 5. The Crucifixion is represented in the Syrian Rabbula Gospel Book of 586 (Florence, Biblioteca Laurenziana, Plut. I. 56) where Christ also wears the long robe usual in eastern iconography. In Insular books the Crucifixion is represented in the St. Gall Gospel Book (no. 44) and the Southampton Psalter (no. 74), and a space is left for it in the Book of Kells (no. 52). T. J. Brown and R. L. S. Bruce-Mitford (*Codex Lindisfarnensis*, 1960), argue that the scribe of the manuscript was also the artist and that he also wrote and decorated the Echternach Gospel Book (no. 11). They call him the 'Durham / Echternach calligrapher'. Brown considers he is likely to have been the master of Eadfrith, scribe and artist of the Lindisfarne Gospels (no. 9), but nevertheless suggests a slightly later date than Lindisfarne for the present manuscript. Verey (1969) has shown that the text is

a good Vulgate text belonging to the mixed Italian tradition and that Lowe is incorrect in describing it as Irish. He has also shown that corrections in this manuscript and in the Book of Lindisfarne (no. 9) are entered by the same hand (see Brown, 1972). Though the Crucifixion miniature is so damaged that its original style and quality are not easy to judge, it seems to lack the taut dynamism of the Echternach Gospel Book's symbol pages. It is difficult to accept, therefore, that both are by the same artist, a conclusion also rejected by Henry (1963). Nor do the initials seem particularly close in colour or decorative vocabulary to those in the Echternach Gospel Book. The interlaced lacertine animals can be compared to those in the Lindisfarne Gospels, however, and support the attribution of the present Gospel Book to the Lindisfarne scriptorium made on paleographical and textual grounds.

PROVENANCE: At Chester-le-Street with the community of St. Cuthbert, 10th century. Bound up with a fragment of the Gospel of St. Luke (ff. 103–11) written in the same centre as produced the *Codex Amiatinus* (no. 7), that is Wearmouth/Jarrow, already in the 10th century as shown by entries with the names of Boge the Priest and Aldred the Bishop (bishop of Chester-le-Street, 944–68), on ff. 80, 80*ᵛ, and 106. Durham Cathedral letter mark 'C' and 'de le Spendement', written by Thomas Swalwell (d. 1539), f. 2. The detached leaf was given to Samuel Pepys by the Dean and Chapter in 1700.

LITERATURE: Westwood, *Facsimiles*, 48–9; *New Pal. Soc.*, I, pl. 30; Zimmermann, *Vorkarolingische Miniaturen*, 117, 124–5, 259–60, pls. 221, 222 a, c; M. R. James, *Bibliotheca Pepysiana. A descriptive catalogue of the library of Samuel Pepys. III, Medieval manuscripts*, 1923, 120; E. G. Millar, *The Lindisfarne Gospels*, 1923, 5, 10–11, 19; Micheli, *L'enluminure*, 11, 21–2, pl. 48; Mynors, *Durham*, 15–17, colour frontispiece, pls. 2, 3; Masai, *Origines*, 106, pl. X; C. Nordenfalk, 'Before the Book of Durrow', *Acta Archaeologica*, 18, 1947, 156, fig. 16; Ker, *Catalogue*, 144 (no. 105); *Codex Durmachensis*, figs. 72, 96; *Codex Lindisfarnensis*, 89 ff., 100–6, 245–9, etc., pls. 2, 4, 6, 8, 10, 11, 50 a, b, d, e, f, h; McGurk, *Latin Gospel Books*, no. 13; O.-K. Werckmeister, 'Three problems of tradition in pre-Carolingian figure style', *Proceedings Royal Irish Academy*, 63c no. 5, 1963, 184–9, pl. XXXIII; F. Henry, 'The Lindisfarne Gospels', *Antiquity*, 37, 1963, 100–10; Rickert, *Painting in Britain*, 16, 21; Henry, *Irish Art*, I, 161, 163, 170, 174, 192–3, pls. 62, 99; Werckmeister, *Irisch-northumbrische Buchmalerei*, 42 f., 45, 53–97, pls. 14, 16, 18 a, b, 19a, 20, 21b, 23b–c, 24a, 25; C. D. Verey, *A collation of the Gospel texts contained in Durham Cathedral MSS. A. II. 10, A. II. 16 and A. II. 17*, unpublished M.A. Thesis, Durham, 1969; *C.L.A.*, II, no. 149; Koehler, *Buchmalerei*, 4, 14, 17–19, 21 f., 23, 36–7, 39–41, 57 ff., 66–8, 72, 74, 76, 185–7, 189; T. J. Brown, 'Northumbria and the Book of Kells', *Anglo-Saxon England*, I, 1972, 219–46, pls. II a, b, IV a, b, Vb, VI c, d, e; Henry, *Kells*, 150, 163, 167, 180, 182, 207, 213, 226, figs. 3, 13c, 18; Nordenfalk, *Celtic*, 24, 56–7, pls. 13, 14.

11. Paris, Bibliothèque Nationale MS lat. 9389
Gospel Book (Echternach Gospels)
335×255 mm., ff. 223
Late 7th or (?) early 8th century.
(?) Northumbria

Ills. 48, 51–56, 59

The illumination consists of Canon Tables, full-page miniatures with the Evangelist symbols, and initials. The Canon Tables begin in the lower right column on f. 2ᵛ and run for twenty-three pages ending on the top half of f. 13ᵛ. They are written in columns with rectangular frames in orange or yellow (cf. Durrow, no. 6). Though simple, the bands are subtly varied and counterbalanced as on the symbol pages.

The major initials to the Gospels, 'Liber' (f. 20, misplaced, see below under FOLIATION), 'Xpi' (f. 19, misplaced), 'Ini' (f. 76), 'Quo' and F (the latter is smaller, both are on f. 116) and 'In' (f. 177) are placed in the left-hand column of the double column layout with the continuation lettering placed on panels of orange dots. The initials are only half or quarter of a page in height. They are decorated with interlace, fret, spiral, and other patterns of great intricacy and minuteness. The predominant colour is yellow. Black, pinkish orange, and orange are also used. There are smaller initials for each Ammonian section in black outlined with orange dots. Those for Matthew XXVIII, 1, V (f. 71), Luke XXIV, 1, 'Un' (f. 170ᵛ), and John XX, 1 'Un' (f. 219) are slightly larger as are also the initials for the lists of chapters, '*Interpretatio nominum*', and Preface to each Gospel. The N for Jerome's letter to Damasus (f. 1) is a six-line initial decorated with interlace and spirals and coloured with yellow. Flaws in the parchment are decorated with orange dots. One on f. 17 is in the shape of a duck.

The symbols are labelled: *Imago hominis* (f. 18ᵛ), *Imago leonis* (f. 75ᵛ), *Imago vituli* (f. 115ᵛ), and *Imago aquile* (f. 176ᵛ). The Man is shown frontally (seated?) with a bar throne behind him. He holds a book up before him with the opening words of the Gospel written on it. The drapery is broken up into paired ovoid shapes which are coloured in bands of purple, orange, and yellow. The figure is set in the centre of a cross whose outer squares are filled with interlace in yellow and pale orange running without interruption into the surrounding narrow rectangular frame. Small colour alternations in yellow and purple mark the centre of the frame at the sides and at top and bottom. The page combines, therefore, symbol and cross-carpet page (see also below FOLIATION). The same is true, though less obviously, of the other symbol pages. The Lion (f. 75ᵛ) is, in heraldic terms which seem quite appropriate, rampant with tongue protruding from open jaws. He is set within and upon an irregular orange cross with four corner squares

in purple. The outer framing orange rectangle merges into the cross at the sides. The animal is painted in yellow and pinkish orange with black dots on his head and muzzle. The Calf (f. 115ᵛ) is smaller, and, though walking to the right, appears static after the vigorous movement of the Lion; it is set within and over another pattern formed of cross shapes in orange, this time more symmetrical in design. The colouring is yellow and pinkish orange, with thigh, shoulder, and neck outlined in abstract loops (cf. Durrow, no. 6). The Eagle (f. 176ᵛ), shown in profile with wings folded, is a textured mosaic of minute coloured dots and lines representing the feathers. The background pattern is adjusted to enclose the Eagle like a template, actually touching tail, head, and chest, while forming, as it were, a perch below it. The same effect of enclosure is found on the Matthew and Mark pages. On the Luke page the figure's movement is as it were arrested by the pattern.

The symbols are linked with those in the Book of Durrow (no. 6) being 'terrestrial' types without books or haloes. They are very similar indeed to the two surviving symbols from the Cambridge Gospel Book (no. 12). If Nordenfalk is correct in his hypothesis that the symbols are to be connected with those found in the Persian Diatessaron manuscript (fig. 14), then they are closer to the supposed archetype than those in Durrow, especially the leaping Lion and the profile Eagle.

The illumination is one of the high points of Insular calligraphic virtuosity applied to the stylization of natural objects. The limited chromatic range with its abrupt contrasts further emphasizes the dynamic vigour of the designs. At the same time there is a tendency to symmetry and balance which makes itself felt on all the pages. Even on the Lion page where the orange cross shapes are least regular, the four regular corner squares seem to be placed deliberately to restore stability, and are emphasized by the use of purple found nowhere else on the page. In this way the aesthetic seems comparable to that of the Book of Lindisfarne (no. 9) where there is a similar tension between dynamic forms which, whether abstract or natural, have their own vigorous life, and the forces of containment and balance that hold them in check. The tension in these pages is tangible, as if at any moment the symbols will explode from their containing frames. At the same time there is the constant Insular ambiguity between object and interval, background and foreground.

The close connection with Durrow especially in the symbol pages has meant that there has been a tendency to attribute the one to the same centre as the other, whether Iona or Northumbria. Nordenfalk (*Early Medieval* and *Celtic*) inclines to consider the Gospel Book an Irish product of the late 7th century (*c.* 690). He suggests that the tonsure of the Matthew symbol, which is so strongly emphasized, is to be connected with the controversy between the Roman and Celtic churches on this subject. He draws attention to the fact that St. Willibrord's teacher, Egbert (d. 729), succeeded in converting the Irish of Iona to accept the Roman tonsure and calendar ('Diatessaron', 134. For Egbert see also W. Levinson, *England and the Continent in the eighth century*, 1946, 52–3). Lowe says of the manuscript: 'written in Northumbria, or possibly in a Continental centre with close Anglo-Saxon connections such as Echternach'. Brown (*Codex Lindisfarnensis*) has argued that the same scribe ('the Durham/Echternach calligrapher') wrote the Durham Gospel Book (no. 10) and that both manuscripts were produced at Lindisfarne, the present one perhaps for presentation to St. Willibrord. He also suggests that scribe and artist are one, and the close connection between script and illumination, for example the script on the Man's book (f. 18ᵛ) and the inscriptions on all the symbol pages, make this plausible (cf. Eadfrith, the scribe/artist of the Lindisfarne Gospels, no. 9). It is less easy, however, to accept that the artist of the Durham Gospel Book is the same as the artist here (cf. no. 10).

If the manuscript was written at Lindisfarne and is contemporary with the Book of Lindisfarne, or possibly even later, the artist must have been consciously faithful to an earlier tradition in his type of Canon Tables, his smaller initials to the Gospels and in his terrestrial symbols. The third possibility, that the manuscript was produced at the newly founded monastery of Echternach seems less likely. A colophon copied presumably from the exemplar (f. 222ᵛ) refers to a revision of the Gospel text in 558 from an exemplar of the priest Eugippius, perhaps identifiable as Abbot of a monastery near Naples.

PROVENANCE: Contents written on f. 1 as in other Echternach manuscripts, 15th century. Brought to Paris with other Echternach manuscripts c. 1802 after the secularization of the monastery at the French Revolution. Perhaps to be connected with the Frisian mission of St. Willibrord (658–739) who founded Echternach in 698. The flyleaf (f. 223) with a cryptogram on the verso: *Codex iste fuit in domo Tomadii d'este . . . 1433* is smaller and different in texture, and would seem to be a single leaf reused in rebinding with no significance for the history of the manuscript. In any event no person of this name is recorded by Cosenza or by D. Fava, *La Biblioteca Estense*, 1925.

FOLIATION: There are a number of pages cancelled in the first three gatherings of the manuscript. The collation is: 1^{10-1} (2 cancelled, no gap in text), 2^{10-2} (3 and 7 cancelled, no gaps in text), 3^{10-3} (1, 5, 6 missing). The leaf missing at the beginning of gathering 3 (between ff. 17–18) might have contained a carpet page or a four-symbol page (cf. the Harburg Gospel Book, no. 24 and the Trier Gospel Book, no. 26); but there is no sign of any offset. The bifolium at the centre of the gathering which is missing contained Matthew II, 8–IV, 4. The two bifolia, ff. 19, 22, and ff. 20, 21, have been placed in the reverse order in rebinding so that the present f. 19 should follow not precede the present f. 20, and the text of f. 22ᵛ (*paraliticos*, IV, 24) is followed by the text of f. 21 (*et curavit eos*, IV, 24), i.e. the correct order is ff. 20, 19, 22, 21.

LITERATURE: Westwood, *Facsimiles*, 58–9, pl. 21; Comte J.-F.-A. de Bastard d'Estang, *Peintures et ornements des manuscrits*, 1832–69, pls. 76–7; L. Delisle, *Le Cabinet des manuscrits de la bibliothèque nationale*, III, 1881, 231, pl. XIX. 8: Zimmermann, *Vorkarolingische Miniaturen*, 22, 31, 36, 95, 105, 122–7, 276–7, pls. 255–8, 260a, 261a; H. Degering, 'Handschriften aus Echternach und Orval in Paris', *Aufsätze Fritz Milkau gewidmet*, 1921, 48–85; K. Pfister, *Irische Buchmalerei*, 1927, pls. 36–7; A. Goldschmidt, *German illumination*, I, 1928, pl. 3; W. R. Hovey, 'Sources of the Irish illuminative art', *Art Studies*, 6, 1928, 118, fig. 29; Saunders, *English Illumination*, 11; Kenney, *Sources*, no. 460; C. Nordenfalk, 'On the age of the earliest Echternach manuscripts', *Acta Archaeologica*, 3, 1932, 57; Kendrick, *Anglo-Saxon*, 139 ff., 149, 163, pl. LV, LIX. 2; C. Nordenfalk, *Die spätantiken Kanontafeln*, 1938, 207 n. 1; Micheli, *L'enluminure*, 21–3, 26 n. 5, 44, 47, 113, pls. 24, 26, 63; Masai, *Origines*, 99, 106 f., 125, etc., pls. VIII, IX. 1–2; *C.L.A.*, V, no. 578; Duft, Meyer, *St. Gall*, figs. 15, 18, 95; Nordenfalk, *Early Medieval*, 113, 124, pls. pp. 112–13; *Codex Durmachensis*, figs. 20, 23, 32, 48, 60, 95, 99; *Codex Lindisfarnensis*, 89 ff., 96–7, 103–4, 158, 187, 246–9, pls. 3, 5, 7, 9, 12–14, 19d, 26 e–h, 33d, 50c; McGurk, *Latin Gospels Books*, no. 59; O.-K. Werckmeister, 'Three problems of tradition in pre-Carolingian figure style', *Proceedings of the Royal Irish Academy*, 63c no. 5, 1963, 175–89, pls. XXVII, XXXI; Rickert, *Painting in Britain*, 17, pl. 8b; Henry, *Irish Art*, I, 140, 172, 175–8, 181, 184, 186, 193, 201, 222, pl. V, fig. 33; Werckmeister, *Irisch-northumbrische Buchmalerei*, 7 ff., 53, 56, 60 f., 64 f., 69, 77, 79 ff., 164, pls. 1, 4, 6a, 12, 21a, 22b, 23a, 24b; R. L. S. Bruce-Mitford, 'The reception by the Anglo-Saxons of Mediterranean Art following their conversion from Ireland and Rome', *Settimane di studio del Centro italiano di studi sull'alto medioevo*, Spoleto, 14, 1967, 799, pl. XXXIV; C. Nordenfalk, 'An illustrated Diatessaron', *Art Bulletin*, 50, 1968, 134–5, pls. 24 a–d; C. Nordenfalk, *Codex Caesareus Upsaliensis*, 1971, 27, 37, 47, 138; Koehler, *Buchmalerei*, 14, 18–24, 32 ff., 35, 36 f., 38–41, 54 ff., 58, 67–8, 76, 185, 187, 189 f.; T. J. Brown, 'Northumbria and the Book of Kells', *Anglo-Saxon England*, I 1972, 219–46; M. Schapiro and seminar, 'The miniatures of the Florence Diatessaron', *Art Bulletin*, 55, 1973, 509, 527–8, fig. 20; C. Nordenfalk, 'The Diatessaron once more', *Art Bulletin*, 55, 1973, 538, 542–3, fig. 4; Henry, *Kells*, 151, 153, 167, 171 n., 180, 226, fig. 25; Nordenfalk, *Celtic*, 10, 20, 24, 48–53, fig. VIII, pls. 9–12.

EXHIBITED: *Kunst des frühen Mittelalters*, Bern, 1949, no. 2, pl. 3; *Ars Sacra. Kunst des frühen Mittelalters*, Munich, 1950, no. 2; *Les Manuscrits à peintures du VIIᵉ au XIIᵉ siècle*, Paris, 1954, no. 23; *Werdendes Abendland an Rhein und Ruhr*, Essen, 1956, no. 228. See also V. H. Elbern, *Das erste Jahrtausend. Tafelband*, 1962, pls. 181–2; *Saint Willibrord*, Echternach, 1958, no. 162, pls. II, XLV; *Karl der Grosse*, 1965, no. 395.

**12. Cambridge, Corpus Christi College
MS 197B, ff. 1–36 (formerly pp. 245–316).
London, British Library Cotton MS Otho C. V**
Gospel Book (fragment)
285×212 mm., 36 ff. in Cambridge and
64 mounted fragments of originally 109 or
110 ff. in London
Late 7th to early 8th century. (?) Northumbria

Ills. 49, 57, 58

The London leaves, which were damaged in the fire
at Ashburnham House in 1731, contain parts of
Matthew and Mark. The illumination remaining
consists of a part of the Lion and the initial 'In' of
St. Mark (ff. 27, 28) They are discoloured, but the
main colours were apparently orange and yellow.
The inscription of the Lion remains in part: *(im)ago
le(o)nis*. There was also originally an *Imago hominis*
before St. Matthew (see Smith). The Cambridge
leaves contain parts of Luke and John with the Eagle
and initial *In principio* (ff. 1, 2). The colours are
orange, yellow and green. The Eagle is enclosed in
a frame with an outer band of orange and an inner
of green with crosses enclosing it like a template
(cf. the Echternach Gospel Book, no. 11). The Ammonian sections are marked with small initials with
blobs of yellow or green and orange dots.
Both symbols are very close to those in the Echternach Gospel Book and the manuscript was presumably made in the same centre (cf. no. 11). The *In
principio* initial page, cut by a former binder at the
top, is similar in design to those in the Book of
Lindisfarne (no. 9) and the Durham Gospel Book
(no. 10). Lowe attributed the book to 'an important
English centre familiar with Irish calligraphy'. He
thought this was probably in Northumbria. He also
suggested that the fragments of Canon Tables in B.L.
Royal 7. C. XII, ff. 2, 3, come from a similar or even
the same Gospel Book. They show an offprint of an
archway (f. 3) for which see under the Book of Kells
(no. 52, see also the reconstruction in *Codex Lindisfarnensis*, fig. 34). They are prefixed to an 11th-
century Aelfric, *Homilies*, which belonged to Cardinal
Wolsey (d. 1530), f. 2.

PROVENANCE: T. Smith (1696) records a tradition
that the Cotton manuscript belonged to St. Augustine, Apostle of the English, though he says there is
no evidence to support it; a note in the Cambridge
fragment connects it too with St. Augustine. Archbishop Tanner suggested that the manuscript might
be the Red Book of Eye, Suffolk, known from
Leland's description. The Cambridge fragments are
now separate but were formerly bound up with texts
written in the 15th and 16th centuries and were
bequeathed to the College by Archbishop Matthew
Parker (d. 1575). The Cotton fragment (Sir Robert
Cotton, d. 1631) came to the British Museum in
1753.

LITERATURE: T. Smith, *Catalogus librorum manu-
scriptorum Bibliotecae Cottonianae*, 1696, 72; J.
Goodwin, *Evangelia Augustini Gregoriana* (*Cambridge
Antiquarian Society*, II, no. xiii), 1847, pls. I–VII;

Westwood, *Facsimiles*, 49–51; *Catalogue of ancient
manuscripts in the British Museum, II. Latin manuscripts*, 1884, 20; M. R. James, *The Ancient
Libraries of Canterbury and Dover*, 1903, lxvii–
lxviii; *id. A descriptive catalogue of the manuscripts
in the library of Corpus Christi College, Cambridge*,
1910, 474–5; Zimmermann, *Vorkarolingische Miniaturen*, 32, 123–4, 277–8, pls. 259, 266; Micheli,
L'enluminure, 21–3, 47, 65, pls. 25, 49; Duft, Meyer,
St. Gall, fig. 25; P. McGurk, 'Two notes on the Book
of Kells', *Scriptorium*, 9, 1955, 105–7; *Codex Durmachensis*, figs. 42, 100; *Codex Lindisfarnensis*, 92,
190–1, pl. 39b, fig. 34; McGurk, *Latin Gospel Books*,
no. 2; Henry, *Irish Art*, I, 162, 174–6, 178, 184,
192, pls. 97, 100, J, fig. 33; Werckmeister, *Irisch-
northumbrische Buchmalerei*, 8, 10, 64 f., 85 n. 382,
pl. 18c, *C.L.A.*, II, no. 125; Koehler, *Buchmalerei*,
20, 36–41, 187, 190; Henry, *Kells*, 180, 226.

EXHIBITED: *Matthew Parker's Legacy*, Corpus
Christi College, Cambridge, 1975, no. 2, pl. 2.

13. Cologne, Dombibliothek Cod. 213
Collectio Canonum
332×230 mm., ff. 143
Early 8th century. Northumbria

Ills. 60, 61

The illumination consists of a whole page frontispiece with initial D and border (f. 1), and other
larger initials on ff. 2ᵛ, 4ᵛ, 10, 11, 16, 19, 23, 27ᵛ,
32, 36ᵛ, 48, 59. The decoration is of interlace, bird
interlace, spiral, and animal and bird-head motifs.
The bird interlace (f. 1) can be compared with that
in the Lindisfarne Gospels (no. 9) and the bird-head
terminals with those in the Salaberga Psalter (no.
14). The initial D (f. 2ᵛ) with a turning bird is a
design often copied later in Insular and also in
Romanesque art (Pächt, 1963).

PROVENANCE: The inscription *Sigbertus scripsit*
(f. 143), presumably the same scribe who wrote his
name in Cologne, Dombibl. 212, shows the manuscript was already at Cologne in the 8th century.

LITERATURE: P. Jaffé, W. Wattenbach, *Ecclesiae
Metropolitanae Coloniensis Codices Manuscripti*, 1874,
95; A. Chroust, *Monumenta Palaeographica*, 1909–17,
pl. 299; Zimmermann, *Vorkarolingische Miniaturen*,
121, 273–5, pls. 252–3, 254 d, e; Micheli, *L'enluminure*,
22, 47, 123, 132, 134, 140, pls. 51, 59–61; Åberg,
Occident, 98, 117, figs. 69, 84. 2–3; V. H. Elbern,
'Die Dreifaltigkeitsminiatur im Book of Durrow',
Wallraf-Richartz Jahrbuch, 17, 1955, 27, fig. 21;
Ker, *Catalogue*, 139 (no. 98*); *C.L.A.*, VIII, no.
1163; *Codex Lindisfarnensis*, 283; O. Pächt, 'The
Pre-Carolingian roots of early Romanesque art',
*Romanesque and Gothic Art. Studies in Western Art,
Acts of the 20th International Congress of the History
of Art*, I, ed. M. Meiss *et al.*, 1963, 73, pl. XXI. 13;
Henry, *Irish Art*, I, 174, pls. 63, 101; Henry, *Kells*,
207, 214, 226, fig. 13.

EXHIBITED: *Werdendes Abendland an Rhein und Ruhr*, Essen, 1956, no. 282. See also V. H. Elbern, *Das erste Jahrtausend. Tafelband*, 1962, pl. 227; *Karl der Grosse*, no. 393, pl. 43.

14. Berlin, Deutsche Staatsbibliothek MS Hamilton 553

Psalter (Salaberga Psalter)
345 × 250 mm., ff. 64
First half of 8th century. Northumbria

Ills. 62–65

The liturgical and three-part divisions of the Psalter are marked by initials, f. 2, Psalm 1; f. 13, Psalm 26; f. 20ᵛ, Psalm 38; f. 27, Psalm 51; f. 27ᵛ, Psalm 52; f. 34, Psalm 68; f. 41, Psalm 80; f. 47, Psalm 97; f. 48, Psalm 101; f. 52ᵛ, Psalm 109. They are decorated with interlace and other patterns and animal and bird forms. On f. 24 an O (Psalm 46) contains a frontal face. There are also initials at Psalm 17, f. 8 (cf. no. 29) and Psalm 32, f. 16. The colours are bright yellow, greyish blue, greyish green, and brick red, and according to E. A. Lowe are similar to those used in the Lindisfarne Gospels (no. 9). Lowe considered the manuscript to have been written in Northumbria. It was badly cropped in binding perhaps *c.* 1685 when a note says it was restored.

PROVENANCE: At the monastery of St. John, Laon, in the Middle Ages (inventory of the treasury, 12th century, f. 26ᵛ), and seen there by Mabillon. Connected in the 17th century with the foundress, Salaberga, who, however, died in 675. 10th Duke of Hamilton (1767–1852), before 1819. Bought by the Berlin Library in 1883.

LITERATURE: J. Mabillon, *De re diplomatica*, 1681, 358A, pl. VIII; Zimmermann, *Vorkarolingische Miniaturen*, 35, 119–20, 272–3, pls. 249–50; *New Pal. Soc.*, II, pls. 33–5; Saunders, *English Illumination*, 4; H. Degering, *Lettering*, 1929 (2nd edn., 1965), pl. 36; Micheli, *L'enluminure*, 48, pls. 57–8; *C.L.A.*, VIII, no. 1048; *Codex Lindisfarnensis*, 283; *Deutsche Staatsbibliothek, Geschichte und Gegenwart, 1661–1961*, ed. H. Kunze *et al.*, I, 1961, 342, pl. 2; H. Boese, *Die lateinischen Handschriften der Sammlung Hamilton zu Berlin*, 1966, 270–1; E. Rothe, *Mediaeval Book Illumination in Europe*, London, 1968 (Berlin, DDR, 1966), 184, 234, colour pl. 4.

EXHIBITED: *Karl der Grosse*, no. 394.

15. Leipzig, Universitätsbibliothek MSS Rep. I, 58ᵃ and Rep. II, 35ᵃ

Gospel Book (fragment)
295 × 218 mm., ff. 1 (I, 58ᵃ)+5 (II, 35ᵃ)
First half of 8th century. (?) Northumbria

Ills. 67, 86

The fragment (II, 35ᵃ) contains Matthew I, 2–VI, 4. The illumination consists of initials 'Xpi' (f. 1ᵛ) decorated with bird heads and orange dots. The single leaf (I, 58ᵃ), now used as a pastedown, has a Canon Table 'm n ' arch with interlace, animal masks as imposts, and panels of animal interlace. Micheli, who first published it, related it to the Northumbrian group. Lowe dates the fragment to the first half of the 8th century: 'written presumably in Northumbria'. Presumably, the single leaf and the fragment come originally from the same Gospel Book.

PROVENANCE: According to the Leipzig catalogues of 1737 and 1752 the fragment (Rep. II, 35ᵃ) was formerly bound up with Rep. II, 35ᵇ which belonged to Niederaltaich, Bavaria.

LITERATURE: Micheli, *L'enluminure*, 47, pl. 11; *C.L.A.*, VIII, no. 1229 and *Supplement*, 1971, 11 (no. **1229).

16. Durham, Cathedral Library MS A. II. 16, ff. 1–23, 34–86, 102, and Cambridge, Magdalene College, Pepysian MS 2981 (18)

Gospel Book (incomplete)
350 × 245 mm., ff. 79
(?) First half of 8th century. Northumbria

Ill. 85

These leaves containing parts of Matthew, all of Mark and parts of Luke, are written in uncial script. Ff. 24–33 and 87–101 (*C.L.A.*, II, no. 148b) are written in Insular majuscule and contain most of the remainder of Matthew and Luke (both begin incomplete and there is no decoration in this part). The text shows affinity with the Echternach and Durham Gospel Books (nos. 10, 11) in Matthew and Mark respectively (Verey, 1969). Folios 103–34 (*C.L.A.*, II, no. 148c) which contain most of St. John's Gospel (this also begins incomplete) have a text related to that in the *Codex Amiatinus* (no. 7) and are written in the late 8th century in Anglo-Saxon majuscule evidently to complete the earlier text of the other three Gospels.
Of the decoration only three initials survive. The I for the beginning of St. Mark (f. 37) runs the whole length of the page with five panels of fine interlace white on black. The terminals are a frontal human head at the top (cf. the Barberini Gospel Book, no. 36) and a biting animal head at the bottom with touches of orange and yellow. There are also smaller initials to the preface to St. Mark, M (f. 34) in black with orange dots, and for the list of chapters, A (f. 34ᵛ) with an animal head. The style has been compared by Koehler to that of the Durham Cassiodorus (no. 17).

PROVENANCE: Documents written early 12th century on f. 60ᵛ and a Papal Bull on f. 101ᵛ concern Durham. Identifiable in the Durham catalogue of 1391 as *Quattuor Evangelia de manu Bedae*. The detached leaf was given to Samuel Pepys by the Dean and Chapter in 1700.

LITERATURE: Westwood, *Facsimiles*, 8–9; *New Pal. Soc.*, I, pls. 54–6; Zimmermann, *Vorkarolingische*

Miniaturen, 24, 306, pl. 327; M. R. James, *Bibliotheca Pepysiana. A descriptive catalogue of the library of Samuel Pepys. III, Medieval manuscripts*, 1929, 119; Mynors, *Durham*, 18–20 (no. 7), pls. 5–7; Micheli, *L'enluminure*, 26, 90, pl. 216; Masai, *Origines*, 106, pl. XL. 1; *Codex Lindisfarnensis*, 91; Lowe, *English Uncial*, 20, pl. XVII; McGurk, *Latin Gospel Books*, no. 10; C. D. Verey, *A collation of the Gospel texts contained in Durham Cathedral MSS. A. II. 10, A. II. 16, A. II. 17*, unpublished M.A. Thesis, Durham, 1969; *C.L.A.*, II, no. 148a; Koehler, *Buchmalerei*, 13, 187 n. 10.

17. Durham, Cathedral Library MS B. II. 30

Cassiodorus, Commentary on the Psalms
420×295 mm., ff. 266
Second quarter of 8th century. Northumbria

Ills. 74, 75

The surviving illumination consists of two full-page miniatures preceding Psalms 51 and 101. The first (f. 81ᵛ) shows David enthroned (*David Rex*) holding a harp in his left hand. He has a green halo and his cloak is dull mauve. His throne consists of two narrow uprights framed in orange and filled with interlace partly coloured orange and green and reserved on black. The uprights have biting beast terminals. There are three cross-bars. Above and inside the throne are patterns of dots in concentric circles.
The frame has broad panels of interlace and animal interlace. The narrow outer framing bands are dull mauve with interlace motifs in orange and green at the corners. Other colours are orange, green, yellow, and black. They are countercharged in the Insular manner, for example green and orange on the beasts in the side panels.
The second miniature (f. 172ᵛ) shows a standing figure with a spear in his left hand held across the body and an orange ring held up in his right hand, which is inscribed *David*. His cloak is dull mauve. He stands on a long scaly snake-like creature with animal heads with open mouths and teeth at each end. The background is patterned with dots in concentric circles (a compass hole in the centre of each). The frame has interlace corner motifs, very broad panels of interlace pattern at top and bottom and at the sides, and fret pattern at the corners. They are reserved on black and framed in orange, mauve, or yellow. Nordenfalk (1977) attributes this miniature with its flattened drapery style to a second artist. He also points out that the border can be compared to that of the first miniature of the Valenciennes Apocalypse (no. 64). He argues, therefore, that the present manuscript was made at Wearmouth/Jarrow. The beginning of the manuscript, which probably included another portrait and an initial, is missing. It was replaced in the 12th century, as was also the last leaf (f. 265). On f. 5ᵛ an initial B, seven lines tall, is decorated with interlace and beast heads in black with orange-dot outline. There are a few other black initials of larger size, some with orange dots.
This is an early example of the marking of the threefold division of the Psalter with miniatures, a prac-

tice taken up by later Anglo-Saxon artists in the 11th century (e.g. in the Athelstan and Cotton Tiberius Psalters, both from Winchester, Temple, *Anglo-Saxon*, nos. 5, 98). The figure on f. 172ᵛ recalls the iconography of Christ trampling on the beasts (Psalm 91) which is also found in several of the later Anglo-Saxon Psalters, as well as on the Ruthwell and Bewcastle crosses (cf. F. Saxl, 'The Ruthwell Cross', *Journal of the Warburg and Courtauld Institutes*, 6, 1943). It is possible that the present miniature is adapted from such a Christ figure rather than a David figure.
Though they are stylized the figures retain a classical feeling in the signs of contraposto poses (especially the standing figure) and in their drapery forms. It seems probable that the models were 6th-century Italian miniatures and that means that the exemplar could quite possibly have come from Cassiodorus' own scriptorium (cf. the *Codex Amiatinus*, no. 7). A Psalter, written at Mondsee before 778, with prefatory standing figures of David and Christ based on earlier models is now Montpellier, Bibliothèque de l'Université, MS 409 (see *Karl der Grosse*, no. 450).

PROVENANCE: In the Durham cathedral catalogues of the late 12th century and of 1391. A 14th-century inscription reads *de manu Bedae* (f. 1ᵛ).

LITERATURE: Westwood, *Facsimiles*, 77–8, pls. 17–18; *Pal. Soc.*, I, pl. 164; Zimmermann, *Vorkarolingische Miniaturen*, 118–20, 271–2, pls. 222b, 247–8; Saunders, *English Illumination*, pl. 22a; Kendrick, *Anglo-Saxon*, 133, 138, pl. LIV; Mynors, *Durham*, 21–2 (no. 9), pls. 8–10; Micheli, *L'enluminure*, 27, 88, pls. 70–1; W. Oakeshott, *Classical Inspiration in Medieval Art*, 1959, 26–7, 123, pl. 46b; *Codex Lindisfarnensis*, 91, 171 n. 2, 286; Lowe, *English Uncial*, 24, pl. XXXVIIIc; H. Steger, *David Rex et Propheta*, 1961, 154–5; Rickert, *Painting in Britain*, 18, pl. 10a; D. H. Wright, *The Vespasian Psalter (Early English manuscripts in facsimile*, XIV), 1967, 72 n. 3; *C.L.A.*, II, no. 152; Koehler, *Buchmalerei*, 13, 22, 68, 87, 188; Henry, *Kells*, 163, 226; Nordenfalk, *Celtic*, 10, 85, 87, pls. 27, 28.

18. Leiden, Universiteitsbibliotheek MS Voss. Lat. F. 4, ff. 4–33

Pliny, Natural History
410×290 mm., ff. 30
First half of 8th century. (?) Northumbria

Ills. 66, 68, 69

The text is a fragment containing parts of Books II to Book VI. The illumination consists of initials to the lists of chapters and openings of books (ff. 9, 9ᵛ, 20, 20ᵛ, 29ᵛ, 30). They show great calligraphic verve and fantasy. They are in black with spirals, animal hind-quarters and, particularly striking, human hands as terminals. Lowe compares an initial in the Durham Cassiodorus (no. 17) to the initial T on f. 20ᵛ. Other leaves bound with the fragment contain Paul the Deacon, 9th century (ff. 1–3) and Peter of Poitiers 12th–13th century (ff. 34–7).

PROVENANCE: *A rendre a Monsieur de la Vergne,* 16th century, f. 4. Bound with other fragments (ff. 1–3) from St. Denis, Paris. *P. 43* (f. 1) in the hand of Paul Petau. Later belonged to Queen Christina of Sweden (d. 1689) and Isaac Vossius (d. 1688).

LITERATURE: É. Chatelain, *Paléographie des classiques latins*, II. 2, 1896, 13, pl. CXXXVIII; Micheli, *L'enluminure*, 67 n.; *C.L.A.*, X, no. 1578; L. D. Reynolds, N. G. Wilson, *Scribes and Scholars*, 1968, 78, 184, pl. XII; K. A. de Meyier, *Codices Vossiani Latini, Pars I. Codices in folio*, 1973, 6–8.

19. Leningrad, Public Library Cod. Q. v. I. 18
Bede, Historia ecclesiastica
270 × 190 mm., ff. 162
c. 746. Wearmouth/Jarrow

Ill. 83, 84

The illumination consists of an initial to each book. The most important are to Books I and II. For the former a B (f. 3ᵛ) has plant forms in the upper and lower bowls and continuation capitals ornamented with bands of pink and orange. The plant scroll has naturalistic features which suggest an ultimately eastern Mediterranean model. For Book II an H (f. 26ᵛ) contains a half-length haloed figure carrying a book in his draped left hand and a cross in his right hand. The initial is painted in unexpectedly bright colours, the halo and the saint's underrobe being pale yellow, his cloak slate-blue and his book pinky-red. The figure retains much of the contraposto of classical art in its turning posture. On the other hand the Insular tradition of schematization is apparent in the drapery and facial features. The figure is thus related in style to the tradition of the Lindisfarne Gospels (no. 9) and the Cuthbert Coffin (fig. 5), though not so extreme as either. The continuation capitals 'IS' are again ornamented with bands, this time of pink and blue. Other smaller initials occur in the text, e.g. on f. 29ᵛ, with animal-head terminals and grid patterns in which the Insular principle of 'articulation of the background interspaces as a contrasting ornament' (Schapiro) is seen. Minor initials in a similar style are found in another Bede, *Historia ecclesiastica*, B.L., Cotton Tiberius A. XIV, probably copied from the present manuscript (*C.L.A.*, Supplement, no. 1703).
A later (late medieval?) hand has written *Augustinus* on the halo of the saint (f. 26ᵛ). However, Chapter I of Book II starts with the year 605 in which Gregory the Great died and is entirely concerned with the Pope. St. Augustine is not mentioned, though the narrative of his mission does continue in Chapter II. It seems much more likely, therefore, that the artist intended the portrait to be St. Gregory as suggested by Meyvaert (1964) who points out that cross and book seem to have been papal attributes and that there is a record of a portrait of Gregory represented with them.
The initial A to Book III (f. 48ᵛ) is over erasure. It is in powder gold outlined in orange and is probably a later addition, as is also the A of Book IV and the S of Book V. On f. 161ᵛ there is a sketch of some interlace and an inscription, both perhaps late 11th to early 12th century.
The inscription *Beda famulus Xpi indignus* once thought to be autograph (f. 161) has been shown to be an addition. Retrospective numbers of years in the margins opposite Bede's chronological recapitulation on f. 159 recto and verso suggest the date 746 (Wright, 1961) which is accepted as probable by Lowe who also considers Wearmouth/Jarrow the likely place of origin.
Though on a modest scale the illumination is important both because it is apparently securely dated and placed at Wearmouth/Jarrow and also because it is one of the earliest examples of the use of the historiated initial (cf. no. 29). Moreover, it is significant that Bede's text, as opposed to a liturgical or biblical manuscript, should receive figure illustration which must have been invented for it, not copied from a Mediterranean model unless, possibly, an illustrated World History provided a direct or indirect prototype for the figure (that such a manuscript was known in Northumbria seems to be indicated by some of the scenes on the Franks Casket, cf. J. Beckwith, *Ivory Carvings in Early Medieval England*, 1972, 14 ff., 117).
Even if the artist took his figure from some earlier source, the way he has chosen to illustrate his text is original and significant for the future. If the identification is correct (see above), he has represented in the initial H the protagonist of the ensuing chapter. The illustration is, therefore, neither a narrative scene, nor an author portrait of Bede incorporated in the initial. It is rather a form of 'word illustration' taking up the first sentence of the chapter *His temporibus . . . beatus Papa Gregorius* (for medieval word illustration cf. O Pächt, *The Rise of Pictorial Narrative in twelfth-century England*, 1962, p. 55. The best-known example is the 9th-century Utrecht Psalter. See F. Wormald, *The Utrecht Psalter*, 1953). The use of the form of the historiated initial is thus motivated by the medieval wish to integrate the text, thought of as a physical object represented by lines of script, and its illustration. The historiated initial is used occasionally by Carolingian artists and becomes widespread in the Romanesque period. The other early Insular examples of the historiated initial, those in the Vespasian Psalter (no. 29), are different in that they contain narrative scenes; but there, too, the object is similar, to integrate text and picture.

PROVENANCE: Count Achille III de Harlay (d. 1712) with his arms on the binding. Passed to St. Germain-des-Prés, Paris, in 1755 or 1762. Acquired from there by Pierre Dubrowski, a Russian nobleman attached to the embassy in Paris, probably in 1791. Given by him to the Public Library, St. Petersburg, in 1805.

LITERATURE: A. Staerk, *Les Manuscrits latins du Vᵉ au XIIIᵉ siècle conservés à la Bibliothèque Impériale de Saint-Pétersbourg*, I, 1910, 52–3, pl. XIV, II, pl. L;

Zimmermann, *Vorkarolingische Miniaturen*, 145, 309–10, pl. 332a; O. Dobiăs-Roždestvenskaia, 'Un manuscrit de Bède à Leningrad,' *Speculum*, 3, 1928, 314–21, pls. I–III; O. Arngart, *The Leningrad Bede* (Early English Manuscripts in Facsimile, II), 1952; Ker, *Catalogue*, 158 (no. 122); E. A. Lowe, 'A Key to Bede's scriptorium. Some observations on the Leningrad manuscript of the *Historia Ecclesiastica Gentis Anglorum*', *Scriptorium*, 12, 1958, 182–90, pls. 17, 19, 20, 21c; M. Schapiro, 'The decoration of the Leningrad manuscript of Bede', *Scriptorium*, 12, 1958, 191–207, pls. 23 a, b; Lowe, *English Uncial*, 9, 13, 23, pl. XXXVIIIa; D. H. Wright, 'The date of the Leningrad Bede', *Revue Bénédictine*, 71, 1961, 265–73, pls. I–IV; P. Meyvaert, 'The Bede "signature" in the Leningrad colophon', *Revue Bénédictine*, 71, 1961, 274–86; M. Bévenot, 'Towards dating the Leningrad Bede', *Scriptorium*, 16, 1962, 365–9; P. Meyvaert, *Bede and Gregory the Great* (Jarrow Lecture), 1964, 3–4, pl. I; D. H. Wright review of P. H. Blair, *The Moore Bede in Anglia*, 82, 1964, 113–15; *C.L.A.*, XI, no. 1621; D. H. Wright, 'The Italian stimulus on English art around 700', *Stil und Überlieferung. Akten des 21. Internat. Kongress für Kunstgeschichte. Bonn, 1964*, I, 1967, 91, pl. 7/1; B. Colgrave, R. A. B. Mynors, eds., *Bede's Ecclesiastical History of the English People*, 1969, xliv, lxi; Henry, *Kells*, 205 n. 226.

EXHIBITED: *Great Britain. U.S.S.R.*, London, Victoria and Albert Museum, 1967, no. 1.

20. London, British Library Royal MS 1. B. VII
Gospel Book
273 × 214 mm., ff. 155
First half of 8th century. (?) Northumbria

Ills. 70–73

The illumination consists of Canon Tables on twelve pages (ff. 9–14ᵛ) and initials to the Gospels, 'Li' (f. 15), X (f. 15ᵛ), I (f. 55), Q (f. 84), I (f. 130ᵛ), There are smaller initials for the Prefaces and chapter lists, N (f. 1), P (f. 2ᵛ), E (f. 3ᵛ), M (f. 4ᵛ), Z (f. 5), M (f. 52), E (f. 52ᵛ), L (f. 78ᵛ), J (f. 128). The Canon arcades which have 'm' arches, are plain black lines, but the capitals and imposts are made up of interlace, profile human heads in pairs adorsed, and bird and animal motifs. They appear to be traced through from rectos to versos. The colours used in the Canon Tables and initials are yellow, pinkish orange, and olive green. Some initials have continuation lettering on coloured panels, e.g. ff. 15ᵛ, 55. Orange dots are used to outline the initials. The Gospel text is similar to that of the Book of Lindisfarne and there are the same tables of lections including the Neapolitan feasts. T. J. Brown (*Codex Lindisfarnensis*) argues that the Gospel Book is an independent copy of the same exemplar which was probably a 6th-century Neapolitan Gospel Book (cf. no. 9). Lowe says the manuscript was written in England probably in Northumbria. The Canon Tables are different from those in the Book of

Lindisfarne (cf. no. 9) and the illumination of the initials with its limp interlace and crude bird heads is much less accomplished than in other Northumbrian manuscripts such as the Cologne Canons (no. 13) and the Salaberga Psalter (no. 14). Looking purely at the illumination one would be tempted to consider it a continental copy of Insular work. However, this is unlikely since the manuscript was certainly in England in the 10th century.

PROVENANCE: On f. 15ᵛ is a record of a manumission of one Eadhelm by King Athelstan, written c. 925. Wanley says the Gospel Book belonged to Christ Church, Canterbury, but gives no evidence.

LITERATURE: *Catalogue of ancient manuscripts in the British Museum, II. Latin manuscripts*, 1884, 19–20, pl. 16; F. G. Kenyon, *Facsimiles of Biblical manuscripts in the British Museum*, 1900, pl. XII; Zimmermann, *Vorkarolingische Miniaturen*, 121, 275, pl. 254; G. F. Warner, J. P. Gilson, *Catalogue of Western Manuscripts in the Old Royal and King's Collections*, I, 1921, 10–11, IV, pl. 6; Micheli, *L'enluminure*, 26, 46, 103, pls. 128, 215; Ker, *Catalogue*, 316–17 (no. 246); *Codex Lindisfarnensis*, 33, 43–6, 47 ff., 190, pl. 33 f.; McGurk, *Latin Gospel Books*, no. 28; *C.L.A.*, II, no. 213.

21. Lichfield, Cathedral Library
Gospel Book (Book of St. Chad)
308 × 235 mm., pp. 236
(?) Second quarter of 8th century

Ills. 50, 76–82

The illumination consists of two Evangelist portraits, St. Mark (p. 142) and St. Luke (p. 218), a carpet page (p. 220) preceding the opening of St. Luke, initial pages, St. Matthew, 'Lib' (p. 1) and 'Xpi' (p. 5), St. Mark, *Initium* (p. 143), St. Luke, *Quoniam* (p. 221), and a page with the four Evangelist symbols preceding the St. Luke carpet page (p. 219). Four pages of text are framed (cf. nos. 10, 52, 54), the Genealogy of Christ in St. Matthew (pp. 2–4) and the last page of St. Matthew (p. 141). The text ends at St. Luke III, 9 and the rest of Luke and the whole of St. John are missing. Presumably the manuscript would originally have had Canon Tables and Prefaces, as well as portrait, four-symbol page and carpet page for each Gospel. The leaves were cut into singletons in an earlier rebinding and the collation established by Powell (1965) does not seem decisive as to what is missing.

St. Mark (p. 142) sits on a cushion holding a book in front of him with both hands. He has a halo and wears a short beard. His robes are striped in violet, mauve, and a third colour (or perhaps a base for gilding) which now looks a dull orange, but which has mostly flaked away. To his right is an inkstand and behind him a throne of flat bars whose uprights are formed of quadrupeds which interlace with the two mauve cross bars. Of these the upper bar ends in half circles at each side, which not only fill the space with a typical Insular *horror vacui*, but also enclose the figure in a manner comparable with the grid patterns of the Echternach Gospel Book (no. 11). Above the saint's head is his symbol, a profile Lion without wings, but holding a book. The frame is a continuous band of fret pattern in black and white between pink bars.

The St. Luke has a similar type of frame whose corners are marked, however, with squares of interlace. The throne uprights end in animal masks. The saint's robes are painted in stylized bands and circles of mauve, violet, blue-green and, originally, the same colour as that which has flaked off in the St. Mark page. He holds a yellow cross in his left hand and a blue-green flowering staff in his right hand. It seems as if he also has a book cradled between his arms. His symbol, the Calf, is placed above his large violet halo: its wings extend behind the frame and its horns overlap it. It has no book.

The four symbols on p. 219 are arranged about a cross: (reading clockwise from the top left) the winged Man, the Lion, the Eagle, and the Calf. All are winged, full-length, and none carry books. They are all ornamented with dot patterns which are so faded on the Man and the Eagle that they are hardly visible. The Lion and the Calf are rotated so that they fit into the rectangle. The frame is again a continuous band of fret pattern.

The cross-carpet page (p. 220) is a square-armed cross filled with interlaced lacertine and bird ornament, and set on a ground of similar ornament. There are interlace motifs at the four corners of the frame; further ornamental motifs extend at the sides and top and bottom of the frame. The initial pages have frames on three or four sides (the L and the Q), ending in an animal's head above and its feet below. The continuation lettering is in black on coloured, framed panels. The Matthew page has suffered very much and seems to have been retouched (particularly the beading in the centre of the L), but the 'Xp' page is in better condition and gives more of an idea of the original splendour of the ornamental pages. The frames of the panels containing the continuation lettering of the St. Luke opening (p. 221) are formed of animals who bite their own bodies or the animal below, thus linking each panel with the next. There are a number of smaller initials in black with orange dots, some ornamented with interlace and fret ornament and some coloured with blobs of yellow, orange, purple, and mauve. There are also some enlarged, two-line initials: V for Matthew XXVI, 20, 'Ihs' for Matthew XXVII, 11, and V for Matthew XXVIII, 1, and also for the *Pater noster* which is inserted on p. 217.

The colouring of the manuscript seems now muted and many of the patterns and parts of the figures appear as if drawn in black ink and left blank. But this is a false impression, since the pigments have suffered from abrasion, flaking, and damp. The main surviving colour is one which in its lighter shade looks violet and in its darker mauve. Greenish blue, light blue, and brown are also used. The light blue is striking and on the 'Xp' page in particular it provides a vivid contrast with the yellow.

The quality of the illumination is very high. It contains a great variety of ornament finely executed and used with imagination, including trumpet, fret, key, spiral, interlace, animal, bird, and rosette patterns. Originally, when it was complete, the manuscript must have been the equal of any of the Insular Gospel Books with a programme of illustration richer even than the Book of Lindisfarne (no. 9), if, as seems likely, each Gospel was preceded by a portrait, a four-symbols page, a cross-carpet page, and an initial page. There is, of course, no way of knowing what type of Canon Tables it had.

The Evangelist portraits presumably depend ultimately on a late antique model in which the frontal figure was enthroned on a backed chair of which the arms were formed of lions (St. Matthew). The thrones are similarly stylized into a grid pattern in the Trier Gospel Book portraits of St. Mark and St. Luke (no. 26). It is uncertain whether the Insular artists themselves combined unaccompanied portraits (cf. the Barberini Gospel Book, no. 36) with full-length symbols (cf. the Books of Durrow and Echternach, nos. 6 and 11); or whether they depended on an early Christian tradition of accompanied portraits separate from that seen in the 6th-century Gospel Book of St. Augustine (Corpus Christi College, MS 286, fig. 23, cf. no. 30) in which the symbol is half-length and related to the Evangelist in an architectural setting. The Lichfield portraits can be compared to the Matthew and Luke in the St. Gall Gospel Book (no. 44), whilst the four-symbols page also occurs in the Books of Durrow (no. 6), Kells (no. 52) and Armagh (no. 53), and in the Trier and Macdurnan Gospel Books (nos. 26, 70).

The manuscript is also linked in certain ways, especially in the design of the initials and the cross-carpet page, and in the ornament, particularly the interlaced birds and the lacertine animals, with the Book of Lindisfarne (no. 9). The patterns of dots in circles on the symbols of the four-symbols page also recall the Durham Cassiodorus (no. 17). It is not clear whether such links are due to Northumbrian influence, or to a common decorative tradition lying behind both the Lichfield and the Northumbrian manuscripts, possibly to be placed at Iona or in Ireland, evidence of which, however, does not otherwise survive. For the moment both origin and date of the manuscript remain problematic.

PROVENANCE: A Latin inscription, early 9th century, on p. 141 states that the manuscript was exchanged for his best horse by Gelhi, son of Arihtiud, who offered it to God and on the altar of St. Teilo. Various other entries are in Welsh, some copying much earlier documents, late 8th to early 9th century, pp. 18, 19, 141, 216–18. The place-names and the mention of the altar of St. Teilo suggest that the Gospel Book was then at Llandeilo-fawr, Carmarthenshire, (rather than at Llandaff as often stated, cf. M. Richards). It apparently reached Lichfield in the 10th century (Richards suggests under Athelstan, *c.* 934). On p. 1 *Wynsige presul* no doubt refers to the Bishop of Lichfield (*c.* 963 to 973–5) and in the margin of p. 4 there is a contemporary note concerning

Leofgar, Bishop of Lichfield (1020–7). *Textus evangelii Sancti Ceaddae*, 15th century, p. 1 (St. Chad, first Bishop of Lichfield, died in 672). Walter Higgins, precentor of Lichfield, rescued the volume at the siege of Lichfield in 1647. It was returned to the Cathedral by Frances, widow of William Seymour, Duke of Somerset, in 1673.

LITERATURE: W. J. Rees, *The Liber Landavensis*, 1840, 271–6, pls. VI, VII; Westwood, *Palaeographia*, no. 12; id., *Facsimiles*, 56–8, pl. XXIII; *Pal Soc.*, I, pls. 20–1, 35; F. H. A. Scrivener, *Codex S. Ceaddae Latinus*, 1887, pls. 1–3; H. Bradshaw, *Collected papers*, 1889, 283, 458–61, 483–4; J. G. Evans, J. Rhys, *The text of the Book of Llan Dăv reproduced from the Gwysaney Manuscript*, 1893, xlii ff., pls.; W. M. Lindsay, *Early Welsh Script*, 1912, 1 ff., pls. I, II; H. E. Savage, 'The story of St. Chad's Gospels', *Transactions of the Birmingham Archaeological Society*, 41, 1915, 5–21, pls. I, III, V, VI; Zimmermann, *Vorkarolingische Miniaturen*, 20, 31, 116–18, 269–70, pls. 245–6; E. G. Millar, *The Lindisfarne Gospels*, 1923, 18–19, pls. 38–9; K. Pfister, *Irische Buchmalerei*, 1927, pl. 35; W. R. Hovey, 'Sources of the Irish illuminative art', *Art Studies*, 6, 1928, 111, 116–17, figs. 18, 23; Saunders, *English Illumination*, 12, pls. 8, 9; Kenney, *Sources*, no. 468; L. J. Hopkin-James, *The Celtic Gospels*, 1934, ix ff., frontispiece and pls. facing pp. x, 161; Kendrick, *Anglo-Saxon*, 137–9, pl. LIII; Micheli, *L'enluminure*, 16–18, pls. 27, 43, 46; N. R. Ker, 'The migration of manuscripts from the English medieval libraries', *The Library*, 4th ser., 23, 1942, 4; Masai, *Origines*, 58, pls. XIX, XX; Duft, Meyer, *St. Gall*, figs. 4, 14, 22, 33–4, 39, 44–5, 48, 51, 55–6, 58, 70, 75, 82; Ker, *Catalogue*, 158 (no. 123); *Codex Durmachensis*, figs. 34, 76, 112; *Codex Lindisfarnensis*, xxiv, 187, 257–8, pls. 19e, 27 k, l, 50g, 51d, 53d, 54; McGurk, *Latin Gospel Books*, no. 16; F. Henry, 'The Lindisfarne Gospels', *Antiquity*, 37, 1963, 100–10; Rickert, *Painting in Britain*, 10, 16–17, pl. 8a; R. Powell, 'The Lichfield St. Chad's Gospels: Repair and Rebinding, 1961–2', *The Library*, 5th ser., 20, 1965, 259–76, pls. I–IX; Henry, *Irish Art*, I, 106, 162, 174, 176, 183–7, 190–2, 194–7, 199, 202, 209, 218, 220, 224, pls. 89, 98, 102–3, 105, 107, F, H, I; M. Werner, 'The four Evangelist Symbols page in the Book of Durrow', *Gesta*, 8, 1969, 3–17, fig. 6; *C.L.A.*, II, no. 159; Koehler, *Buchmalerei*, 14, 19, 22, 29, 41–5, 55, 66 ff., 78; M. Richards, 'The Lichfield Gospels (Book of St. Chad)', *The National Library of Wales Journal*, 18, 1973, 135–46; Henry, *Kells*, 151–2, 155, 160, 163, 167, 180, 182–3, 188, 191, 198–9, 205, 207–8, 212–13, 226, figs. 5, 26, 45, 61; Nordenfalk, *Celtic*, 76, 79, 81, 83, fig. VI, pls. 23–6.

22. Maeseyck, Church of St. Catherine, Trésor, s.n., ff. 1–5

Gospel Book (fragment)
240 × 184 mm., ff. 5
Early 8th century. North England (? York)

Ills. 87–95

The fragment consists of a singleton and two bifolia now bound with another fragmentary Gospel Book (no. 23). The illumination consists of an Evangelist portrait, unidentifiable since there is no text and no symbol (f. 1), and Tables for Canons II–X (Matthew) on eight pages (ff. 2–5ᵛ).

The bearded Evangelist is seated on a throne facing to the right and turning in three-quarter view. He writes in a book which he holds with his veiled left hand. He is placed under an arch with leaf motifs extending from the capitals. There is an outer panel frame of interlace with corner pieces of interlaced birds.

The Canons are out of order, the correct order being ff. 3, 3ᵛ, 5ᵛ, 5, 2, 2ᵛ, 4, 4ᵛ and the numbers for Canon II–III only are entered on the first two folios (ff. 3, 5). They are 'm n' arches, each with a bust figure in a roundel at the top. The Canons would probably have been on twelve pages originally and the figures are identifiable as the twelve Apostles. Under the lower arches are abbreviated Evangelist symbols without wings, books or haloes, while birds perched on plants extend from the outer capitals of the main arches. A wealth of filling patterns are found on the columns, some of them of naturalistic leaf-forms, birds (cf. the Book of Lindisfarne, no. 9), or illusionistic fluting, others of abstract interlace. Comparing the Evangelist with the portrait heads of the Canons shows that they are by the same artist and must have belonged to the same book. The colours used are now rather pale possibly due to deterioration. They are orange, blue, and olive-green.

The artist of the Evangelist portrait must have had a good model, perhaps Italo-Byzantine, since the figure is bearded and there is no symbol. The Insular ingredients are the exterior frame and perhaps the pattern on the throne, which may reflect native wooden construction methods. It has been compared to that on the 10th-century tower of Earls Barton, Northants (Schapiro, 1959). Nordenfalk, commenting on the artist's ability to understand and reproduce late antique forms, has compared the portrait to the classicism of the Ruthwell and Bewcastle crosses. Since the manuscript cannot on paleographical grounds have been made at the great Northumbrian centres, he makes the attractive suggestion that it might perhaps be connected with St. Wilfrid of York (d. 709). Other scholars (Lowe, Wright) consider the book more likely to have been made on the Continent, though it is not clear when it reached Aldeneyck.

The Canon Tables are of the type named 'Apostolic' by Nordenfalk and he has shown that this type is likely to have originated in Constantinople in the 4th century. They also occur in the Trier Gospel Book (no. 26) and the Gospel Book bound with the present manuscript (no. 23). Again this suggests a good model with eastern connections. The symbols are presumably an intrusion from some different model (cf. the Book of Kells, no. 52, where the problem of the origin of the 'beast Canon Tables' is discussed). They also occur on the opening page of the Barberini Gospel Book (no. 36) which has other features in common with the present manuscript, particularly in the type of frame of the Evangelist portrait, in the plant motifs, in the absence of Evangelist symbols and in the writing bearded Evangelist.

PROVENANCE: Bound with another Gospel Book fragment which was apparently at Aldeneyck from an early date (see no. 23).

LITERATURE: Nordenfalk, *Early Medieval*, 122, pl. opp. p. 120; M. Schapiro, 'A note on the wall strips of Saxon churches', *Journal of the Society of Architectural Historians*, 18, 1959, 124–5, fig. 3; D. H. Wright review of Nordenfalk in *Art Bulletin*, 43, 1961, 253; McGurk, *Latin Gospel Books*, no. 44; C. Nordenfalk, 'The Apostolic Canon Tables', *Gazette des Beaux-Arts*, 6ᵉ pér., 62, 1963, 20, fig. 2; *C.L.A.*, X, no. 1559. See also no. 23 for other references.

23. Maeseyck, Church of St. Catherine, Trésor, s.n., ff. 6–132
Gospel Book (fragment)
240 × 184 mm., ff. 128
First half of 8th century. Northumbria or (?) Continental centre under Northumbrian influence
Ills. 96–107

The manuscript is only a fragment bound up with another fragmentary Gospel Book (no. 22). The illumination consists of Canon Tables on twelve pages (ff. 6–11ᵛ) and simple initials for the Prefaces, Chapter lists, and the Four Gospels, 'Lib' (f. 15ᵛ), 'Xpi' (f. 16), 'In' (f. 56), Q (f. 77), 'In' (f. 112). It does not seem that there were ever Evangelist portraits.

The Canon Tables are 'm n' arches with bust medallions of the Apostles at the crown of the main arch beginning with St. Peter with his keys (f. 6ᵛ, reversed, it should be f. 6, Canon I, 1) and St. Paul (f. 6, reversed, it should be f. 6ᵛ, Canon I, 2), and followed by SS. Andrew (f. 7), James the Less (f. 7ᵛ), John (f. 8), Bartholomew (f. 8ᵛ), James the Greater (f. 9, the medallion is now missing), and Thomas (f. 9ᵛ, the medallion is also missing). Then follow the zooanthropomorphic symbols of the four Evangelists in roundels in the same position, half-length, winged, and carrying books (ff. 10–11ᵛ).

The figure style is more linear than that of the Gospel fragment bound in with the present manuscript (no. 22), and the filling patterns of the Canons use the Insular repertoire of interlace, fret, etc. The 'Apostolic' Canon Tables can be compared with those in the attached fragment (no. 22) and in the Trier Gospel Book (no. 26), though they do not appear to be directly copied from either.

Origin and date of the Gospel Book are both uncertain. Lowe assigns the manuscript to an Anglo-Saxon centre with Northumbrian connections, or possibly to Northumbria itself, in the first half of the 8th century. On f. 128ᵛ is a prayer for the scribe 'pro laboratore hujus operis'.

PROVENANCE: By tradition written by the founders

of Aldeneyck, Harlindis, and Reglindis in the early 8th century (cf. *Acta Sanctorum*, March, III, 388). Presumably at Aldeneyck from an early date and transferred from there by the Canons of Notre Dame to the church of St. Catherine, Maeseyck to which they moved in 1570.

LITERATURE: J. Gielen, 'L'Évangéliaire d'Eyck lez Maeseyck du VIIIᵉ siècle', *Bulletin des commissions royales d'art et d'archéologie*, 30, 1891, 19–28, pls. I–III; D. de Bruyne, 'L'Évangéliaire du VIIIᵉ siècle conservé à Maeseyck', *Bulletin de la société d'art et d'histoire du diocèse de Liège*, 17, 1908, 385–92, 2 pls.; Zimmermann, *Vorkarolingische Miniaturen*, 66, 128, 142–3, 303–4, pls. 318–30; W. Koehler, 'Die Denkmäler der karolingischen Kunst in Belgien', *Belgische Kunstdenkmäler*, ed. P. Clemen, 1923, 3, fig. 3; Micheli, *L'enluminure*, 29, 49–50, pls. 37, 159; E. de Moreau, *Histoire de l'église en Belgique*, I, 1945, 338, pl. IXb, II, 1947, 313 f.; A. Boeckler, 'Die Kanonbogen der Ada-Gruppe und ihre Vorlagen', *Müncher Jahrbuch der bildenden Kunst*, N.F. 5, 1954, 18–19, fig. 19; E. Rosenbaum, 'The Vine Columns of Old St. Peter's in Carolingian Canon Tables', *Journal of the Warburg and Courtauld Institutes*, 18, 1955, 4, 8, 15; Nordenfalk, *Early Medieval*, 122; *Codex Lindisfarnensis*, 193–6, pls. 35d, 37d, 40a; McGurk, *Latin Gospel Books*, no. 44; C. Nordenfalk, 'The Apostolic Canon Tables', *Gazette des Beaux-Arts*, 6ᵉ pér. 62, 1963, 20; *C.L.A.*, X, no. 1558; Henry, *Irish Art*, II, 60, 63–4, 67, 85–86, pl. IV; Koehler, *Buchmalerei*, 16, 188–9; Henry, *Kells*, 167, 183, 187, 198, 214, 226, figs. 16, 39. See also under no. 22.

EXHIBITED: *Art Mosan. Trésors d'Art de la Vallée de la Meuse et arts anciens du pays de Liège*, Liège, 1951–2, nos. 203–6; *Werdendes Abendland an Rhein und Ruhr*, Essen, 1956, no. 272. See also V. Elbern, *Das erste Jahrtausend. Tafelband*, 1962, pl. 226; *Saint-Willibrord*, Echternach, 1958, no. 168, pl. XX; *Karl der Grosse*, 1965, no. 392, pl. 42; *English Illuminated Manuscripts 700–1500*, Brussels, 1973, no. 1, pl. 1.

24. Harburg über Donauwörth, Schloss Harburg, Fürstlich Öttingen-Wallerstein'sche Bibliothek Cod. I. 2. 4°. 2 (*olim* Maihingen)
Gospel Book
245 × 180 mm., ff. 159
Early 8th century. Echternach
Ills. 115, 116, 119–124, 126

The illumination consists of Canon Tables (ff. 7–12) and initials to the four Gospels, L (f. 16), X (f. 16ᵛ), 'In' (f. 55), Q (f. 83), 'In' (f. 127). There are smaller initials to the Prefaces and Chapter lists, P (f. 3), N (f. 5), M (f. 52ᵛ), 'Et' (f. 53ᵛ). Preceding St. John (f. 126ᵛ) is a cross-carpet page with interlace outer border. The cross is filled with fret patterns and set on a blank ground. In the four corners there are symmetrical irregular shapes filled with fret patterns.

Folio 2 has a square filled with the words *Evangelia veritatis* in capitals with a pair of birds above, and on f. 157ᵛ there is a lion with the inscription *Ecce leo stat super* (. . . erased). Below the lion is an acrostic poem giving by the first and last letters of each line the words *Laurentius vivat senio*.

Probably this refers to the scribe of Echternach charters dated between 704 and 711 and of Paris, B.N., lat. 10837, ff. 2–33 (*C.L.A.*, V. no. 605). The script cannot be attributed to Laurentius himself, however, and the explanation is probably that it is by a disciple. The script is very close to that of the so-called Calendar of St. Willibrord (Paris, B.N., lat. 10837, ff. 34–41, 44, *C.L.A.*, V, no. 606a). This is datable before 728 since it contains an autograph inscription by St. Willibrord and probably *c.* 717 since there is a cross in the margin of the Paschal table opposite that year. The Calendar also has simple initials related to those in the present manuscript and in the Echternach Gospel Book, no. 11 (see H. A. Wilson, 'The Calendar of St. Willibrord', *Henry Bradshaw Society*, 55, 1918, for plates). Zimmerman also drew attention to the similarity of design between the major initials in the present manuscript and those in the Echternach Gospel Book (no. 11). Patterns of dots are used with the major initials to integrate them with the script and more thickly as a ground for the minor initials.

Though using the Insular repertoire of pattern, the initials and decoration appear more restrained. Interlaced birds similar to those found in the Book of Lindisfarne (no. 9) fill the L (f. 16), and the cross-carpet page is a simpler version of the first carpet page there (f. 2ᵛ). Possibly it is a copy of a lost carpet page in the Echternach Gospel Book (cf. no. 11). The marbling on the columns, though reduced to Insular calligraphic patterns (e.g. f. 10), and the naturalistic birds and the lion in a landscape setting, clearly show late antique influence. Nordenfalk (1932) suggested that the birds and lion might be 9th-century Carolingian additions.

The Gospel Book later received portraits by the Ottonian artist known as the 'Master of the Registrum Gregorii' of which only the St. Mark survives. It bears an offset of the initial 'In' (f. 55), and is now at the Archiepiscopal Seminary, St. Peter, Schwarzwald, MS 25 (cf. C. Nordenfalk, 'The chronology of the Registrum Master', *Kunsthistorische Forschungen Otto Pächt zu ehren*, 1972, 65 with earlier literature). Titles were added at this date in rustic capitals in gold (f. 83) and silver (f. 123ᵛ), and gold was added to various initials.

PROVENANCE: *Ex libris A. Gaertler a. 1809*, f. 159. Very probably obtained from Echternach by Dom J.-B. Maugérard *c.* 1785–90. Later purchased by Prince Ludwig of Oettingen.

LITERATURE: W. Wattenbach, 'Sur un Évangéliaire à miniatures d'origine irlandaise dans la bibliothèque princière d'Oettingen Wallerstein', *Revue Celtique*, 1, 1870–2, 27–31, 2 figs.; Zimmermann, *Vorkarolingische Miniaturen*, 25, 125–6, 279–80, pls. 260b, 261b, 262b, 263–5, 266 a, b, c, d; Kenney, *Sources*, no. 459; C. Nordenfalk, 'On the age of the earliest Echternach manuscripts', *Acta Archaeologica*, 3, 1932, 57–62, fig. 2; Micheli, *L'enluminure*, 44–5, 66, pls. 6, 62, 64; Masai, *Origines*, 126, pl. IX. 4; Duft, Meyer, *St. Gall*, fig. 91; Ker, *Catalogue*, 348 (no. 287*); *C.L.A.*, VIII, no. 1215; *Codex Durmachensis*, fig. 93; *Codex Lindisfarnensis*, 90–1, 283; McGurk, *Latin Gospel Books*, no. 72; Henry, *Irish Art*, I, 173, 178–9, 181–2, 193–4, pls. 106, VII; *Irish Art*, II, 85, 97; Henry, *Kells*, 151, 155, 167, 180, 182, 226, fig. 26.

EXHIBITED: *Karl der Grosse*, 1965, no. 400.

25. Freiburg-im-Breisgau, Universitätsbibliothek Cod. 702
Gospel Book (fragment)
304×262 mm., ff. 2
Early 8th century. (?) Echternach

Ills. 117, 118

The fragment contains the preface and list of chapters for St. Luke. The preface (f. 1–1ᵛ) is written in a cross set within a rectangle with the rubric *Incipit | Argume | Secundum | Lucam* written in the corner squares which are decorated with dot patterns. There is an initial L decorated with bird interlace, spirals and dots (f. 1) and a Z decorated with spirals (f. 2ᵛ).

The fragment is related paleographically to the Echternach Gospels (no. 11) and the initial L can be compared to that in the Schloss Harburg Gospel Book (no. 24). The manuscript may therefore have been made at Echternach. If even the prefaces were decorated in this way, it must have been illuminated on a considerable scale.

PROVENANCE: Found in a rent-roll of the Benedictine abbey of Tholey, near Trier. Bought by Freiburg in 1913.

LITERATURE: A. Dold, 'Eine kostbare Handschriften-reliquie', *Zentralblatt für Bibliothekswesen*, 52, 1935, 125–35, pls. 1, 2; Micheli, *L'enluminure*, 44; *C.L.A.*, VIII, no. 1195; *Codex Durmachensis*, fig. 90; *Codex Lindisfarnensis*, 283; Lowe, *English Uncial*, 20, pl. XVI; McGurk, *Latin Gospel Books*, no. 67.

EXHIBITED: *Kunst des frühen Mittelalters*, Bern, 1949, no. 3; *Ars sacra. Kunst des frühen Mittelalters*, Munich, 1950, no. 3; *Werdendes Abendland an Rhein und Ruhr*, Essen, 1956, no. 229; *Saint-Willibrord*, Echternach, 1958, no. 164; *Karl der Grosse*, 1965, no. 396.

26. Trier, Domschatz Codex 61 (Bibliotheksnummer 134)
Gospel Book
c. 300×245–50 mm., ff. 207
Second quarter of 8th century. (?) Echternach

Ills. 108–114, 125, 127

The illumination consists of a four-symbols page (f. 1ᵛ), the Tetramorph page (f. 5ᵛ), a miniature of SS. Michael and Gabriel holding a plaque with the incipit of St. Matthew (f. 9), Canon Tables on ten pages (ff. 10–14ᵛ, originally twelve, a page is missing between ff. 13–14), and portraits of the first three Evangelists, St. Matthew (f. 18ᵛ), St. Mark (f. 80ᵛ), and St. Luke (f. 125ᵛ). There are smaller initials for the Prefaces and Chapter lists, P (f. 2), N (f. 6), M (f. 76), Z (f. 119), A (f. 123), I (f. 172) and larger initials for the Gospels, L (f. 19), 'Xp' (f. 20), I (f. 81), Q and F (f. 126ᵛ) and I (f. 176). There are also initials of Merovingian type made up of birds, fish and even human forms (f. 110ᵛ). At the end of St. John's Gospel is a horizontal panel filled with foliage (f. 204).

The Gospel Book was written by two scribes, one Anglo-Saxon, who signs his name 'Thomas' (ff. 5ᵛ, 11, 125ᵛ), the other Continental, who is writing 'uncial of a French type' (Lowe).

On the four-symbols page (f. 1ᵛ) a haloed, bust, figure with a book is in the centre medallion of a cross filled with interlace which runs continuously into the frame of the page. The symbol of St. Matthew, inscribed *homo*, holds a scroll and (?)stands before a bar structure which presumably originates from the representation of a throne (cf. f. 18ᵛ and e.g. the Lichfield Gospel Book, no. 21). The other three symbols (inscribed *leo*, *vitulus*, and *aquila*) are full-length terrestrial types comparable to those in the Book of Durrow (no. 6) and the Echternach Gospel Book (no. 11). At the corners of the frame are human heads. Other four-symbols pages are found in the Book of Durrow (no. 6), the Lichfield Gospel Book (no. 21), the Books of Kells and Armagh (nos. 52, 53) and the Macdurnan Gospel Book (no. 70).

The miniature of the Tetramorph (f. 5ᵛ) is placed opposite St. Jerome's Preface to Pope Damasus. It is inscribed *Matheus Evang.*, *Marcus Evang.*, *Lucas Evang.*, and *Johannis* (sic) *Evang.* A frontal bearded human figure who holds a flabellum (liturgical fan) and a knife crossed in front of his chest (cf. the Lichfield Gospel Book, no. 21), stands with his feet pointing to the right as in the Man symbol in the Book of Durrow (no. 6). He has no wings or halo. In front of him are as it were suspended the legs and paws of the Lion, the talons of the Eagle, and the legs and hooves of the Bull-calf. Presumably this representation, for which there appears to be no parallel, is intended as a visual symbol of the unity of the four Gospels. Nordenfalk (1977) notes that the Gospel harmony of Ammonius of Alexandria had a similar emphasis on St. Matthew's Gospel, but considers the miniature here an Insular invention. The frame is of interlace and chequer pattern with corner and side pieces of animal heads and interlace.

The two Archangels who are inscribed *Scs Michael* and *Scs Gabriel* are mirror images of each other. Their classical pose suggests an early Christian prototype (cf. the Angels flanking the Virgin in the mosaics at S. Apollinare Nuovo, Ravenna, c. 500; Nordenfalk (1977) also compares a coin of Constantine with two winged victories). This might also

have provided the model for the Apostolic Canon Tables. Nordenfalk (1963) has shown that this type of Canon Table containing bust medallions of Christ and the Apostles goes back to a 4th-century Constantinopolitan recension, though the placing of the roundels on the summit of the arches is perhaps an Insular feature (cf. the Maeseyck Gospel Books, nos. 22, 23). The Apostles are not labelled except for Thomas (f. 11), but the series starts with St. Peter with his key (f. 10). Naturalistic birds perched on curving leaves flank the main arches and the columns of the arches are shown as if fluted or marbled, which also suggests a good early model in illusionistic style. Some Insular patterns are also used, however, for instance the biting animal heads in the columns and the interlace bases.

St. Matthew (f. 18ᵛ) appears to stand in front of a bar throne (cf. f. 1ᵛ) and holds a book in his veiled left hand. He is bearded but has no halo. There is an inscription *Imago Sci Mathei Evang.* The frame is of interlace extending into the miniature to form a cross in which the figure is as it were, imprisoned (cf. the Echternach Gospel Book, no. 11). St. Mark (f. 80ᵛ) and St. Luke (f. 125ᵛ) are both haloed and St. Luke is bearded. They have bar thrones behind them and are presumably seated, since they have footstools. St. Mark holds a scroll and St. Luke a book, and on both pages a second book seems to float without a bookstand to the right. In the upper part of each page to the right is a half-length, winged symbol, the Lion and the Calf respectively, without haloes, but holding books. The frames are of panels filled with patterns and more elaborate interlace at the corners and the centre of each side. Zimmermann attributed the Canon Tables, the four-symbols page, the Archangels with the Matthew title-page, and the Matthew portrait, as well as the initials in Merovingian style to a Continental artist, and the rest to the Anglo-Saxon scribe Thomas. However, 'Thomas' is written by the Apostle medallion on f. 11 (the other portraits are not labelled) and it seems questionable whether the differences of style observable in the full-page miniatures and the Canon Tables are not rather a result of different models (cf. Nordenfalk, 1977).

Nordenfalk (1977) considers the model for the Canon Tables and the page with the Archangels to have been an Italian Gospel Book of the 6th or 7th century. A comparison of the initials, especially the L (f. 19) with those in the Echternach Gospel Book suggests the artist was familiar with that book too (no. 11, ill. 52). If it once contained a four-symbol page, it could also have been the source for the four-symbol page in the present manuscript. The St. Matthew is perhaps adapted from the representation of St. Matthew's symbol on the same page. The other two seated Evangelists are also in Insular style, but cannot derive from the Echternach Gospel Book. Presumably another Insular Gospel Book was available, one which contained rather faithful copies of a set of late antique Evangelist portraits who were not writing and the bindings of whose codices were represented in the same sort of detail as in the early 5th-century illustrations of the *Notitia Dignitatum*, known to us through Renaissance copies. A similar arrangement of the symbols beside or facing the Evangelists is seen in the Cutbercht Gospel Book (no. 37) and the St. Gall Matthew portrait (no. 57). It is questionable whether they were present in the late antique portraits or whether they are an Insular addition.

PROVENANCE: A Mass of the Feast of St. Potentinus is added, f. 5, 11th–12th century: . . . *sancti confessoris tui Potentini qui in praesenti requiescit ecclesia*. This shows the Gospel Book was then in the Premonstratensian Abbey Church of Steinfeld in the Eifel. It is uncertain when and how it reached Trier.

LITERATURE: Westwood, *Facsimiles*, 72–7, pls. XIX, XX, LII. 3; Zimmermann, *Vorkarolingische Miniaturen*, 11, 36–7, 75, 126–30, 133, 281–5, pls. 258 d–e, 267–79; K. Pfister, *Irische Buchmalerei*, 1927, pl. 38; A. Goldschmidt, *German illumination*, I, 1928, 6, pls. 4–8; Kenney, *Sources*, no. 487; N. Irsch, *Der Dom zu Trier*, 1931, 326–8, fig. 214; C. Nordenfalk, 'On the age of the earliest Echternach manuscripts', *Acta Archaeologica*, 3, 1932, 57–62; C. Nordenfalk, 'Vier Kanonestafeln eines spätantiken Evangelienbuches', *Göteborgs Kungl. Vetenskaps-och Vitterhets-Samhälles handlingar*, V, ser. A, Bd. 6, no. 5, 1937, 22 f., 27, 30, 33 f., pls. 9, 10, fig. 3e; C. Nordenfalk, *Die spätantike Kanontafeln*, 1938, 175, 179 ff., 218 n. 1, Beil. B, pls. 74–83; Micheli, *L'enluminure*, 44–5, 50, pls. 32, 65, 158; Åberg, *Occident*, 96, 101, figs. 65, 76.6; A Boeckler, 'Formgeschichtliche Studien zur Adagruppe', *Bayerische Akademie der Wissenschaften, Abhandlungen, phil.-hist. Klasse*, N.F. 42, 1956, 28 f., pl. 23b; H. Schnitzler, *Rheinisches Schatzkammer*, I, 1957, 21 (no. 2), pls. 6–9; Nordenfalk, *Early Medieval*, 124; *C.L.A.*, IX, no. 1364; *Codex Durmachensis*, figs. 22, 39, 49, 57, 66, 94; *Codex Lindisfarnensis*, 158, 283, pl. 26 i–l; McGurk, *Latin Gospel Books*, no. 76; C. Nordenfalk, 'The Apostolic Canon Tables', *Gazette des Beaux-Arts*, 6e pér., 62, 1963, 20, 31, figs. 1, 14; Henry, *Irish Art*, I, 174, 178, 180–1, 194–5, pl. VI; D. H. Wright, 'The Italian stimulus on English Art around 700', *Stil und Überlieferung in der Kunst des Abendlandes. Akten des 21. Internat. Kongress für Kunstgeschichte, Bonn, 1964*, I, 1967, 84 ff., pl. 7/4; Werckmeister, *Irisch-northumbrische Buchmalerei*, 7 n. 8, 13, 15, pl. 2a; M. Werner, 'The four Evangelist Symbols page in the Book of Durrow', *Gesta*, 8, 1969, 3–17, fig. 8; R. B. K. Stevenson, 'Sculpture in Scotland in the 6th–9th centuries A.D.', *Kolloquium über spätantike und frühmittelalterliche Sculptur*, II, 1970, 65–75, pl. 49.4; A. Kurzeja, *Der älteste Liber Ordinarius der Trierer Domkirche*, 1970, 8–10; C. Nordenfalk, *Codex Caesareus Upsaliensis*, 1971, 27, 95, 142 n. 4, fig. 47; Koehler, *Buchmalerei*, 187; Henry, *Kells*, 167, 191, 226; Nordenfalk, *Celtic*, 88, 90, 93, pls. 29–31.

EXHIBITED: *Werdendes Abendland an Rhein und Ruhr*, Essen, 1956, no. 287. See also V. H. Elbern, *Das erste Jahrtausend. Tafelband*, 1962, pls. 234–7; *Saint-Willibrord*, Echternach, 1958, no. 163, pl. XIX; *Karl der Grosse*, 1965, no. 401, pl. 48.

27. Gotha, Forschungsbibliothek Cod. Memb. I. 18
Gospel Book
310 × 260 mm., ff. 232
Mid 8th century

Ills. 128–132

The illumination remaining consists of initials for St. Mark, 'In' (f. 78) and St. Luke, 'Quo' (f. 126), which are decorated with interlace, a biting animal head (the Q) and red dots. Three other initials for St. Matthew and St. John have been cut out (ff. 13, 14 and 195ᵛ). There are smaller initials for the Prefaces and Chapter lists, N (f. 1), P (f. 3), A (f. 5ᵛ), M (f. 6ᵛ), G (f. 7), M (f. 74), E (f. 75), P (f. 118ᵛ), and P (f. 194).
The origin of the manuscript is uncertain. Nordenfalk has compared the initials to those in the Trier Gospel Book (no. 26). Presumably it was produced in a Continental centre under strong Anglo-Saxon influence.

PROVENANCE: Probably from Murbach, near Colmar, Vosges. Sold by Dom J.-B. Maugérard (cf. no. 24) to Duke Ernest II of Gotha Altenburg between 1795 and 1802.

LITERATURE: L. Traube, R. Ehwald, 'Jean-Baptiste Maugérard', *Abhandlungen der historischen Klasse der Kgl. Bayer. Akademie der Wissenschaften*, 32.2, 1904, 355; C. Nordenfalk, 'On the age of the earliest Echternach manuscripts', *Acta Archaeologica*, 3, 1932, 57 n. 1, fig. 1; Micheli, *L'enluminure*, 46; *C.L.A.*, VIII, no. 1205; McGurk, *Latin Gospel Books*, no. 69; E. Rothe, *Mediaeval Book Illumination in Europe*, London, 1968 (Berlin, DDR, 1966), 184, 235, pl. 6; R. Schipke, *Die Maugérard-Handschriften der Forschungsbibliothek Gotha*, 1972, 30–2.

28. Stuttgart, Württembergische Landesbibliothek Cod. Bibl. 2° 12
Psalter
305 × 210 mm., ff. 93
(?) Mid 8th century. (?) Echternach

Ills. 140–142

The illumination consists of large initials for the tripartite division of the Psalter, B, Psalm 1 (f. 1), Q, Psalm 51 (f. 32) and D, Psalm 101 (f. 63). The bowls of the B are constructed of fish and there is a plant scroll inside (cf. the Leningrad Bede, no. 19). The continuation lettering is in white on coloured panels, the 'e' of *Beatus*, Psalm 1, having an animal mask as in the Canterbury group (nos. 29–33), and the Barberini Gospel Book (no. 36). The Q is made up of two fish with a leaping beast as tail and plant forms inside the bowl. The D is constructed of three fish. Both these initials also have continuation lettering on panels. There are also initials to each Psalm many of them constructed of fish. The colours used are red, violet, yellow, blue, and brown.
The illumination is of great interest because it shows

a presumably Anglo-Saxon artist working on the Continent (cf. Nordenfalk, 1974) and transforming the decorative vocabulary of Merovingian illumination. The birds, fish, and animals combined like matchsticks to form the letters in Continental examples are here given life and movement in accordance with the Insular dynamic aesthetic (cf. O. Pächt's remarks on 'The pre-Carolingian roots of early Romanesque art', *Romanesque and Gothic Art. Studies in Western Art. Acts of the 20th International Congress of the History of Art*, ed. M. Meiss *et al.*, I, 1963, 68).

PROVENANCE: The litany, now lost, suggested the manuscript was in use at Echternach. It was cut out by Baron Hüpsch who then split the manuscript into three parts which he sold separately to Herzog Karl Eugen von Württemberg in 1787–8.

LITERATURE: A. Schmidt, 'Baron Hüpsch in Köln als Inkunabelsammler und Händler', *Wiegendrucke und Handschriften. Festgabe Konrad Haebler zum 60. Geburtstage*, 1919, 47 ff.; C. Nordenfalk, 'On the age of the earliest Echternach manuscripts', *Acta Archaeologica*, 3, 1932, 58; A Dold, *Lichtbild-Ausgabe des Stuttgarter altlateinischen Unzialpsalters*, 1936 (repr. from *Römische Quartalschrift*, 42, 1934, 251–77, pls. XXVI–XXX); *C.L.A.*, IX, no. 1353; Lowe, *English Uncial*, 23, pl. XXXIV; C. Nordenfalk, 'Corbie and Cassiodorus', *Pantheon*, 32, 1974, 231 n. 1.

EXHIBITED: *Kunst des frühen Mittelalters*, Bern, 1949, no. 4; *Ars sacra. Kunst des frühen Mittelalters*, Munich, 1950, no. 4; *Saint-Willibrord*, Echternach, 1958, nos. 165–7, pl. XXI; *Karl der Grosse*, 1965, no. 399.

29. London, British Library Cotton MS Vespasian A. 1

Psalter (Vespasian Psalter)
235×180 mm., ff. 153
Second quarter of 8th century. Canterbury,
St. Augustine's

Ills. 143–146, fig. 7

The remaining illumination consists of a miniature showing King David and his musicians (f. 30ᵛ, but originally probably a frontispiece), and initials to each Psalm. There are more elaborate initials, two of which are historiated and all of which have continuation lettering, to Psalms 17 (f. 21ᵛ), 26 (f. 31), 38 (f. 42), 52 (f. 53), 68 (f. 64ᵛ), 80 (f. 79ᵛ), 97 (f. 93ᵛ), 109 (f. 110) and 118 (f. 115ᵛ). These mark the liturgical division of the Psalter into eight parts, except for Psalm 17. There appears to be no special reason for the emphasis on this Psalm, which is, however, also given a special initial in the Salaberga Psalter (no. 14).

The historiated initials are those to Psalms 26 and 52, the former, a D, showing David and his friend Jonathan who stand holding spears and shaking

hands (f. 31), and the latter, a D, showing David as shepherd rescuing a lamb from the lion (f. 53). Some of the larger initials are on colour backgrounds with birds, animals, and interlace filling the interstices (see f. 64ᵛ especially). The initial B of Psalm 1 is missing and since we know from the 15th-century description of Thomas of Elmham that the Psalter contained a representation of Samuel, it was probably historiated with the scene of Samuel annointing David. Another page is lost between ff. 141 and 142, the beginning of the Canticles, and an offprint shows that this was a carpet page. The colours used are rich and varied, including gold and silver, blue, green, yellow, red, red-orange, violet, and white. Wright has suggested that the main scribe is also the artist.

Wright has compared the illustrations, particularly the scene of David and his musicians, with those in the Khludov Psalter, a mid 9th-century Byzantine manuscript (Moscow, Historical Museum, Gr. 129), and concludes that both go back to a common early Christian model. He thinks the immediate model of the Vespasian Psalter is likely to have been an Italian 6th-century work, perhaps from a centre under Byzantine influence such as Ravenna. Such a book might have been brought to England by Theodore of Tarsus when he came from Rome to England in 669. In addition there are various oriental decorative motifs, especially the plant forms on f. 30ᵛ, which may derive from imported textiles.

If the historiated initials pre-date, as seems likely, the example in the Leningrad Bede (no. 19, ill. 84), they are probably the earliest surviving example of a formula for uniting text and illustration which was to remain in use throughout the Middle Ages. Here they contain narrative scenes which in the exemplar are likely to have been either marginal or prefatory full-page miniatures.

The style suggests that the Psalter is the earliest member of an important group of manuscripts from southern England, in which artists tend to preserve more of the style of their Mediterranean models than do either their Northumbrian or their Irish contemporaries (cf. the Durham Cassiodorus, no. 17). Wright has argued for a date in the second quarter of the 8th century preceding the Stockholm *Codex Aureus* (no. 30). Nordenfalk (1977) considers that the same artist worked on the Stockholm *Codex Aureus*. Kuhn's attempt to locate this and the related manuscripts in Mercia has not been generally accepted (see Sisam, 1956–7, and under *Provenance*).

PROVENANCE: Identifiable with the Psalter described by Thomas of Elmham as being kept on the high altar of St. Augustine's, Canterbury, when he wrote his history *c.* 1414–18. The Canterbury origin is confirmed by paleographic and textual evidence of the 11th century and earlier. Borrowed from Sir William Cecil, Lord Burghley, by Matthew Parker, Archbishop of Canterbury, in 1566. Sir Robert Cotton, 1599, and passed with his library to the British Museum in 1753.

LITERATURE: Westwood, *Palaeographia*, no. 40;

id., *Facsimiles*, 10–14, pl. 3; *Pal. Soc.* I, pls. 18–19; *Catalogue of ancient manuscripts in the British Museum, II. Latin manuscripts*, 1884, 8–11, pls. 12–15; F. G. Kenyon, *Facsimiles of Biblical manuscripts in the British Museum*, 1900, pl. X; M. R. James, *The ancient libraries of Canterbury and Dover*, 1903, lxv–lxvi, 501; G. F. Warner, *Illuminated manuscripts in the British Museum*, 1903, pl. 3; *Schools of illumination. Reproductions from manuscripts in the British Museum*, I, 1914, 8, pls. 6, 7; Zimmermann, *Vorkarolingische Miniaturen*, 120, 131, 133–4, 289–91, pls. 286–8; J. Brøndsted, *Early English Ornament*, 1924, 102–4, 109, 112, 122 n. 1, 124, figs. 84, 85b; *British Museum. Reproductions from Illuminated Manuscripts, Series IV*, 1928, 7, pl. I; Kendrick, *Anglo-Saxon*, 159 ff., 181, pl. LXV. 2; Micheli, *L'enluminure*, 31, 33, pl. 15; S. M. Kuhn, 'The Vespasian Psalter and the Old English Charter hands', *Speculum*, 18, 1943, 458–83, pl. I; S. M. Kuhn, 'From Canterbury to Lichfield', *Speculum*, 23, 1948, 591–629, pls. I, IIb; C. Nordenfalk, 'A note on the Stockholm *Codex aureus*', *Nordisk Tidskrift för Bok- och Biblioteksväsen*, 38, 1951, 147 ff.; K. Sisam, 'Canterbury, Lichfield and the Vespasian Psalter', *Review of English Studies*, N.S. 7, 1956, 1–10, 113–31; *ib.*, N.S. 8, 1957, 370–4; S. M. Kuhn, 'Some early Mercian manuscripts', *ib.*, N.S. 8, 1957, 355–70; Ker, *Catalogue*, 266–7 (no. 203); W. Oakeshott, *Classical Inspiration in Medieval Art*, 1959, 36–8, 124, pl. 51a; Lowe, *English Uncial*, 8, 21–2, pls. XXVI–XXVII; H. Steger, *David Rex et Propheta*, 1961, 155–7, pl. 3; Rickert, *Painting in Britain*, 18–19, 49, pl. 10b; S. M. Kuhn *ed.*, *The Vespasian Psalter*, 1965; D. H. Wright, *The Vespasian Psalter* (Early English Manuscripts in Facsimile, XIV), 1967; *id.*, 'The Italian stimulus on English art around 700', *Stil und Überlieferung in der Kunst des Abendlandes. Akten des 21. Internat. Kongress für Kunstgeschichte, Bonn, 1964*, I, 1967, 90, pl. 5/2; R. L. S. Bruce-Mitford, 'The reception by the Anglo-Saxons of Mediterranean Art following their conversion from Ireland and Rome', *Settimane di studio del Centro italiano di studi sull'alto medioevo, Spoleto*, 14, 1967, 822–5, pls. XXXVII–XXXVIII; *C.L.A.*, II, no. 193; Koehler, *Buchmalerei*, 16, 24, 78, 87, 118, 192; Nordenfalk, *Celtic*, 95, pl. 32.

30. Stockholm, Royal Library MS A. 135

Gospel Book (Codex Aureus)
395×314 mm., ff. 193.
Mid 8th century. Canterbury

Ills. 147, 152–159

The illumination consists of incomplete Canon Tables on eight pages (ff. 5–8^{v}) and Evangelist portraits of St. Matthew (f. 9^{v}) and St. John (f. 150^{v})—those of St. Mark and St. Luke are missing. There are initials to the Prefaces *Novum Opus* (f. 1) and *Plures* (f. 2) with decorated continuation lettering, and whole decorated initial pages for St. Matthew, L (f. 10) and 'Xpi' (f. 11), St. Luke, Q (f. 97), and St. John I (f. 151). Other decorated initials are at Luke XXII, 1, *Adpropinquabat autem* (f. 141) and for the preface to St. John (f. 149); the initial I to St. Mark (f. 63) is simpler.

The Canon Tables (Canons I–VIII) are 'm n' arches filled with a variety of patterns. On ff. 6–7 the outer capitals and bases are replaced with medallions with half-length figures of saints holding books.

The text of the Gospels is written on alternating purple-stained and white folios, the script on the former being white or gold. Silver and red are also used. Various geometrical line patterns, including crosses and the 'Chi Rho', are introduced into the text, either by varying the colours of the inks, or by introducing dividing lines, or by the use of geometric ornament. Nordenfalk (1951) has shown that this pattern making on the script pages is probably derived from the *Carmina figurata* of Porfyrius, court poet of Constantine. Porfyrius was known to Bede and there is a reference to a copy which Lullus, Archbishop of Mainz, wanted and which Bishop Cuthbert, probably the Archbishop of Canterbury (740–60), had not yet returned. The colouring of the manuscript is very rich, and the extensive use of gold and of blue is particularly striking. Colours are shaded preserving still something of the late antique illusionistic style, for example the marble columns of St. Matthew's arch.

The Gospel Book is generally assigned to Canterbury (though Kuhn has argued for Mercia and Masai tentatively proposed York), and dated slightly later than the Vespasian Psalter (no. 29). The Evangelist portraits are of a different type from those in the Book of Lindisfarne (no. 9) or the Irish tradition (nos. 44–9), and go less far in transforming the late antique style of their Mediterranean models. Insular ornament is used but is more confined, less invasive, for example the interlace on St. Matthew's throne. It seems likely that the model was the so-called Gospels of St. Augustine (Cambridge, Corpus Christi College MS 286, fig. 23) in which the formal arrangement of frontal Evangelist with symbol in the tympanum above is the same. The Gospels of St. Augustine is a sixth-century Italian Gospel Book which was preserved at St. Augustine's Canterbury in the Middle Ages, and which by tradition had been brought to England by St. Augustine himself. Unfortunately only the portrait of St. Luke is preserved so no direct comparison is possible. In both Gospel Books the Evangelists do not write and St. Luke is shown seated out of doors with small plants flanking his throne, which are found also, though more formalized, in the Stockholm St. Matthew.

Wormald, however, notes stylistic differences which suggest that if the St. Augustine Gospel Book was indeed used as model, other models were also available (cf. also the discussion by Koehler, 1972). Thus the drapery with its tubular folds, he suggests, recalls rather more the fifth-century *Virgilius Romanus* (Vat. Lat. 3867), and the colouring is also different from that in the St. Augustine Gospels. These differences might perhaps be explained, however, by the influence of the pictorial vocabulary of the earlier Vespasian Psalter (no. 29), which depends on a different type of Mediterranean model. The colouring of the Psalter is similarly rich in its use of shaded blue and pink (the colour of the Virgil is again different). It seems far-fetched to posit another late antique Gospel Book at Canterbury with similar iconography but in a different style.

Nordenfalk (1977) distinguishes two artists in the book, of whom the first executed the Canon Tables on ff. 5 and 8 and probably the St. Matthew (f. 9ᵛ) and who, he considers, was probably also responsible for the frontispiece of the Vespasian Psalter (no. 29). The way in which the continuation lettering is placed on bands of gold and is decorated with small animals, birds, interlace and other motifs in the interstices, is similar to that of the initial pages of the Vespasian Psalter (no. 29), the Royal Gospel Book (no. 32), the Barberini Gospel Book (no. 36) and the Book of Cerne (no. 66).

PROVENANCE: According to an inscription on f. 11, the Gospel Book was obtained from a heathen army for gold by the Aldorman Aelfred and given by him and his wife, Werburg, to Christ Church, Canterbury (printed *Sweet's Anglo Saxon Reader*, revised edn. by Dorothy Whitelock, 1970, no. XXXV). Aelfred is usually identified with an earl who made his will between 871 and 889 (*Sweet's Reader*, no. XXXIV), but Ker notes that the script of the inscription looks earlier and resembles that of Canterbury charters of *c.* 830–40. On f. 1 an inscription, 10th century (?), asks for prayers for Ceolheard, Niclas, Ealhun, and Wulfhelm aurifex. The Gospels later belonged to Jerónimo Zurita, the Spanish scholar (1512–80); the Carthusians of Aula Dei, Saragossa; Gaspar de Guzmán, Conde-Duque de Olivares (d. 1645); and his son, Gaspar de Haro, Marqués d'Eliche. It was acquired for the Swedish Royal Library from the last named by Johan Gabriel Sparwenfeldt in Madrid in 1690 (his note, f. 3.).

LITERATURE: Westwood, *Facsimiles*, 1–7, pls. I, II; J. Belsheim, *Codex aureus sive quattuor Evangelia ante Hieronymum Latine translata*, 1878, pls. I–IV; Zimmermann, *Vorkarolingische Miniaturen*, 128, 131–5, 139, 286–9, pls. 204a, 280–6; J. Brøndsted, *Early English Ornament*, 1924, 109–13, 122 ff., figs. 92, 94; Saunders, *English Illumination*, 14; W. Koehler, *Die Karolingischen Miniaturen. Die Schule von Tours*, I, 1, 1933 (reprinted 1963), 76–8; Kendrick, *Anglo-Saxon*, 136, 139, 148, 159, pl. LXV.1; Micheli, *L'enluminure*, 31–2, 62, 93, pls. 17, 133; Åberg, *Occident*, 98, fig. 72; Masai, *Origines*, 29, 62 f., 119, 124 f., 132, pls. XXXVI–XXXVIII; S. M. Kuhn, 'From Canterbury to Lichfield', *Speculum*, 23, 1948, espec. 592–8, pl. Ia; C. Nordenfalk, 'A note on the Stockholm *Codex Aureus*', *Nordisk Tidskrift för Bok- och Biblioteksväsen*, 38, 1951, 145–55, figs. 3–7, 10, 13; A. Boeckler, 'Die Evangelistenbilder der Adagruppe, *Münchner Jahrbuch der bildenden Kunst*, 3rd ser., 3/4, 1952–3, 122–6, fig. 2; F. Wormald, *The miniatures in the Gospels of St. Augustine, Corpus Christi College MS. 286*, 1954, 9 ff., 14, pls. XV, XVIb; K. Sisam, 'Canterbury, Lichfield and the Vespasian Psalter', *Review of English Studies*, N.S. 7, 1956, 7–8, 115 f.,

and *ib.*, 8, 1957, 370–4; S. M. Kuhn, 'Some early Mercian manuscripts', *Review of English Studies*, N.S. 8, 1957, 355–70, espec. 364–6; Ker, *Catalogue*, 456 (no 385); Nordenfalk, *Early Medieval*, 124–5, 139, colour plate p. 123; W. Oakeshott, *Classical Inspiration in Medieval Art*, 1959, 36–8, 124, pls. 52 a, b; Lowe, *English Uncial*, 8, 21–2, pl. XXVIII a, b; H. Buchthal, 'A Byzantine miniature of the fourth Evangelist and its relatives', *Dumbarton Oaks Papers*, 15, 1961, 135–6, fig. 10; McGurk, *Latin Gospel Books*, no. 111; Rickert, *Painting in Britain*, 19, pl. 11a; D. H. Wright, *The Vespasian Psalter* (Early English Manuscripts in Facsimile, XIV), 1967, 57–8, 63, 68, 79, pl. Vp; *C.L.A.*, XI, no. 1642; Koehler, *Buchmalerei*, 16, 22, 24, 78 ff., 104, 118, 112 f., 184; Henry, *Kells*, 155 n., 204, 215, 219, 224, fig. 56; Nordenfalk, *Celtic*, 10, 19, 26, 96–106, pls. 33–8.

EXHIBITED: *Gyllene Böcker. Illuminerade medeltida handskrifter i dansk och svensk ägo*, Nationalmuseum, Stockholm, 1952, no. 8, pls. II, III; *Karl der Grosse*, 1965, no. 397, pls. 44–5.

31. New York, Pierpont Morgan Library MS M. 776

Psalter (Lothian Psalter)
300–5 × 225–30 mm., ff. 88
Mid 8th century. (?) Southern England

Ills. 148–151

The manuscript has been mutilated and there are at least twenty-seven leaves missing, twenty-one from the beginning of the Psalter containing Psalms 1–31, 2, and six from within the text. Each Psalm is introduced by an initial and there are also major initials surviving to Psalms 38 (f. 7), 68 (f. 27), 80 (f. 40), and 118 (f. 66). For these there is continuation lettering with the letters set in panels (ff. 7, 27) and decorated with interlace, spirals, animal, human, and other motifs. Originally the liturgical and tripartite division of the Psalter will have been emphasized by similar initials, as is clear from offsets from the missing pages. The colours used are orange, green, yellow, purple, light blue, pink, and gold.

There are some close similarities with the initials of the Vespasian Psalter (no. 29) and the arrangement of the continuation lettering in panels also recalls the Canterbury group. However, it is also possible that the manuscript was produced in the central or western part of England, where the Old English glosses were added in the 9th or 10th century. The use of lines of red dots in patterns also recalls the Book of Prayers in the British Library, possibly from Mercia (no. 35). The quality of the illumination is high and many of the Psalm initials are imaginative (e.g. ff. 13, 34 with human heads, f. 20 with human hand and f. 78 with fish).

PROVENANCE: A calendar, probably for Lincoln use, is prefixed (ff. viii–x), and extracts from the four Gospels are copied (f. 89), 15th century. Notes and names on flyleaves, 16th–17th centuries, are connected with Lincoln where the manuscript was used as an oath book from the early 16th century at the latest. Sir Richard Ellis of Nocton, Lincs., d. 1742, and from him by descent to the Marquess of Lothian, Blickling Hall, Norfolk. Sold, American Art Association, New York, 27 January 1932, no. 1.

LITERATURE: *New Pal. Soc.*, I, pls. 231–2; Zimmermann, *Vorkarolingische Miniaturen*, 120–1, 273, pl. 251; Saunders, *English Illumination*, 4; S. de Ricci, W. J. Wilson, *Census of Medieval and Renaissance Manuscripts in the United States and Canada*, II, 1937, 1502, 2320; *The Pierpont Morgan Library. Review of the activities and acquisitions of the library from 1930 through 1935*, 1937, 15–6, 92; S. M. Kuhn, 'From Canterbury to Lichfield', *Speculum*, 23, 1948, 609; R. Weber, *Les Psautiers latins* (Collectanea Biblica Latina, X), 1953, xiii, 3, etc.; Ker, *Catalogue*, 348 (no. 287); Nordenfalk, *Early Medieval*, 125; *C.L.A.*, XI, no. 1661; D. H. Wright, *The Vespasian Psalter* (Early English Manuscripts in Facsimile, XIV), 1967, 61 n. 3, 63–4, 68.

EXHIBITED: *Illuminated Books of the Middle Ages and Renaissance*, Baltimore, 1949, no. 1, pl. I; *Liturgical manuscripts for the Mass and the Divine Office*, Pierpont Morgan Library, New York, 1964, no. 44, pl.; *Mediaeval and Renaissance Manuscripts*, Pierpont Morgan Library, New York, 1974, no. 1, pl.; *Anglo-Saxon Vernacular Manuscripts in America*, Pierpont Morgan Library, New York, 1976, no. 10, pl. 11.

32. London, British Library Royal MS 1. E. VI and Canterbury, Cathedral Library Additional MS 16

Gospel Book (fragment of a Bible)
467×345 mm., ff. ii+78
Later 8th century. Canterbury

Ills. 160–164

The illumination consists of Canon Tables complete on five pages (ff. 4–6), an *incipit* page for St. Luke (f. 43) and smaller initials, Z (Chapter lists for St. Luke, f. 42), and F (Chapter lists for St. John, f. 68). The openings of the other three Gospels are lost, but there are fine pages of large ornate display script in gold and silver on purple stained pages on ff. 1ᵛ, 30 (preceding St. Mark), and 44 (preceding St. Luke) and in orange on plain vellum on f. 28ᵛ (*explicit* of St. Matthew).

The *incipit* page of St. Luke is also stained purple (f. 43). In the lunette of the arch is a half-length figure of St. Luke's symbol, the Calf, and above in a circular medallion affixed to the arch is a blessing figure, presumably representing the Evangelist. The colours used are gold, silver, orange, green, and yellow. On f. 30ᵛ a portrait of St. Mark has been added by an Anglo-Saxon artist in the early 11th century (see Temple, *Anglo-Saxon*, no. 55, pl. 172).

It looks as if the clouds in the lunette of f. 43 and perhaps the symbol and the Evangelist were repainted at this time by the same artist.

The Canon Tables are richly ornamented with panels of interlace, fret pattern, animal and plant ornament. There are also filling designs in orange dots with interlace and animals.

The iconography of the St. Luke *incipit* recalls the so-called Gospel Book of St. Augustine (Cambridge, Corpus Christi College MS 286), a 6th–century Italian manuscript believed to have been brought to England by St. Augustine of Canterbury (fig. 23). The symbol is almost identical. A later adaptation is in the Book of Cerne (no. 66). Other features, particularly some of the ornament of plants and animals reserved in white on the Canon Tables and the lettering in panels, are reminiscent of the Vespasian Psalter (no. 29), the Stockholm *Codex Aureus* (no. 30) whose Evangelist portraits also appear to copy the Gospel Book of St. Augustine, and the related group.

Of great interest are the inscriptions on ff. 1ᵛ, 30, and 44 which show that there were once miniatures at the beginning of the manuscript and preceding St. Mark and St. Luke. The first (f. 1ᵛ) reads: *Haec est speciosa quadriga luciflua animae spiritus gratia per os agni Dei inlustrata in quo quattuor proceres consona voce magnalia Dei cantant.* The miniature, emphasizing the concordance of the four Gospels as is common in other Insular manuscripts (nos. 6, 21, 26, 52, 53, 70), probably showed the Lamb of God surrounded by the four symbols. The second inscription (f. 30) reads: *Hic Jesus baptizatus est ab Johanne in Jordane caelis apertis Spiritu Sancto in specie columba* (sic) *discendente super eum voceque paterna filius alti throni vocicatus* (sic). The miniature must have represented the Baptism. The third inscription (f. 44) reads: *Hic Gabriel angelus Zachariae sacerdoti in templo domini apparuit almumque praecursorem magni regis ei nasciturum praedixit.* This miniature must have shown the Annunciation of the birth of the Baptist to Zaccharias.

Pages with symbols surrounding the Lamb are found in a number of Carolingian manuscripts, particularly of the Tours school (J. Hubert, J. Porcher, W. F. Volbach, *Carolingian Art*, pls. 120–1) and also in the Gospel Book from St. Amand in Valenciennes, (*ib.*, pl. 171). The Baptism and the Annunciation to Zaccharias are found in historiated initials at the beginning of the Gospels of St. Mark and St. Luke in the Soissons and Harley Gospel Books of the Charlemagne Court school (*ib.*, pl. 71).

The lost miniatures seem to have been full page. All four Gospels begin imperfectly, but the missing text is short. McGurk (1962), therefore, reconstructs the original sequence as of four pages all on rectos with the versos blank, first the description of the miniature, second the miniature, third the initial page with symbol and Evangelist, and fourth the remaining introductory text of the Gospels written in large capitals. The two purple pages still surviving for St. Luke (ff. 43, 44) have presumably changed places. The manuscript is too tightly bound for collation, but all four introductory pages may have been singletons. The first three pages certainly and the fourth probably will have been stained purple. In St. Mark and St. Luke the four pages preceded the Gospel text. In St. John, however, offsets show that the description and the miniature were separated from the initial page by the Chapter list. There are no offsets of the St. Matthew pages, but there may well have been an extra initial page of the 'Xpi' as in other Insular manuscripts.

The first of two quire numerations in the Gospel Book runs from LXXX to LXXXVIII and this, as well as the large size of the manuscript, have led to the supposition that this is part of a Bible and not a separate Gospel Book. Thomas of Elmham in his history of St. Augustine's written c. 1414–18 described a 'Biblia Gregoriana' in two volumes as having certain leaves inserted which were coloured purple or rose (James, *Ancient Libraries*) and which, when held up to the light, gave a wonderful reflection. It seems likely (cf. James, McGurk as against Warner and Gilson), that the present manuscript was part of that Bible, though already separated from it in the 15th century (see under PROVENANCE). If so the Bible would have been the equal in magnificence of the *Codex Amiatinus* (no. 7), and like it was probably based on an early Christian prototype, from which would have come its monumentality, and such features as the purple stained pages, the classicizing inscription pages, and perhaps the cycle of scenes. Lowe considers that a detached leaf in the Bodleian Library, Oxford (MS Lat. bibl. b. 2(P), *C.L.A.*, II, no. 244, Pächt and Alexander, III, no. 4), which contains Acts XVIII, 27–XXI, 12 is part of the same manuscript. The text of the Canterbury leaf contains John XI, 38–XII, 34 and follows directly the last leaf of the Royal manuscript.

PROVENANCE: Pressmark *Distinctio III Gradus I* and *ex libris* of St. Augustine's, Canterbury, 14th century, f. ii. The *secundum folium*, however, does not correspond with the Gospel Book listed under this pressmark in the 15th-century catalogue, which, moreover, was a glossed book (James, *Ancient Libraries*). Presumably the manuscript was by then kept in the church. The Bodleian leaf was found in the binding of MS Bodley 381, an 11th-century manuscript also from St. Augustine's. John, Lord Lumley, f. iᵛ, whose collection passed into the Royal library after his death in 1609.

LITERATURE: Westwood, *Palaeographia*, no. 21; *id.*, *Facsimiles*, 39–42, pls. XIV–XV; *Pal. Soc.*, I, pl. 7; *Catalogue of ancient manuscripts in the British Museum, II. Latin manuscripts*, 1884, 20–2, pls. 17–18; M. R. James, *The ancient libraries of Canterbury and Dover*, 1903, lxiv–lxv, lxvii, 208 (no. 190), 500, 516; *British Museum. Reproductions from Illuminated Manuscripts*, Series III, 1908, 9, pl. III; Zimmermann, *Vorkarolingische Miniaturen*, 131, 134–5, 139, 143, 291–3, pls. 289–92; G. F. Warner, J. P. Gilson, *Catalogue of Western Manuscripts in the Old Royal and King's Collections in the British Museum*, I, 1921, 20, IV, pl. 14; J. Brøndsted, *Early English Ornament*, 1924, 104, 106, 108, 117 ff., 122 n. 1, 127, 138, 159,

figs. 86, 88, 98, 99, 100; Saunders, *English Illumination*, 14, pl. 15; A. Schardt, *Das Initial*, 1938, 43, pl. (p. 44); Kendrick, *Anglo-Saxon*, 148, 162 ff., 168, 184, 188, pl. LXVI; Micheli, *L'enluminure*, 31–2, 51, 62, 114, pl. 16; Åberg, *Occident*, 74, figs. 53. 1–2; W. Urry, *Annual Report of the Friends of Canterbury Cathedral*, 21, 1948, 33 ff.; S. M. Kuhn 'From Canterbury to Lichfield', *Speculum*, 23, 1948, 612–13; F. Wormald, *The miniatures in the Gospels of St. Augustine*, 1954, 8–9, pl. XIVb; K. Sisam, 'Canterbury, Lichfield and the Vespasian Psalter', *Review of English Studies*, N.S. 7, 1956, 7; S. M. Kuhn, 'Some early Mercian manuscripts', *Review of English Studies*, N.S. 8, 1957, 364; Nordenfalk, *Early Medieval*, 125; P. McGurk, 'An Anglo-Saxon Bible fragment of the late eighth century', *Journal of the Warburg and Courtauld Institutes*, 25, 1962, 18–34, pls. 4, 5; D. H. Wright review of P. H. Blair, *The Moore Bede* in *Anglia*, 82, 1964, 116 f.; Rickert, *Painting in Britain*, 19–20, pl. 16; D. H. Wright, *The Vespasian Psalter* (Early English Manuscripts in Facsimile, XIV), 1967, 57–8, 68, 79; F. Wormald, 'Bible illustration in medieval manuscripts', *The Cambridge History of the Bible*, ed. G. W. H. Lampe, 2, 1969, 310–11; *C.L.A.*, II, nos. 214, 244 and *Supplement*, 1971, 5; Koehler, *Buchmalerei*, 16–17, 24, 188.

33. London, British Library Cotton MS Tiberius C. II

Bede, Historia ecclesiastica
272 × 216 mm., ff. 157
Late 8th century. (?) Southern England

Ills. 134, 165

The illumination consists of initial letters and continuation lettering to each of the five books, Book I, B (f. 5ᵛ), Book II, H (f. 34ᵛ), Book III, A (f. 60ᵛ), Book IV, 'In' (f. 94), and Book V, S (f. 126). The most elaborate initial is the first which has panels of interlace, key pattern, and animal and plant scroll reserved on black, and in the centre of the letter a white cross and four small grotesque beasts on grounds of green and orange. The text is continued in white ribbon lettering with animal and bird heads, on three panels, the first orange framing yellow, the second yellow framing orange, and the third green framing yellow. In the third panel the letters are alternately orange and white. The letters overlap and interlace with the frame, and the two lower panels are joined by interlace at the right. The B is outlined by a double row of orange dots.

The H of Book II contains a bird on a plant scroll and the continuation lettering is in black with colour blobbing and some animal heads but no panelling. Another bird occurs in the A of Book III. Here the continuation lettering is white on a green panel framed in orange. The first and the last letters, T and R, have mask heads which bite the frame. The last two initials have similar panels of continuation lettering, that on f. 126 with a human head. The chalice forms breaking into interlace on f. 94 should also be noted. The colours used are the same as on f. 5ᵛ.

Many small initials occur in the text with colour blobbing, outline dots, animal and interlace terminals, those to the lists of chapters rather larger and more elaborate.

The type of initials, many of the specific motifs and the use of lettering on panels link the manuscript with the Vespasian Psalter (no. 29) the Stockholm *Codex Aureus* (no. 30) and the Royal Gospel Book (no. 32), for which a Canterbury origin seems assured. The manuscript may perhaps have belonged to Lindisfarne shortly after it was written (see under PROVENANCE), but it seems unlikely that it was made there. Kendrick suggested a Mercian origin linking it with the Book of Cerne (no. 66), and Kuhn attributed the whole group to Mercia.

The form of initial decoration evolved here is taken up and further elaborated in Anglo-Saxon initials of the 10th and 11th centuries (cf. Temple, *Anglo-Saxon*, 11). On ff. 4ᵛ–5 are later (? 12th-century) pen sketches.

PROVENANCE: In Bede's preliminary letter an almost contemporary hand has written *nostro* between the words *patre* and *et antistite cudberchto*, f. 4. This may suggest that the manuscript then belonged to the congregation of St. Cuthbert at Lindisfarne (Ker, 1957).

LITERATURE: Westwood, *Facsimiles*, 79–80, pl. 52, figs. 7, 9; *Pal. Soc.*, I, pl. 141; *Catalogue of ancient manuscripts in the British Museum, II. Latin manuscripts*, 1884, 78–9, pl. 19; Zimmermann, *Vorkarolingische Miniaturen*, 135, 138, 141, 144, 294, pls. 291–2; J. Brøndsted, *Early English Ornament*, 1924, 109, 112, 114 n. 1, 120–2, 122 n. 1, 124, fig. 101; Saunders, *English Illumination*, 15, pl. 16; Kendrick, *Anglo-Saxon*, 153, 168, 199, pl. LXIX. 2; Micheli, *L'enluminure*, 31, 33, 51, 65–6; S. M. Kuhn, 'From Canterbury to Lichfield', *Speculum*, 23, 1948, 613–19; K. Sisam, 'Canterbury, Lichfield and the Vespasian Psalter', *Review of English Studies*, N.S. 7, 1956, 8–9; *ib.*, N.S. 8, 1957, 370; S. M. Kuhn, 'Some early Mercian manuscripts', *ib.*, N.S. 8, 1957, 366–8; Ker, *Catalogue*, 261 (no. 198); D. H. Wright, review of P. H. Blair, *The Moore Bede* in *Anglia*, 82, 1964, 116 f.; Rickert, *Painting in Britain*, 20, pl. 15; D. H. Wright, *The Vespasian Psalter* (Early English Manuscripts in Facsimile, XIV), 1967, 68, 79; B. Colgrave, R. A. B. Mynors ed., *Bede's Ecclesiastical History of the English People*, 1969, xlii; *C.L.A.*, II, no. 191; Koehler, *Buchmalerei*, 188.

34. Paris, Bibliothèque Nationale MS lat. 281, 298

Gospel Book (Codex Bigotianus)
345–50 × 262–75 mm., ff. 265
Late 8th century. (?) Southern England

Ills. 166–168

Latin 281 contains 216 folios and the remaining 49 folios containing St. John with the colophon bound out of place at f. 1 are in lat. 298. The illumination consists of initials of eight to ten lines in height for each Gospel, Matthew, L (f. 7), Mark, I (f. 86), Luke, Q (f. 137) and John, I (f. 2 of lat. 298). The manuscript has suffered from damp and has also been defaced. The fillings of the initials and the letters of the opening words of Matthew, Luke, and John, which were set on coloured panels and which seem to have been of leaf gold, have been scraped off. Colours remaining are blue, olive green, brown, orange, and black. The Q (f. 137) has panels in the stem and the bowl containing birds and animals with interlace, and inside the bowl of the letter is a biting lion head with a dolphin in its jaws. The colours used are orange, green, and blue with a few traces of gold remaining. The I (f. 2 of lat. 298) has similar panels filled with animals and birds. The Canon Tables, originally following f. 4 of lat. 281, have been lost. It is not clear if Evangelist portraits ever existed. There appear to be offprints of colour on ff. 86, 137, but the collation is not decisive.

Lowe calls the general aspect of the script 'south English'. The use of continuation lettering on panels and the animal decoration link the Gospel Book with the Canterbury group of the Vespasian Psalter (no. 29).

PROVENANCE: *Ex libris* of the Benedictine abbey of La Trinité, Fécamp, 15th century, f. 1ᵛ of lat. 298. Jean Bigot with his bookplate, lat. 281, first half 17th century. Acquired with the Biblioteca Bigotiana for the Royal Library in 1706.

LITERATURE: L. Delisle, *Le cabinet des manuscrits de la bibliothèque nationale*, III, 1881, 214, pl. X; Zimmermann, *Vorkarolingische Miniaturen*, 289, pls. 285 b, c; J. Brøndsted, *Early English Ornament*, 1924, 108–9, 111–13, 122 n. 1, 124, fig. 93; Kenney, *Sources*, no. 495; Micheli, *L'enluminure*, 50–1, pl. 73; *C.L.A.*, V, no. 526; Lowe, *English Uncial*, 22, pls. XXX–XXXI; McGurk, *Latin Gospel Books*, no. 58; G. Nortier, *Les bibliothèques médiévales des abbayes bénédictines de Normandie*, 1971, 6, 19, 26.

35. London, British Library Royal MS 2.A.XX

Book of Prayers
233 × 170 mm., ff. 52
Second half of 8th century. (?) Mercia

Ill. 133

The illumination consists of the initials *Liber* in gold and silver outlined in orange (f. 1) and an 'In' in black ink with animal cross-bar with some green and orange colouring (f. 17). Smaller initials are filled with colour and outlined with red dots. Paleographic evidence supports a Mercian origin according to Lowe. There seems to be some influence from the south English school (nos. 29, etc.) seen also in the Book of Cerne (no. 66).

PROVENANCE: Old English glosses, 10th century, suggest a Mercian origin. John Theyer, Cowpers Hill, Glos., with his notes, one dated 1649. Probably the *Precationes quaedam charactere saxonico 4°* in Patrick Young's catalogue of the manuscripts of Worcester Cathedral (ed. I. Atkins, N. R. Ker, 1944, no. 309).

LITERATURE: *Catalogue of ancient manuscripts in the British Museum, II. Latin manuscripts*, 1884, 60, pl. 21; A. B. Kuypers, *The Book of Cerne*, 1902, 200–25; G. F. Warner, J. P. Gilson, *Catalogue of Western Manuscripts in the Old Royal and King's Collections in the British Museum*, I, 1921, 33–6, IV, pl. 18; Kenney, *Sources*, no. 576; Ker, *Catalogue*, 317–18 (no. 248); *C.L.A.*, II, no. 215; Temple, *Anglo-Saxon*, 11, fig. 4.

36. Rome, Vatican, Biblioteca Apostolica MS Barberini Lat. 570

Gospel Book
340 × 250 mm., ff. 153
Second half of 8th century.

Ills. 169–178

The illumination consists of Canon Tables, Evangelist portraits and initial pages. The Canons are on twelve pages (ff. 1–6ᵛ), but only the first seven pages have the arches inserted (ff. 1–4). Some faint traces sketched in ink are visible on f. 6ᵛ. The arches are of the 'm' form with four columns, so that the last is left blank in Canons II, III, and IV. Their decoration is incomplete. The first page (f. 1) shows the four Evangelist symbols under the arches, half-length, erect, haloed, and holding books. They face towards each other in pairs. The columns and arches are filled with interlace except for the centre column. Here the capital is a frontal human face and there is a filling of lacertine animals with interlacing tails. Half-way down a frontal squatting naked figure holds his beard with his left hand and touches his genitals with his right. Pairs of lacertine animals threaten his head and his genitals. The inclusion of such a figure in this context is unexplained. For the symbols under the arches see the Maeseyck Gospel Book (no. 22) and the Book of Kells (no. 52). The colours used are orange, greenish blue, blue, lilac, and yellow. The columns of the other Canons are coloured in orange and yellow but left blank.

The four Evangelist portraits, St. Matthew (f. 11ᵛ), St. Mark (f. 50ᵛ), St. Luke (f. 79ᵛ), and St. John (f. 124ᵛ) show bearded figures seated in a landscape without symbols. Each is inscribed. St. Matthew dips his pen to the right and has a lap-board (see Metzger, 1968, for the representations of this early form of writing desk). The miniature has a frame of panels of interlace and interlacing lacertine animals. There is a corner motif at the bottom left corner and sketches for similar motifs at the top corners. St. Mark (f. 50ᵛ) is also frontal, writing on a scroll held across his lap. He wears a pink robe with a purple cloak with the folds indicated in orange. The background is green above and yellow below. The panels of the frame are not filled in. St. Luke (f. 79ᵛ) sits with legs crossed facing three-quarters to the right. He also writes on a scroll held across his lap. He wears a blue cloak over a yellow mantle. The background is pink above and green below. The frame is again incomplete and not even the panels are indicated. St. John (f. 124ᵛ) is a frontal enthroned figure writing in a book on his lap and turning his head slightly to the right. He wears an orange cloak over a purple mantle. The frame panels are again blank except for the centre panel below, in which an animal is sketched apparently drinking. The date of this, as also its significance, is uncertain. On f. 11 the St. Matthew figure and the plant scroll are traced through from the verso (cf. Macgregol Gospel Book, no. 54). Perhaps this and the animal on f. 124ᵛ were done at the same date.

The initial pages are St. Matthew, L (f. 12), a relatively small letter with continuation lettering on coloured panels; 'Xpi' (f. 18), a magnificent whole-page monogram with the text continued in capitals below; St. Mark, 'Ini' (f. 51), the monogram and *incipit* filling the left-hand column of script; St. Luke, Q (f. 80), the uncial letter filling the left column and the text continuing as ribbon lettering of intertwining lacertine animals in white and black on colour grounds in the right column; St. John, 'In' (f. 125), the monogram is again placed in the left column and the text continues as ribbon lettering of lacertine animals in the right column, though the last panel at the bottom extends into the left column. On all the initial pages there are very intricate patterns of orange dots which form a more or less regular frame to the initials and also fill all the spaces. Striking frontal human masks are placed at the top of the shafts of the St. Mark monogram (f. 51) and below at the right is a half-length winged angel. The tail of the Q of St. Luke (f. 80) is a large biting animal head. There is a great wealth of animal, interlace, trumpet, spiral, and other patterns, and the colours are rich, varied and often bright (blue, violet, orange). On the 'Xpi' page there is a plant scroll inhabited by birds at the left and vegetable forms occur elsewhere (cf. nos. 37, 40, and the Book of Kells, no. 52). There are a number of small relatively plain initials for the Prefaces and Chapter lists. There are also initials and calligraphic embellishments in the text, especially on ff. 24ᵛ ff. and ff. 85 ff.

Though incomplete the decoration is of very high quality. Unfortunately there is no indication of date, of where the Gospel Book was made, or even of its later history. It has been attributed to Northumbria (Henry, see PROVENANCE), southern England and Mercia (Kendrick). A date in the second half of the 8th century seems generally agreed upon. The continuation lettering of lacertine animals on panels recalls the Canterbury group (e.g. no. 29). But this style evidently spread elsewhere, as is shown by the Book of Cerne (no. 66) to which the present manuscript has also been compared. Both the figure style and the decoration show a greater indebtedness to late antique Mediterranean sources than does the Book of Cerne, however. It seems doubtful if, even taking the later date of Cerne into account, the two books can be attributed to the same centre.

Some similarities with the first Maeseyck Gospel Book (no. 22) should be noted (cf. Koehler). Both books have Evangelist symbols in the Canon Tables and the frame of the Maeseyck Evangelist portrait is rather similar in the design of interlace and lacertine animal panels to that of the St. Matthew portrait here. Though the portrait there is of a different type and placed on a different type of throne under an arch, he is also bearded and there is no symbol. If the suggestion that the Maeseyck portrait is a product of York is correct, the Barberini Gospel Book could possibly be so too, though considerably later in date. The comparison of the foliage scroll on the 'Xpi' page (f. 18) with that on the bowl (fig. 11) found at Ormside, Westmorland, though, of course, not necessarily produced in that area, is also striking (cf. Kendrick, 151–2).

Iconographically the absence of symbols and the fact that the Evangelists are bearded suggest a model with Eastern connections. The combination of landscape elements with what in origin is perhaps a wall or screen in front of which the Evangelist sits, is also reminiscent of Byzantine Evangelist portraits. It has, however, become so misunderstood that it is unlikely to be a direct copy; and such a hypothetical early Eastern model could already have been transformed in an Italo-Byzantine milieu (cf. Boeckler). The Carolingian Godescalc Gospel lectionary (Paris, B.N., n. acq. lat. 1203, J. Hubert, J. Porcher, W. F. Volbach, *Carolingian Art*, 1970, pls. 64–5, 276–8) has some parallel features, e.g. bearded Evangelists, plant scrolls, and the type of throne, though symbols are included there. A rare feature, also apparently Eastern, is the drape spread over the thrones. The three-quarter face Luke portrait should also be compared with the Luke portrait in the Book of Lindisfarne (no. 9), who is also writing on a scroll, as well as to the only surviving portrait, St. Mark, in the 6th-century Greek Gospel Book in Rossano.

PROVENANCE: On f. 153 is written: *Ora pro wigbaldo*, apparently the scribe. Henry has proposed an identification with Hygebeald, Bishop of Lindisfarne 781–802, but it seems very doubtful if the name is the same. The *Biblioteca Barberina* founded mainly by Francesco Barberini (1597–1679) was bought by Pope Leo XIII for the Vatican in 1902.

LITERATURE: Zimmermann, *Vorkarolingische Miniaturen*, 25, 34, 128, 140–2, 300–2, pls. 313–17; *New Pal. Soc.*, II, pls. 58–60; J. Brøndsted, *Early English Ornament*, 1924, 115–16, fig. 97; Saunders, *English Illumination*, 8, 12; *C.L.A.*, I, no. 63; A. Schardt, *Das Initial*, 1938, 35, pl. p. 38; Kendrick, *Anglo-Saxon*, 144 ff., 157, 163, 165, 182, 188–90, pls. LVI–LVII; Micheli, *L'enluminure*, 28–30, 33, 49, 56, pls. 66, 75; H. Swarzenski, *Art Bulletin*, 24, 1942, 288; A. Boeckler, 'Die Evangelistenbilder der Adagruppe', *Münchner Jahrbuch der bildenden Kunst*, 3rd ser., 3/4, 1952–3, 125; E. Rosenbaum, 'The Vine Columns of Old St. Peters in Carolingian Canon Tables', *Journal of the Warburg and Courtauld Institutes*, 18, 1955, 4, 8; id., 'The Evangelist portraits of the Ada School and their models', *Art Bulletin*, 38, 1956, 83, fig. 8;

McGurk, *Latin Gospel Books*, no. 137; Rickert, *Painting in Britain*, 20, 24–5, pls. 11b, 12; Henry, *Irish Art*, II, 60–4, 67, 73, 78, 85–6, 91, pls. 34, IVb, Va; B. M. Metzger, 'When did scribes begin to use writing desks?', *Historical and Literary Studies, Pagan, Jewish and Christian*, 1968, 131–2; Koehler, *Buchmalerei*, 16, 24, 100, 188; Henry, *Kells*, 163, 167, 183, 198, 204–5, 209–10, 214, 226, figs. 12, 13 a, f, 15, 16, 28, 31, 32, 66.

EXHIBITED: *Il libro della Bibbia*, Biblioteca Apostolica Vaticana, 1972, no. 14, colour plate.

37. Vienna, Nationalbibliothek Cod. 1224
Gospel Book (Cutbercht Gospel Book)
310×238 mm., ff. 205
Late 8th century. (?) Salzburg

Ills. 180–187

The illumination consists of Canon Tables, Evangelist portraits, and initial pages. The Canon Tables now on eight pages (ff. 18–21v) were originally on twelve (Canons II and III were on a bifolium now missing between ff. 18v–19). They are 'm n' arches in which the architectural forms are flattened out, and include a large repertory of patterns, some of Mediterranean origin, others more obviously of Insular inspiration. On the first page (f. 18) the four Evangelists are represented under the subsidiary arches, half-length in pairs and holding books between them. All are bearded except St. John, and they are labelled above their haloes.

The four Evangelists are shown seated, St. Matthew (f. 17v) with hand to chin facing right with his book on a bookstand; St. Mark (f. 71v) holding a book, facing to the right and accompanied by a half-length lion holding a book; St. Luke (f. 110v) holding a scroll and turning to the right with hand raised; St. John (f. 165v) frontal, holding a scroll and with a lectern to the right. St. John is unbearded and has a tonsure, as has St. Mark; the others are all bearded. The frames are square except for St. Mark's which is arched. All have panels of interlace, zoomorphic and other ornament.

There are initials with interlace and other ornament, St. Matthew, L (f. 16, Matthew I, 1–17 is placed here and followed by the portrait of the Evangelist and the Canon Tables), 'Xpi' (f. 22), St. Mark, 'In' (f. 72), St. Luke, Q (f. 111), St. John, I (f. 166). Accompanying the last is the half-length symbol of St. John, the Eagle, carrying a book. There are also minor initials for the Chapter list of St. John, 'In' (f. 14) and the Preface to St. Luke, L (f. 105).

The colours used are predominantly orange, green, pale yellow, pale blue, black, and chocolate. The paint is often thick and has flaked in places, for example on St. Mark's feet.

Folios 1*–4*, prefixed to the manuscript, contain the capitulary and on the verso of the last leaf (f. 4*v) is the inscription of the scribe, Cutbercht: *Cutbercht scripsit ista IIII evangelia. praecat nos omnia oramus pro anima tua* (sic). He was probably an Anglo-Saxon scribe working at Salzburg. The illuminator was clearly able to draw on Insular sources, for example in his 'Xp' initial which can be compared to that in the Barberini Gospel Book (no. 36), and quite possibly he was therefore Cutbercht himself. At the same time Merovingian motifs appear, particularly in the Canon Tables (Wright). This and comparison with other Salzburg manuscripts suggest a date at the end of the 8th century. A similar set of Evangelist portraits is found in the *Codex Millenarius* (Kremsmünster), a Gospel Book probably written at Mondsee in the late 8th century, though the St. John portraits are somewhat different. None of the Evangelists write and the poses of St. Matthew—reflective—St. Luke—teaching—and St. John—holding a scroll—recall late antique pagan author and philosopher portraits. For example the St. John can be compared with the Virgil portraits in the *Virgilius Romanus* (Vat. Lat. 3867, 5th century, cf. Saxl, Oakeshott).

Wright suggests that the model for both Gospel Books may have been a Gospel Book made at Ravenna in the first half of the 6th century. There is textual support for this in the presence of the anti-Marconite preface to Luke in both Gospels. Wright also supposes that the model had Evangelist portraits on versos with their symbols on the opposite rectos. Holter has drawn attention to parallels in Greek Gospel Books for the profile portraits. These would not have had Evangelist symbols and the symbols would have had to be combined with them at some stage (cf. the discussion of the Book of Lindisfarne, no. 9). Wright may be correct in assuming that they had already been incorporated in the model and Ravenna would be a likely place for this merging of Eastern and Western features. The Evangelist portraits in the mosaics of San Vitale are not similar, however, and it is hard to see why the artist of the Cutbercht Gospel Book should have omitted the symbols for Matthew and Luke if they were in his model. It may rather be that he and the artist of the *Codex Millenarius* attempted to combine symbols from some other source with a set of portraits without symbols. It should also be noted that the chalice given to Kremsmünster by Duke Tassilo between its foundation in 777 and his death in 788 has portraits of seated Evangelists with symbols of a different type (see Neumüller, Holter, fig. 13).

PROVENANCE: The names *Rutrud* and *Liutker* are on f. 2. It has been noted that an Irishman, Virgilius (Feirgil), who had been trained at Iona, was Bishop of Salzburg from the mid 8th century to his death in 784. No. 46 in the catalogue of the Salzburg Cathedral library by Johannes Holveld of 1433–5. Transferred to the Hofbibliothek in 1806.

LITERATURE: G. Swarzenski, *Die Salzburger Malerei von den ersten Anfängen bis zur Blütezeit des romanischen Stils*, 1908, 1913 (repr. 1969), 1–3, pls. I–VI; Zimmermann, *Vorkarolingische Miniaturen*, 30, 128, 137–40, 297–300, pls. 297–312; H. J. Hermann, *Die frühmittelalterlichen Handschriften des Abendlandes* (*Die illuminierten Handschriften und Inkunabeln der*

Nationalbibliothek in Wien, I), 1923, 50–6, pls. XI–XX; J. Brøndsted, *Early English Ornament*, 1924, 106, 113–15, 124, 138 n. 1, 249 n. 1, 250, figs. 89, 95, 96; K. Pfister, *Irische Buchmalerei*, 1927, pl. 40; A. Goldschmidt, *German illumination*, I, 1928, pl. I; Saunders, *English Illumination*, 8; Kendrick, *Anglo-Saxon*, 143–4, 146, 190, pl. LVIII; A. Schardt, *Das Initial*, 1938, 39, 43, pl. pp. 40–2; Micheli, *L'enluminure*, 32, 50, 55–7, 61, 63, 71, 88, 113, 139, 170, pls. 18–20, 38, 40, 209; F. Saxl, 'The Ruthwell Cross', *Journal of the Warburg and Courtauld Institutes*, 6, 1943, 19, pl. 6e; Masai, *Origines*, 119, pl. XXXIX; Nordenfalk, *Early Medieval*, 125; W. Oakeshott, *Classical Inspiration in Medieval Art*, 1959, 38–9, 125, pl. 54; W. Neumüller, K. Holter, *Der Codex Millenarius*, 1959, *passim*, figs. 9–10, 21–2, 50–3; McGurk, *Latin Gospel Books*, no. 42; *C.L.A.*, X, no. 1500; D. H. Wright, 'The *Codex Millenarius* and its model', *Münchner Jahrbuch der bildenden Kunst*, 3rd ser., 15, 1964, 37–54, figs. 1, 3, 5, 8; Rickert, *Painting in Britain*, 20, pl. 9a; K. Holter in *Cyrillo-Methodiana. Zur Frühgeschichte des Christentums bei den Slaven, 863–1963*, ed. M. Hellmann, *et al.*, 1964, 180 ff., figs. 12, 16, 17; K. Holter, 'Der Buchschmuck in Süddeutschland und Oberitalien', *Karl der Grosse. Lebenswerk und Nachleben*, III, ed. W. Braunfels, H. Schnitzler, 1965, 110, fig. 103; F. Unterkircher, *European illuminated manuscripts in the Austrian National Library*, 1967, 20–1, pl. 2; O. Mazal, *Himmels- und Weltenbilder*, 1973, 26–8, 32–4, pls. 1–2; W. Neumüller, K. Holter, *Codex Millenarius* (Codices selecti, 45), 1974, 19, 29–30.

EXHIBITED: *Ars sacra. Kunst des frühen Mittelalters*, Munich, 1950, no. 5; *Karl der Grosse*, 1965, no. 452, pls. 72–3.

38. Hereford, Cathedral Library MS P. I. 2
Gospel Book
227 × 170 mm., ff. 135
Late 8th century. (?) Western England or Wales
Ills. 197–199

The illumination consists of three initial pages, to St. Matthew, 'Lib' (f. 1), St. Mark, 'Ini' (f. 36) and St. John, 'In p'. (f. 102). Pages are missing for the 'Xpi' initial in Matthew (ff. 1–2) and the opening of St. Luke (ff. 59–60). The initials are decorated with panels of interlace, fret, spiral, and other patterns, and they have animal head and leg terminals. The three initial pages have narrow frames. There are also smaller initials for Matthew XXVI, 30, *Et* (f. 31ᵛ) and XXVIII, 1, *Vespere* (f. 35), for Mark XIV, 26, *Et ymno* (f. 55ᵛ) and XVI, 2, *Et* (f. 59), for Luke IV, 1, *Ihs autem* (f. 65b) and XXIV, 1, *Una autem* (f. 100), and for John XVIII, 1, *Haec cum* (f. 128ᵛ) and XX, 1, *Una autem* (f. 131ᵛ). The colours used are restricted to yellow and orange. The manuscript is interesting as a less sumptuous version of the great illuminated Gospel Books, following the general design of their initial pages (cf. the Book of St. Chad, Lichfield, no. 21, to which it is also textually related), but with an impoverished ornamental vocabulary. The attribution to western England or Wales rests solely on the later ownership, as there is nothing closely comparable.

PROVENANCE: Documents in Anglo-Saxon written in the mid 11th century (ff. 134–5) refer to Herefordshire. The second concerns a land transaction of 1043–6. *Ex libris* of the Cathedral, 15th century, f. 135ᵛ.

LITERATURE: Westwood, *Facsimiles*, 61–2; *New Pal. Soc.*, I, pls. 233–4; W. M. Lindsay, *Early Welsh Script*, 1912, 41–3; Zimmermann, *Vorkarolingische Miniaturen*, 24, 307, pl. 328; A. T. Bannister, *A descriptive catalogue of the manuscripts in the Hereford Cathedral Library*, 1927, 98–9; L. J. Hopkin-James, *The Celtic Gospels*, 1934, ix ff., pl. facing p. ix; Micheli, *L'enluminure*, 24, pl. 44; Duft, Meyer, *St. Gall*, figs. 5, 16, 26; Ker, *Catalogue*, 156 (no. 119); *Codex Durmachensis*, figs. 25, 102; McGurk, *Latin Gospel Books*, no. 15; Henry, *Irish Art*, I, 198; *C.L.A.*, II, no. 157; Koehler, *Buchmalerei*, 14–15; Henry, *Kells*, 226.

EXHIBITED: *Illustrated catalogue of illuminated manuscripts*, Burlington Fine Arts Club, London, 1908, no. 2, pl. 10.

39. Leningrad, Public Library Cod. F. v. I. 8
Gospel Book
349 × 242 mm., ff. 214
Late 8th century. (?) Northumbria
Colour Frontispiece, Ills. 188–195

The illumination consists of Canon Tables and initials. The Canon Tables are on twelve pages (ff. 12–17ᵛ). They are very richly ornamented with panels of animal, vegetable and abstract pattern. On f. 12ᵛ, 13ᵛ, and 14ᵛ, the frames, though not the filling ornament, are identical, and pricking holes in the parchment suggest that they have been traced through from the rectos. On f. 16 the twin upper arches and the bases of the columns are formed of curved animals. The patterns in the panels of the arches are carefully arranged and except on ff. 15, 15ᵛ, symmetrical. For example on f. 12 the top centre panel is of fret pattern, whilst the other panels of interlace or animal ornament alternate and balance each other, a b c b a, b a b a b, a b a b a. The capitals and bases continue this alternation of animal and abstract interlace.
The major initials are to St. Matthew, *Liber* (f. 18), St. Mark, 'Ini' (f. 78), St. Luke, Q (f. 119) and St. John, 'In' (f. 177). They have frames on the outer three sides, Matthew and John of panels with interlace and animal patterns, Mark and Luke of interlace patterns in dots with square corner pieces. There is decorated continuation lettering, and patterns of dots are used as background filling, to outline the capitals, and as panel divisions.
There are smaller initials for the Prefaces and Chap-

ter lists, N (f. 1), P (f. 3), E (f. 5ᵛ), M (f. 6ᵛ), and G (f. 7ᵛ), and also for *Xpi autem* (f. 19ᵛ). The colours used are rich and varied, including green, orange, yellow, brown, blue, and mauve. The blue is especially striking and invites comparison with the St. Gall Gospel Book (no. 44). The illumination has been ascribed to three hands (*Karl der Grosse*, 1965) the first, ff. 1, 12–17ᵛ, 18, the second, ff. 78, 119 and the third, f. 177.
There is no indication of the early provenance of the Gospels and it has been ascribed to both north and south England. E. A. Lowe attributes it to Northumbria on the grounds of textual similarities with the Book of Lindisfarne (no. 9) and the *Codex Amiatinus* (no. 7), but notes also Kentish features in the script. Brown (1972) considers it Northumbrian.

PROVENANCE: A later hand has added a note mentioning *Frideger*, f. 213ᵛ. Runes on f. 213. A single leaf of a Sacramentary, bound in, f. 214, late 11th– early 12th century presumably comes from St. Maur-des-Fossés or St. Germain-des-Prés. Listed by Montfaucon (no. 1057) with books bought from St. Maur-des-Fossés by St. Germain. No. 108 in the St. Germain library and acquired from there by Pierre Dubrowski, a Russian nobleman attached to the Embassy in Paris, c. 1791, f. 12, f. 213, etc. Given by him to the St. Petersburg Public Library, in 1805.

LITERATURE: B. de Montfaucon, *Bibliotheca Bibliothecarum*, II, 1739, 1142; Westwood, *Facsimiles*, 52–3, pl. 25; L. Delisle, *Le Cabinet des manuscrits de la bibliothèque nationale*, II, 1874, 54; A. Staerk, *Les manuscrits latins du Vᵉ au XIIIᵉ siècle conservés à la Bibliothèque Impériale de Saint-Petersbourg*, I, 1910, 25–6, II, pls. XXI–XXIII; Zimmermann, *Vorkarolingische Miniaturen*, 24, 35, 126, 143–5, 304–5, pls. 321–6, 329a; Saunders, *English Illumination*, 12; Kendrick, *Anglo-Saxon*, 148, pl. LIX. 3; Micheli, *L'enluminure*, 28–30, 32, 34, 49, 62, 139, 145, pls. 13, 50, 77; M. Schapiro, 'The decoration of the Leningrad manuscript of Bede', *Scriptorium*, 12, 1958, 194, pl. 23e; McGurk, *Latin Gospel Books*, no. 126 and pp. 122–3; D. Wilson, *Anglo-Saxon Ornamental Metalwork 700–1100 in the British Museum*, 1964, 11 f., 20, 70 f., 73 n.; Henry, *Irish Art*, II, 60, 62–3, pl. 35; *C.L.A.*, XI, no. 1605; T. J. Brown, 'Northumbria and the Book of Kells', *Anglo-Saxon England*, I, 1972, 234–5; Henry, *Kells*, 180, 204, 214, 226, fig. 57.

EXHIBITED: *Karl der Grosse*, 1965, no. 398, pls. 46–7; *Great Britain. U.S.S.R.*, London, Victoria and Albert Museum, 1967, no. 2.

40. Oxford, Bodleian Library MS Bodley 426 (S.C. 2327)
Philippus Presbiter, Commentary on Job
292 × 220 mm., ff. 118
Late 8th century. (?) Wessex
Ill. 136

The illumination consists of an initial A (f. 1) with interlace and spiral decoration and some foliage forms (cf. the Barberini Gospel Book, no. 36), and a few other initials decorated with interlace and orange dots, V (f. 2ᵛ), V (f. 61ᵛ). The colours are blue, yellow, orange, and black. Lowe considers an origin in Wessex likely, comparing the script to that of British Library, Cotton Charters VIII. 36.

PROVENANCE: *Ex libris* and pressmark of St. Augustine's, Canterbury, 14th century, f. ivᵛ, and catalogue of late 15th century. Given to the Bodleian by Sir Walter Cope, 1602.

LITERATURE: M. R. James, *The Ancient Libraries of Canterbury and Dover*, 1903, 204 (no. 137), 516; Pächt and Alexander, III, no. 6, pl. I; *C.L.A.*, II, no. 234.

41. London, British Library Harley MS 2965
Book of Prayers (Book of Nunnaminster)
215 × 160 mm., ff. 41
8th to 9th century. Southern England
Ill. 135, 137–139

The book has three smallish initials in black ink sparingly coloured with orange and green, A (f. 4ᵛ) H (f. 11), and D (f. 16ᵛ). They are decorated with animal-head terminals and interlace, and outlined with orange dots. There is also fine decorative display script in orange. Two smaller initials, D and S (f. 37) are in a different style and coloured in blue and yellow.
Similar style initials occur in two other manuscripts from the south, a Gregory the Great, Pastoral Care, which was at Fulda by the 9th century (Kassel, Landesbibliothek, Theol. fol. 32, *C.L.A.*, VIII, no. 1138), and the Corpus Glossary (Cambridge, Corpus Christi College, MS 144, *C.L.A.*, II, no. 122) from St. Augustine's, Canterbury. Since the manuscript was at Winchester in the 10th century it provides an example of the kind of initial decoration that Anglo-Saxon artists had available to copy when book production resumed after the interruptions of the 9th-century Danish invasions.

PROVENANCE: Belonged probably to Ealhswith (d. 909), wife of King Alfred (*ora pro me peccatrice*, f. 41, added first half 10th century), and to St. Mary's Abbey, Winchester (Nunnaminster), founded by her (entry concerning its boundaries added, f. 40ᵛ). Arms of Roscarrock, f. 37ᵛ, and probably belonged to Nicholas Roscarrock, a member of the household of Lord William Howard of Naworth from 1607. Acquired by Robert Harley, 1st Earl of Oxford (1661–1724) from John Warburton, 1720. Purchased by the British Museum, 1753.

LITERATURE: *Pal. Soc.*, I, pl. 163: *Catalogue of ancient manuscripts in the British Museum, II. Latin manuscripts*, 1884, 61–2, pl. 22; W. de Gray Birch, *An ancient manuscript of the eighth or ninth century formerly belonging to St. Mary's Abbey or Nunnaminster, Winchester*, 1889, pl. 1; Kenney, *Sources*, no. 577; Micheli, *L'enluminure*, 33, 65; Ker, *Catalogue*, 308–9 (no. 237); *C.L.A.*, II, no. 199; R. Deshman, 'Anglo-Saxon Art after Alfred', *Art Bulletin*, 56, 1974, 193.

42. Leningrad, Public Library Cod. Q. v. XIV. 1
Paulinus of Nola, Carmina
c. 380 × 210 mm., ff. 22
8th to 9th century
Ill. 179

The drawings on a flyleaf (f. 1) show, above, the Annointing of David by Samuel and, below, David beheading Goliath, with inscriptions *Samuel profeta* and *David, Goeliad*. Between the upper two figures a bust head has been drawn in later, and the shivering drapery style suggests this was by an Anglo-Saxon artist of the later 10th or the 11th century. E. A. Lowe dates the pen-trials on the flyleaf to the 8th century. He attributes the manuscript to the same scriptorium as the Paulinus in the Vatican (Pal. Lat. 235, *C.L.A.*, I, no. 87) and says: 'origin either Ireland or Northumbria, saec. VIII ex.'
The contrast between the movement and activity of the figures and the crude outline style of the drawings proves they must be copies of a good model; and Kurz has compared the two scenes to those found in the Paris Psalter (Bibl. Nat., Gr. 139) a work of the Macedonian Renaissance, early 10th century, especially for the falling figure of Goliath with hands outstretched. The model used by the Insular artist is likely, therefore to be a pre-iconoclastic representation of Eastern origin (cf. the Vespasian Psalter, no. 29). Later Anglo-Saxon representations of the scenes occur in two 11th-century Psalters, B.L. Arundel 155 from Canterbury and B.L. Cotton Tiberius C. VI from Winchester (see Temple, *Anglo-Saxon*, nos. 66 and 98, ills. 220, 307–8).
In spite of their crude style, therefore, the drawings are important as demonstrating the presence of such a model in the British Isles. Their purpose is not certain, but they evidently have no connection with the text. If they are intended as a record of and an aid to the transmission of the model, then they are also of great interest as an early stage in the evolution of the medieval pattern book (cf. Kurz).

PROVENANCE: Brought from the library of the Benedictine abbey of Corbie, where it appears in the 12th-century catalogue, to St. Germain-des-Prés, Paris, in 1638. Acquired by Pierre Dubrowski, a Russian nobleman attached to the Embassy in Paris, *c.* 1791, and given by him to the St. Petersburg Public Library, in 1805.

LITERATURE: A. Staerk, *Les manuscrits latins du Vᵉ au XIIIᵉ siècle conservés à la Bibliothèque Impériale de Saint-Petersbourg*, I, 1910, 222–3, II, pl. 71; Zimmermann, *Vorkarolingische Miniaturen*, 145, 310, pl. 332b; O. Kurz, 'Ein insulares Musterbuchblatt und die byzantinische Psalterillustration',

Byzantinisch-neugriechische Jahrbücher, 14, 1938, 84–93, pl.; *C.L.A.*, XI, no. 1622; M. W. Evans, *Medieval Drawings*, 1969, 21, pl. 5.

43. Oxford, Bodleian Library MS Rawlinson G. 167 (S.C. no. 14890)

Gospel Book (incomplete)
320 × 240 mm., ff. 107
(?) Second half of 8th century. (?) Ireland

Ill. 196

The Gospel Book is mutilated and now contains only parts of St. Luke and St. John. It has also been severely cropped in rebinding. The only illumination surviving is the initial Q to St. Luke (f. 1), which runs the whole length of the page with continuation lettering in bands. There is an interlace frame on three sides with interlace corner pieces. The colours appear to have been orange, yellow, and black, but the page is very rubbed and discoloured. There is also a white which may be a lead-white filler for a purple as in the Lichfield Gospel Book (no. 21, cf. Henry).

The manuscript contains numerous minor initials in black with orange or yellow, sometimes violet, fillings, and orange dotted outline. Initials of larger size mark Luke I, 5, F (f. 1ᵛ), II, 1, F (f. 5), XXII, 1, A (f. 53ᵛ), XXIV, 1, *Una* (f. 60ᵛ), and John II, 1, '*Et*' (f. 74), X, 1, A (f. 83ᵛ) and XX, 1, *Una* (f. 105). The succeeding letters diminish in size in the Insular manner.

The illumination is of fine quality and the manuscript must at one time have been one of the major Insular illuminated manuscripts. Lowe describes the script as 'Irish majuscule' and dates it 'saec. VIII–IX'. The illumination seems particularly close in style to that of the Lichfield Gospel Book (no. 21), however, and also in the design of the Q recalls the Book of Lindisfarne (no. 9). It would be surprising if the manuscript were really so much later in date.

PROVENANCE: The name 'J. Combe' given by Pächt and Alexander, III, no. 1268 is a misreading, of the words (?) *p(er) comve*, perhaps referring to a legal extract in French copied above and perhaps with the date 1614. Bequeathed to the Bodleian by Richard Rawlinson in 1755.

LITERATURE: *New Pal. Soc.*, II, pl. 81; Micheli, *L'enluminure*, 20; McGurk, *Latin Gospel Books*, no. 35; F. Henry, 'The Lindisfarne Gospels', *Antiquity*, 37, 1963, 104–5; Henry, *Irish Art*, I, 162, 196–7, pl. VIII; *C.L.A.*, II, no. 256; Pächt and Alexander, III, no. 1268, pls. CXII–CXIII; Henry, *Kells*, 226.

44. St. Gall, Stiftsbibliothek Cod. 51

Gospel Book
295 × 215–20 mm., ff. 134
Second half of 8th century. Ireland

Ills. 200, 201, 203–208

The illumination consists of Evangelist portraits with initial pages opposite, St. Matthew (p. 2), 'Lib' (p. 3), St. Mark (p. 78), 'Ini' (p. 79), St. Luke (p. 128), Q (p. 129), St. John (p. 208), 'In' (p. 209). In addition a carpet page (p. 6) precedes the Genealogy of Christ with the initials 'Xpi' (p. 7), and there are two miniatures, of the Crucifixion and the Lord's Advent (pp. 266–7).

The Evangelists Matthew and Luke have narrow frames filled with interlace, interlaced animals, key and guilloche patterns, which their feet overlap at the bottom and their symbols interrupt at the top, thus emphasizing the central vertical axis of the compositions. They are tall figures which, since they have bar thrones behind them (cf. the Durham Cassiodorus, no. 17, and the Lichfield Gospel Book, no. 21), must nevertheless be intended to be seen as seated. Their symbols are fitted in above, the Angel frontal, half-length and with a book, the Calf winged, full-length and without halo or book. The St. Mark (p. 78) is accompanied by all four-symbols which are placed in the corners of the frame, from the top left reading clockwise, Eagle, Man (angel), Calf, Lion. The borders are in consequence wider at the sides than at top and bottom. The figure of St. Mark, squat in proportion and with large head and halo, seems to float in the centre rectangle with no throne. The symbols are frontal and as such comparable to those on the Durrow four-symbols page (no. 6). The quadrupeds as it were stand up on their two hind legs with their two front legs crossed before them! St. John (p. 208) has similar proportions to St. Mark; there is no throne, and his feet slightly overlap the border below. The Eagle is fitted in above in profile without halo or book. Koehler considers these two portraits of Mark and John to be by a different hand from that responsible for the rest of the illumination.

The idea of all four symbols accompanying an Evangelist portrait is also found in the Book of Kells (no. 52) and is a conflation of the separate Evangelist portrait and four-symbols page found in the Lichfield Gospel Book (no. 21). The Matthew and Luke as frontal seated figures with symbols above belong to a type already formulated in the 6th-century Gospel Book of St. Augustine (Cambridge, Corpus Christi College MS 286, fig. 23) and copied in the Stockholm *Codex Aureus* (no. 30) and in later Carolingian Gospel Books of the Ada school. These are in an architectural context, however, and the winged symbols are half-length with books and haloes. Similar frontal types of Evangelists with full-length symbols and bar thrones occur in the Lichfield Gospel Book of St. Chad (no. 21). It is not clear if this is a separate early Christian portrait type, or an Insular combination of Evangelist and terrestrial symbol (cf. the discussions of the Books of Lindisfarne and St. Chad, nos. 9, 21).

The other two portraits resemble those in the Books of Mulling (no. 45), and Macdurnan (no. 70), as well as in British Library Gospel Book (no. 46) and the Stowe St. John fragment (no. 47); they are probably, at least in origin, standing types. Moreover since they are basically the same as the Matthew and Luke, it may support the suggestion that the latter are an

Insular conflation of symbols, thrones, and portrait. Koehler comments on the enlargement of the heads and haloes as a means of heightening the effect of spirituality.

The initials have panel frames surrounding but not completely enclosing them. The panels often end in beast heads. A feature of the decoration is the use of dots applied to the frames and initials. In general the ornament is less varied and less fine in quality than that in the earlier Lichfield Gospel Book, though the design of the initial pages is close (compare the 'Xpi' pages, for instance). The colours used are pink, brownish-pink, mauve, yellow, and blue. The palette bears some resemblance to that of the Leningrad Gospel Book (no. 39).

In the Crucifixion miniature (p. 266) the Christ is shown swathed in the colubium as in the Eastern iconography (cf. the Durham Gospel Book, no. 10). Stephaton is on the left holding up the sponge and Longinus with the spear is on the right with the blood from Christ's side spurting into his eye. A pair of frontal half-length angels holding books are on either side above the arms of the cross. The composition is very close to that of the Durham Gospel Book. A Crucifixion miniature was planned for the Book of Kells (no. 52). The scene is also shown in the Southampton Psalter (no. 74).

In the miniature on the opposite recto (p. 267) the half-length Christ, above in the centre, blesses with His right hand and holds a cross and a book. On either side is a full-length angel blowing a trumpet. Below twelve half-length figures with haloes and books and looking up represent the twelve Apostles. The matching narrow frames filled with interlace and key pattern emphasize the connection between the two pictures. This is an early stage in the evolution of the iconography of the Last Judgement (cf. the Turin Gospel Book, no. 61). Christ suffering as Man is contrasted with His triumphant return as Lord and Judge.

There are a number of smaller initials in the text, Matthew XXVIII, 1, V (p. 76), Mark XIV, 17, V (p. 119), Luke I, 5, *Fac* (p. 130), Luke II, 1, *Fac* (p. 134), Luke XXIV, 1, *Una* (p. 203), John X, 1, A (p. 237), John XIII, 1, A (p. 246), John XVIII, 1, H (p. 256), and John XX, 1, U (p. 261).

The manuscript was probably made in Ireland and brought to St. Gall at a later date, no doubt in the 9th century. It is less likely to have been made by Irishmen on the Continent. It is the most important of the later Gospel Books generally accepted as being Irish. Although in some ways it shows a decline from earlier books such as the Lichfield Gospel Book (no. 21), particularly in the ornament, yet in its enrichment with additional miniatures it foreshadows the Book of Kells (unless, of course, Kells is a contemporary production from a different tradition, see no. 52). The stylization of figures and drapery is particularly expressionistic and vigorous (see, for example, the hair and beard of St. Mark), and seems to provide a pattern for the later Irish pocket Gospel Books (nos. 45–7).

PROVENANCE: Not included in the mid 9th-century catalogue of *libri Scottice scripti* at St. Gall. Corrections, and pen-trials in Carolingian minuscule, pp. 1, 128. St. Gall ownership inscription, p. 1, 13th century.

LITERATURE: Westwood, *Facsimiles*, 62–6, pls. 26–28a; Zimmermann, *Vorkarolingische Miniaturen*, 22, 34, 99–102, 240–2, pls. 185–92a; K. Pfister, *Irische Buchmalerei*, 1927, pls. 24–5; Saunders, *English Illumination*, 7, 11; Kenney, *Sources*, no. 486; G.-L. Micheli, 'Recherches sur les manuscrits Irlandais decorés de Saint-Gall et de Reichenau', *Revue archéologique*, 6e sér., 7, 1936, 192–207, figs. 1–2; Kendrick, *Anglo-Saxon*, 136–7; A. Schardt, *Das Initial*, 1938, 31, pl. p. 32; Micheli, *L'enluminure*, 11–12, 19–20, 25, 41, 64–5, 70, 123, 177, pls. 5, 31, 47, and frontispiece; Masai, *Origines*, 122, pl. XXXI; Duft, Meyer, *St. Gall*, 69–71, 87–101, pls. I–XIV, XX–XXV, figs. 1, 3, etc.; E. Kitzinger, 'The Coffin-Reliquary', *The Relics of St. Cuthbert*, ed. C. F. Battiscombe, 1956, 223, 226, pl. XIII. 5; Nordenfalk, *Early Medieval*, pl. p. 108; *Codex Durmachensis*, figs. 13, 14, 19, 27, 41, 62, 74, 108; *C.L.A.*, VII, no. 901; McGurk, *Latin Gospel Books*, no. 117; Henry, *Irish Art*, I, 196–202, 214, pls. 108–9; M. Rickert, *Painting in Britain*, 20–1, 23, pl. 9b; B. Brenk, *Tradition und Neuerung in der christlichen Kunst des ersten Jahrtausends* (Wiener Byzantinische Studien, III), 1966, 68–9, fig. 17; Henry, *Irish Art*, II, 32, 58, 63, 72, 82, 92, 96–9, 161, 169, 172; Werckmeister, *Irisch-northumbrische Buchmalerei*, 80, 101, 134–5; Koehler, *Buchmalerei*, 4, 14–19, 22–4, 41, 43–5, 66–74, 76, 87, 100–1, 184–6, 188; Y. Christe, *La vision de Matthieu XXIV–XXV*, 1973, 53–4, fig. 85; Henry, *Kells*, 152, 155 n., 163, 180, 182–3, 205, 226, figs. 9, 21, 27.

45. Dublin, Trinity College MS A. 1. 15 (60)

Gospel Book (Book of Mulling)
165 × 120 mm., ff. 84
Second half of 8th century.
Ireland (? Tech-Moling)
Ills. 210–212, 214–216, 218

The illumination consists of initials for the Gospels, 'Lib' (f. 13), 'Xpi' (f. 13ᵛ), 'Ini' (f. 36), Q (f. 53) and 'In' (f. 82), all of which are damaged and rubbed. They are decorated with spirals, interlace, animal heads, and other patterns. They fill about a quarter to half the left-hand column on each page. Also three detached Evangelist portraits (formerly pp. 189, 191, 193, now ff. 12ᵛ, 35ᵛ, 81ᵛ) originally preceded each Gospel since there is an offset of former p. 193 on f. 82, as pointed out by W. O'Sullivan. They have now (1977) been replaced in the book and the leaves refoliated. They show frontal Evangelists, haloed and holding books but without symbols. The first dips a pen held in his right hand into an inkwell. The panel frames are filled with interlace and interlaced animals. The colours used include white, blue, green, yellow, ochre, brown, mauve, purple, and cherry red.

The manuscript is one of a group of Irish Pocket Gospel Books and the portraits are very similar in style to those in the British Library Gospel Book (no. 46) and the Stowe St. John (no. 47). Presumably, they are to be seen as standing figures, in spite of the figure dipping his pen. The stylization of the drapery folds, particularly the tube-like folds of the mantle over the arms, is also seen in the portraits of the St. Gall Gospel Book (no. 44).

A surprising feature of the manuscript is the contrast between the comparatively impoverished decorative vocabulary of the borders and initials (even allowing for the latter's condition) and the much higher quality of the portraits.

Eleven leaves of prefatory matter (ff. 1–11, including Canon Tables) may be of slightly later date. A fragment of another Gospel Book with parts of St. Matthew and St. Mark (ff.96–99) was also found in the *cumdach*. It contains an initial 'In' to St. Mark with interlace and beast heads and according to Lowe was probably written in the same scriptorium, 8th to 9th century. For the *cumdach* see H. S. Crawford, 'A descriptive list of Irish shrines and reliquaries. Part II', *Journal of the Royal Society of Antiquaries of Ireland*, 53, 1923, 152, pl. IXa.

PROVENANCE: Colophon, copied presumably from an earlier book, on f. 94: *Nomen h. scriptoris mulling dicitur*. St. Moling (d. 692–7), was the founder of the monastery of St. Mullins (Tech-Moling), Co. Carlow. Liturgical texts and a plan of a monastic enclosure, supposedly of Tech-Moling, are added (ff. 33ᵛ–34, 94ᵛ). Belonged in the 18th century with its *cumdach* to the Kavanagh family at Borris Idrone, Co. Carlow.

LITERATURE: Westwood, *Palaeographia*, no. 19; id., *Facsimiles*, 93; Gilbert, *Facsimiles*, I, xiii, pls. XX–XXI; H. J. Lawlor, *Chapters on the Book of Mulling*, 1897; T. K. Abbott, *Catalogue of the manuscripts of Trinity College, Dublin*, 1900, 8; W. M. Lindsay, *Early Irish Minuscule Script*, 1910, 16–24, pls. VII–VIII; Zimmermann, *Vorkarolingische Miniaturen*, 34, 102–4, 106, 224, pls. 194, 196a; Kenney, *Sources*, nos. 456–7; Micheli, *L'enluminure*, 25, 41; Åberg, *Occident*, 89–90, fig. 60; Duft, Meyer, *St. Gall*, fig. 92; P. McGurk, 'The Irish pocket Gospel Book', *Sacris Erudiri*, 8, 1956, 249–70; F. Henry, 'An Irish manuscript in the British Museum', *Journal of the Royal Society of Antiquaries of Ireland*, 87, 1957, 148 ff., pls. XXVI. 2, XXVII, fig. 2.2; McGurk, *Latin Gospel Books*, nos. 89–90; Henry, *Irish Art*, I, 81, 91, 134–6, 161, 199–200, 202, pl. III, fig. 17; Rickert, *Painting in Britain*, 24; Werckmeister, *Irisch-northumbrische Buchmalerei*, 101 f., 116, pl. 28; Nordenfalk, 'An illustrated Diatessaron', *Art Bulletin*, 50, 1968, 126, pl. 7; *C.L.A.*, II, nos. 276–7; Koehler, *Buchmalerei* 14–15; Henry, *Kells*, 153, 183, 225, fig. 33; Nordenfalk, *Celtic*, 126, pl. 48.

46. London, British Library Add. MS 40618
Gospel Book
130 × 101 mm, ff. 66
Second half of 8th century. Ireland   *Ill. 213*

The only surviving original illumination is a picture of St. Luke (f. 21ᵛ). He is haloed and stands frontally holding a book. He wears a green cloak outlined in orange over a yellow robe. His halo is brownish pink outlined in yellow and overlaps the frame which is pale orange-pink and broader at the sides. On each side three square panels are yellow while two oblong panels contain interlacing lacertine beasts drawn in brown and left uncoloured.

On ff. 23 and 50 the original initials to Luke and John, which were fairly small, have been erased and new ones inserted. At the same date, probably the mid 10th century, the Gospel Book was given new Evangelist portraits of St. Luke and St. John on inserted leaves (ff. 22ᵛ, 49ᵛ, cf. Temple, *Anglo-Saxon*, no. 15, who suggests the additions may have been made at St. Augustine's, Canterbury).

The manuscript belongs to a group of Irish pocket-size Gospel Books in which the Evangelists are usually represented standing and without symbols (cf. nos. 45, 47–9). The portrait of St. Luke is particularly close to the portraits in the Book of Mulling (no. 45).

PROVENANCE: The last page which completes the text (f. 66) was rewritten by 'Eduardus diaconus' in England, 10th century. An erased *ex libris*, 12th or 13th century, is on f. 66ᵛ. William Newman, 1538 (f. 66ᵛ), and Robert Lancaster, 1662 (f. 66ᵛ). Bought for the British Museum at Sotheby's, 1 April 1922, lot 439.

LITERATURE: *New Pal. Soc.*, II, pls. 140–1; *British Museum. Reproductions from Illuminated Manuscripts, Series IV*, 1928, 7, pl. II; Micheli, *L'enluminure*, 25; *Catalogue of Additions to the Manuscripts in the British Museum 1921–5*, 1950, 95–7; P. McGurk, 'The Irish pocket Gospel Book', *Sacris Erudiri*, 8, 1956, 249–70; F. Henry, 'An Irish manuscript in the British Museum', *Journal of the Royal Society of Antiquaries of Ireland*, 87, 1957, 147–66, pls. XXIII–XXV, XXVI.1, XXIX, fig. 2.3; McGurk, *Latin Gospel Books*, no. 20; Henry, *Irish Art*, I, 199, 201, pl. K; *C.L.A.*, II, no. 179.

47. Dublin, Royal Irish Academy MS D. II. 3, ff. 1–11
Gospel of St. John (excerpts)
145 × 114 mm., ff. 11
Second half of 8th century. Ireland

Ills. 209, 220

The illumination consists of a monogram initial *In p(rincipio)* with frame to St. John's Gospel (f. 1). The initials have interlace and animal-head terminals. The frame, broader above and to the right, contains, a fret pattern. Below are two animal heads. There is also a portrait of St. John (f. 11ᵛ). He stands frontally carrying a book. Above his head is his symbol, the Eagle, with wings framing the Evangelist's head. Panels on either side contain interlace patterns. The colours used are yellow, brown, mauve, brownish red, and orange. There is also a stub with a small piece of yellow frame before f. 1 which is conjugate with f. 11. McGurk conjectures this might be the remains of a Luke portrait. Another possibility is that it was a carpet page. The scribe signed his name in ogam: *Peregrinus*.

The squat figure holding his book in front of him with broad framing bands to either side recalls the St. Gall Gospel Book St. John (no. 44). There the Eagle is a profile type, however. The figure can also be compared to the Evangelists in the Book of Mulling (no. 45) and the British Library Gospel Book (no. 46). Like them he appears to be standing and there is a suggestion of contraposto in the placing of the feet.

PROVENANCE: Perhaps written in the same centre as the 'Stowe Missal' (no. 51) which see also for the *cumdach*.

LITERATURE: G. F. Warner, 'The Stowe Missal', *Henry Bradshaw Society*, 32, 1915, viii ff., xxxix–xliii, pls. VII–IX; Kenney, *Sources*, no. 466; Micheli, *L'enluminure*, 25; P. McGurk, 'The Irish pocket Gospel Book', *Sacris Erudiri*, 8, 1956, 249–70; F. Henry, 'An Irish manuscript in the British Museum', *Journal of the Royal Society of Antiquaries of Ireland*, 87, 1957, 151 ff., pl. XXVIIIb; McGurk, *Latin Gospel Books*, no. 82; O.-K. Werckmeister, 'Three problems of tradition in pre-Carolingian figure style', *Proceedings of the Royal Irish Academy*, 63 C, no. 5, 1963, 175 ff., pl. XXXa; Henry, *Irish Art*, I, 43, 161–2, 199–202, 205, pl. 112; Werckmeister, *Irisch-northumbrische Buchmalerei*, 101, 134–5, pl. 38b; *C.L.A.*, II, no. 267; Henry, *Kells*, 153, 183–184, 225.

48. Dublin, Trinity College MS A. 4. 23 (59)
Gospel Book (Book of Dimma)
175 × 142 mm., ff. 74
Second half of or late 8th century. Ireland (Roscrea, Co. Tipperary)

Ills. 219, 222–225

The illumination consists of Evangelist portraits, St. Matthew (p. 2), St. Mark (p. 30), and St. Luke (p. 54), and the Eagle symbol of St. John (p. 104). St. Matthew stands holding a book in front of him. The frame is of panels containing interlace and other patterns. St. Mark is similarly frontal with a book held in front of him, but he is seated on a throne whose uprights terminate in bird heads. The frame is a plain band. St. Luke stands holding a book. His frame is also plain. The colours used are yellow, pink, orange, and green. The Eagle is haloed and one talon is shown holding a book. The frame is again of panels with interlace and fret patterns. The colours

here differ in that blue is used in addition to yellow and orange.

There are initials to each Gospel, 'Li' and 'Xpi' (p. 3), 'Ini' (p. 31), Q (p. 55), and 'In p' (p. 105). There are also larger initials in the text for Mark XIV, 1, *Erat h. Pascha* (p. 48), and John XX, 1, *Una h. Sabbati* (p. 145).

This is one of a group of Irish Pocket Gospel Books (cf. nos. 45–7, 49). The Evangelists show considerable stylization in the way drapery folds become independent forms ornamented with pattern. The ovoid forms particularly recall the Matthew symbol of the earlier Echternach Gospels (no. 11) and Koehler conjectures that the portraits copy faithfully an earlier model. The St. John symbol belongs to the Durrow tradition (no. 6), though the frontal spread-eagled bird is haloed, carries a book, and has acquired an extra pair of wings. In colouring and style it may be compared with the St. Gall Gospel Book (no. 44). A metal *cumdach* made for the manuscript in the mid 12th century survives. See H. S. Crawford, 'A descriptive list of Irish Shrines and Reliquaries. Part II', *Journal of the Royal Society of Antiquaries of Ireland*, 53, 1923, 155–6, fig. 9, and Henry, *Irish Art*, III, 116, 120, pl. 48.

PROVENANCE: The name Dimma stands over an erasure on ff. 15ᵛ, 26ᵛ, and 50, and the entire subscription on f. 74ᵛ is a later addition, the purpose evidently being to ascribe the writing to a scribe contemporary with St. Cronan, founder of Roscrea. Probably written, therefore, at the monastery of Roscrea, Co. Tipperary. Acquired by Trinity College in the early 19th century from Sir W. Bethan.

LITERATURE: Westwood, *Palaeographia*, 19; Westwood, *Facsimiles*, 83–4; Gilbert, *Facsimiles*, I, xii–xiii, pls. XVIII–XIX; T. K. Abbott, *Catalogue of the manuscripts in the library of Trinity College, Dublin*, 1900, 8; W. M. Lindsay, *Early Irish Minuscule Script*, 1910, 12–16, pls. V–VI; Zimmermann, *Vorkarolingische Miniaturen*, 31, 104–5, 108, 245, pls. 195–6; R. I. Best, 'On the *subscriptiones* in the Book of Dimma', *Hermathena*, 44, 1926, 84–100, pls. I, II; Kenney, *Sources*, no. 458; Micheli, *L'enluminure*, 22, 25, pl. 29; Duft, Meyer, *St. Gall*, figs. 64, 94; P. McGurk, 'The Irish pocket Gospel Book', *Sacris Erudiri*, 8, 1956, 249–70; F. Henry, 'An Irish manuscript in the British Museum', *Journal of the Royal Society of Antiquaries of Ireland*, 87, 1957, 150 ff., pl. XXVI. 3; *Codex Durmachensis*, fig. 40; McGurk, *Latin Gospel Books*, no. 88; O.-K. Werckmeister, 'Three problems of tradition in pre-Carolingian figure style', *Proceedings of the Royal Irish Academy*, 63 C, no. 5, 1963, 177–8, 184, pls. XXVIII a–b; Rickert, *Painting in Britain*, 24; Henry, *Irish Art*, I, 161, 199, 201–2, colour pls. G, L; Werckmeister, *Irisch-northumbrische Buchmalerei*, 36, pl. 5a; *C.L.A.*, II, no. 275; Koehler, *Buchmalerei*, 15, 19, 67; Henry, *Kells*, 153, 183–4, 200, 225, fig. 33.

EXHIBITED: *Treasures from Trinity College, Dublin*, London, Burlington House, 1961, nos. 80–1, pls.

49. Fulda, Landesbibliothek
Codex Bonifatianus 3
Gospel Book (Cadmug)
125×112 mm., ff. 66
(?) Second half of 8th century.
(?) Ireland or the Continent

Ill. 228

The illumination consists of framed Evangelist portraits, St. Matthew (f. 1ᵛ), St. Mark (f. 19ᵛ), St. Luke (f. 33ᵛ), and St. John (f. 51ᵛ), with framed initial pages opposite, 'Lib' (f. 2), 'Ini' (f. 20), *Quoniam* (f. 34), 'In' (f. 52). There is also a group of initials 'Xpi' on f. 2ᵛ, and on f. 18ᵛ, the end of St. Matthew, diagonal lines cut the page into four segments containing the colophon and verses about the Evangelist symbols. On f. 65 is the colophon: *Deo Gratias ago Cadmug scribsit.*
The manuscript belongs to a group of Irish Pocket Gospel Books (cf. nos. 45–8). The Evangelists are stylized, identical figures represented frontally with a book in their left hands and a small sceptre in their right. Apparently they are standing, and their feet extend below the frame at the bottom. Each is labelled, *Imago Mathei*, etc. The colours used are red, red-brown, violet, green, and yellow. It is not certain whether the manuscript was produced in Ireland or by Irish monks on the Continent. It has been generally dated in the second half of the 8th century, but Brown (1972) considers it could have been written before St. Boniface's death in 754. In that case the weak style would have to be attributed to provincial workmanship rather than late date. The binding is of dark-red leather with interlace ornament and is similar in technique to that of the Stonyhurst College Gospel of St. John (van Regemorter, 1949).

PROVENANCE: A late 9th- or early 10th-century inscription on f. 65ᵛ records that Abbot Huoggi of Fulda (elected 891) obtained from King Arnulf (d. 899) the restitution of the manuscript which was believed by tradition to have been written by St. Boniface. Fulda *ex libris* of 1776, f. 1ᵛ.

LITERATURE: J. F. Schannat, *Vindemiae literariae, Collectio Prima*, 1723, 217, 224–9, figs.; Westwood, *Facsimiles*, 91–2, pl. LI. 4; C. Scherer, 'Die Codices Bonifatiani in der Landesbibliothek zu Fulda', *Festgabe zum Bonifatius-Jubiläum*, II, 1905, 30–4, fig. 4, pl. 3; W. M. Lindsay, *Early Irish Minuscule Script*, 1910, 4–12, pl. III; Zimmermann, *Vorkarolingische Miniaturen*, 31, 106, 108, 250, pl. 205c; Kenney, *Sources*, no. 491; Micheli, *L'enluminure*, 52–3; B. van Regemorter, 'La reliure des manuscrits de S. Cuthbert et de S. Boniface', *Scriptorium*, 3, 1949, 48; P. McGurk, 'The Irish pocket Gospel Book', *Sacris Erudiri*, 8, 1956, 249–70; F. Henry, 'An Irish manuscript in the British Museum', *Journal of the Royal Society of Antiquaries of Ireland*, 87, 1957, 147–66, espec. 154–5, pl. XXVIIIa; *C.L.A.*, VIII, no. 1198; *Codex Lindisfarnensis*, 85–6; McGurk, *Latin Gospel Books*, no. 68; P. E. Schramm, F. Mütherich, *Denkmale der deutschen Könige und Kaiser*, 1962, 26, 138, pl. 59; Henry, *Irish Art*, I, 199 n. 2; T. J. Brown *ed.*, *The Stonyhurst Gospel of St. John*, 1969, 13, and 45–55 (R. Powell, P. Waters, 'Technical description of the binding'); Koehler, *Buchmalerei*, 15; T. J. Brown, 'Northumbria and the Book of Kells', *Anglo-Saxon England*, I, 1972, 242, 246; Henry, *Kells*, 225.

EXHIBITED: *Werdendes Abendland an Rhein und Ruhr*, Essen, 1956, no. 220. See also V. H. Elbern, *Das erste Jahrtausend. Tafelband*, 1962, pl. 183; *Karl der Grosse*, 1965, no. 391.

50. St. Gall, Stiftsbibliothek Cod. 1395, pp. 426–7
Unidentified text (fragment)
225×182 mm., single leaf
Second half of 8th century. Ireland

Ill. 261

The leaf has an initial P and continuation capitals, *Peccavimus domine peccavimus parcun* (sic), on the recto, and script continuing the prayer and commencing the Litany on the verso. Duft conjectures the page comes from a Psalter, Missal or perhaps Penitentiary. The bowl of the P is filled with a rosette and four panels of animal interlace, and its stem is filled with interlaced birds. The frame which has corner squares has panels of similar patterns and also of interlace. The continuation letters in bands are coloured and have colour infilling. The colours used are orange, purple, yellow, and black. There is apparently no evidence of when the manuscript reached St. Gall.
Panels of bird interlace, first occurring in the Northumbrian manuscripts (no. 9, etc.), are also found in the 'Stowe Missal' (no. 51), and the animal interlace can be compared to that found in the St. Gall Gospel Book (no. 44) and the Irish Pocket Gospel Books (nos. 45–6).

PROVENANCE: The leaf is from a composite volume put together by the Abbey Librarian, I. von Arx, in 1822.

LITERATURE: Westwood, *Facsimiles*, 67–8, pl. 28b; Zimmermann, *Vorkarolingische Miniaturen*, 34, 102, 243, pl. 197b; Kenney, *Sources*, no. 557 (ii); G. L. Micheli, 'Recherches sur les manuscrits Irlandais décorés de Saint-Gall et de Reichenau', *Revue archéologique*, 6ᵉ sér., 7, 1936, 212–14; A. Schardt, *Das Initial*, 1938, 31, pl. on p. 33; Duft, Meyer, *St. Gall*, 76–8, 103–4, pls. XVI, XXVII, fig. 30; *C.L.A.*, VII, no. 988; Henry, *Irish Art*, II, 91.

51. Dublin, Royal Irish Academy MS D. II. 3, ff. 12–67
Sacramentary (Stowe Missal)
145×110 mm., ff. 56
Late 8th century. Ireland

Ill. 217

The illumination consists of an initial P and frame (f. 12) and a number of small decorative initials. The P is composed of fret patterns. The top, bottom, and right of the page are framed with a panel of interlaced birds ending in a beast head above with its hind quarters, legs, and interlacing tail below. The colours used are yellow, black, and brown. The small initials are in black, one or two with interlace terminals or heads enclosed in them—e.g. O (f. 12ᵛ) with profile head.

The Book may have been made at Tallaght or as MacNiocaill argues at Terryglass. It seems to be a product of the same scriptorium as the Gospel fragment (no. 47) but the illumination there is of higher quality. There are almost contemporary additions and insertions in the text with a colophon (f. 37) 'Moel cáich scripsit'.

The *cumdach* (now in the National Museum of Ireland, Dublin) which contained this manuscript and the Stowe St. John (no. 47), bears an inscription stating that it was made by Dunchad O'Taccain, a monk of Clonmacnois, whilst Mac Raith O'Donoghue was King of Cashel, that is between *c.* 1045 and 1052. See H. S. Crawford, 'A descriptive list of Irish Shrines and Reliquaries. Part II', *Journal of the Royal Society of Antiquaries of Ireland*, 53, 1923, 153–4, pl. VIII, and Henry, *Irish Art*, III, 39, 77, 79, 82–3, 88, 95, 118, 120, 190, 208, pls. 28–30.

PROVENANCE: A list of bishops (f. 33) ends with Máel-Rúain, usually identified with the founder of Tallaght, who died in 792. His successor is not in the list. A 14th-century inscription on the *cumdach* refers to an Abbot of Lorrha. Possibly, the manuscript was there or nearby at Terryglass when the *cumdach* (see above) was made. It was still in Ireland in 1735. Acquired in 1819 by the Marquess (later Duke) of Buckingham (hence 'Stowe Missal') and later by the 4th Earl of Ashburnham. Purchased in 1883 at the Ashburnham sale by the British Government and deposited in the Academy.

LITERATURE: Westwood, *Facsimiles*, 88–9; G. F. Warner, 'The Stowe Missal', *Henry Bradshaw Society*, 31–2, 1906, 1915 (vol. I a complete facsimile); T. F. O'Rahilly, 'The history of the Stowe Missal', *Ériu*, 10, 1926–8, 95–109; Kenney, *Sources*, nos. 466, 555; Henry, *Irish Art*, I, 43, 161–2, 199–202, 205; G. MacNiocaill, 'Fragments d'un coutumier monastique irlandais du VIIIᵉ–IXᵉ siècle', *Scriptorium*, 15, 1961, 231–2; F. J. Byrne, 'The Stowe Missal', *Great Books of Ireland* (*Thomas Davis lectures*), 1967, 38–50, pl. 3; *C.L.A.*, II, no. 268.

52. Dublin, Trinity College MS A. 1. 6 (58)
Gospel Book (Book of Kells)
330 × 250 mm., ff. 340
(?) 8th–9th century. (?) Iona

Ills. 231–260

The illumination consists of Canon Tables, initials, symbol-pages, a carpet page, and miniatures. The Canon Tables are on ten pages (ff. 1ᵛ–6), but since ff. 6ᵛ–7 were blank (they were used in the 12th century to enter charters, see below PROVENANCE) they may have been intended originally to fill twelve pages. As far as Canon VIII (f. 5) they are under 'm n' arches and then in grid frames. Canon I (f. 1ᵛ) has four symbols under the main arch and a winged haloed figure holding a book above it. Canon I (f. 2) has four symbols below the main arch. Canon II (f. 2ᵛ) has symbols of Matthew with book, Mark and Luke (with Calf head but Eagle body) under the main arch and a head and shoulders naked figure, bearded and with three crosses in his halo, above the main arch. Canon II (f. 3) has symbols of Matthew with book, Mark and Luke under the main arch, and of Matthew with book in a roundel under the centre subsidiary arch. A small bust figure is above the main arch. Canons II–III (f. 3ᵛ) have symbols of Matthew with book seated on a cushion, Mark and Luke under the subsidiary arches. Canon IV (f. 4) has symbols of Matthew with book, Luke and John under the subsidiary arches, and a bust haloed figure holding a book in each hand over the main arch. Canon V (f. 4ᵛ) has no symbols. Canons VI, VII, and VIII (f. 5) have symbols of Mark and Luke under the main arch, and of Matthew with a flabellum and John holding a book with a human hand over the main arch in the corners. Canons IX and X (Matthew and Mark) (f. 5ᵛ) are placed in a grid of thirty-five squares, five across by seven down. Canon X—Luke and John (f. 6)—is also placed in a grid; above it has twelve squares, four across by three down, and, below, it is undivided horizontally.

The symbols are all winged. They have no haloes and no books except for the John symbol once (f. 5) and the Matthew symbols on ff. 2ᵛ–4. The Canon Tables on ff. 1ᵛ–5 are very richly ornamented with animal, human (e.g. f. 2), and bird interlace, as well as comparatively organic plant scrolls and interlace, trumpet, spiral, fret, and other patterns. The containing forms, circles, arches, rectangular panels, and so on, are strongly emphasized with broad bands of plain colour and often a thick black outline (f. 2). The architectural forms of capitals and imposts are stylized into squares, half-circles, or other flat shapes. A feature not seen in other Insular Canon Tables is the triangular corner pieces on either side of the main arch (ff. 1ᵛ–4ᵛ). On f. 5 the wings of the two symbols are similarly shaped to form a triangle. Grid frames for the Canon Tables are also found in the Books of Durrow (no. 6) and Echternach (no. 11).

There are five pages with Evangelist symbols. The first on f. 1 is damaged. The end of the glossary of St. Matthew fills the left column and the symbols are placed in the right column at right angles to the page, from top to bottom, Man, Lion, Eagle, Calf. They are winged and half-length and hold up books with human hands, i.e. they are zooanthropomorphic. Most probably they are to be connected with the Canon Tables they precede as a form of author portrait (see below). Each of the four Gospels is also preceded by a page with symbols arranged around a cross, f. 27ᵛ (Matthew), f. 129ᵛ (Mark), f. 187ᵛ (Luke; the Matthew and Mark symbols only are here combined with the end of the text of Mark), and f. 290ᵛ (John). Four-symbols pages also occur in the Books of Durrow (no. 6), Chad (no. 21), the Trier Gospel Book (no. 26), the Book of Armagh (no. 53) and in the Macdurnan Gospel Book (no. 70).

The Gospels of St. Matthew and St. John are both introduced by a sequence of four-symbols page, Evangelist portrait and initial page. St. Matthew has in addition a portrait of Christ as well as a carpet page preceding the 'Xp' initial. St. Mark has only a four-symbols page and an initial page and St. Luke only the page with two symbols at the end of Mark, and an initial. It may be, therefore, that a four-symbols page for St. Luke and portraits of St. Luke and St. Mark are missing (see below FOLIATION).

On f. 28ᵛ prefacing St. Matthew a full-length bearded figure holds a book in front of him. To the left and right of his shoulders are lion-heads which indicates a throne in spite of the fact that the position of the figure suggests that he is standing. To his right in a panel is a profile winged Calf and to his left a profile winged Eagle. It seems, therefore, that we have another form of four-symbol page, the Lion being doubled for symmetry, and that the central figure is Matthew in the likeness of his symbol, the Man, as in the Echternach Gospel Book (no. 11) and the Book of Cerne (no. 66), rather than simply as Evangelist portrait.

The Evangelist portrait of St. John (f. 291ᵛ) is bearded and sits frontally holding his book up in his left hand and a huge pen in his right hand. He sits on a high-backed throne on a draped cushion. Above the elaborate panelled frame in the centre is a partly cut off bearded head with draped shoulders. Below in the centre are two feet and on either side in the centre a clenched hand.

Each Gospel has a full-page decorated opening with initial and continuation lettering. On f. 29 the word *Liber* is treated as a monogram. Below in the margin to the left of the L which extends the full length of the page, is an unexplained standing figure with a book (cf. the third figure in the Matthew portrait of the Book of Lindisfarne, no. 9). Henry suggests it is a donor figure. Above to the left is an angel and above the letters 'ib' a third figure, half-length and holding a book. A large roundel above is perhaps a halo. The other initial pages are the 'Xp' (f. 34), the most elaborate in Insular art, with the famous details of the cats and mice and the otter with a salmon; 'Ini', St. Mark (f. 130); Q, St. Luke (f. 188); and 'Inp', St. John (f. 292). All include figures, the St. Mark initial having a seated figure being bitten by a lion, the St. Luke initial a number of small figures interlaced with the letters 'niam', and the St. John initial a frontal three-quarter-length figure with book and a smaller profile figure with book. Each initial has a frame on two or three sides and a great wealth of filling pattern so that the pages have the appearance of carpet pages.

Perhaps this helps to explain the fact, surprising in view of the lavishness of the rest of the illumination, that there is only one carpet-page, whereas there are five in the Book of Lindisfarne (no. 9). It is placed on the recto (f. 33) opposite the miniature of Christ, and precedes the 'Xp' monogram. A double-armed cross is made up of eight circles filled with trumpet and spiral patterns. The frame has corner and side pieces and the filling patterns are mainly zoomorphic and human interlace with fret patterns in the corner squares which are emphasized by their green borders. As usual with the Insular carpet-pages the relationship of the cross and the ground is ambiguous as to whether the cross is superimposed upon or imbedded in the field.

A number of Gospel passages are marked by larger initials and some form of extra framing: Matthew XXVI, 31 *Tunc dicit* (f. 114ᵛ); Matthew XXVII, 38, *Tunc crucifixerant* with groups of small profile half-length figures all facing left inserted in three squares of the frame (f. 124); Mark XV, 25, *Erat autem hora tertia*, with an angel with a book (f. 183); Luke IV, 1, *Jesus autem plenus Spiritu Sancto* (f. 203); and Luke XXIII, 56, *Una autem Sabbati*, with four angels (f. 285). Painted initials in the text are very numerous, and also varied filling decoration appears as line endings. These include pattern, animal forms, birds and even humans, for example the man on horseback (f. 89). Slightly larger initials mark Matthew VI, 9, the *Pater noster* (f. 45), and Luke I, 5, *Fuit in diebus illis* (f. 188ᵛ). On ff. 40 and 212 the initial B of each of the Beatitudes is joined up to the next to form a decorative panel and this also happens for the Genealogy in Luke III, 26–38 (ff. 200–2). The latter ends with a panel of ornament and a figure placed as it were behind it in the centre. Finally there are also initials for the prefatory matter: the Matthew list of chapters, *Nativitas* with panel lettering and frame (f. 8); preface to Matthew, *Mattheus* with figure (f. 12); the Mark list of chapters, *Et erat* (f. 13); preface to Mark, *Marcus Evangelista* (f. 15ᵛ); preface to Luke, *Lucas Syrus natione* (f. 16ᵛ); preface to John, *Hic est Johannes* (f. 18); the Luke list of chapters, *Zacharias* (f. 19ᵛ); the John list of chapters, smaller 'Io' (f. 24); and glossary of Hebrew names, A (f. 26).

The four minatures in the text show the Virgin and Child with four angels in the corners of the frame (f. 7ᵛ, it comes before the Matthew list of chapters); Christ seated on a draped cushion under an arch, bearded and holding a book, with a cross above his head, but no halo, and flanked above by a pair of peacocks and below by four angels (f. 32ᵛ, preceding the Matthew genealogy); the Arrest of Christ showing Him frontal, His arms held by flanking figures, the scene placed under an arch (f. 114, before the narrative in Matthew); and the Temptation (f. 202ᵛ, before the narrative in Luke) showing Christ half-length above a shrine-like object, with two angels above the halo, the Devil to the right, and a crowd of profile figures to the left and below in the frame. A leaf left blank before the Crucifixion narrative in Matthew suggests a miniature was intended here too (f. 123ᵛ). There may also have been miniatures before the passages of text emphasized with initials in Mark (f. 183, Crucifixion narrative) and Luke (f. 285, Resurrection narrative). The end of Luke is also blank and may also have been intended for a miniature (f. 289).

The colours used are of great richness and variety, blue, greenish blue, and a brownish purple being notable. The illumination is unfinished. For example, in addition to the intended miniature on f. 123ᵛ, the features of the angel on f. 29 are not inserted and the frames for the text on ff. 30ᵛ–31, the Matthew genealogy, are sketched, but only partly coloured. Some of the ornament is coarser and it has been conjectured that this was inserted later after a gap in time and, possibly, after the removal of the book to another place (e.g. Canon Table, f. 4ᵛ).

The Book of Kells has been thought to be that referred to by Giraldus Cambrensis who visited Ireland in 1185, as containing 'intricacies so delicate and subtle, so exact and compact, so full of knots and links, with colours so fresh and vivid that you might say all this was the work of an angel and not of a man' (quoted in full, Alton, Meyer, *Codex Cennanensis*, 14–15). It has become one of the most famous of all medieval illuminated manuscipts and for many is the supreme achievement of Insular art. And yet neither its date, nor the place of its origin, nor the sources of its style and iconography are established. Older scholarship dated it to the early 8th century (Zimmermann, 1916). Friend (1939) argued for a later date at the turn of the 8th–9th century. Recently Brown (1972) has reopened the question and argued for an earlier date in the second half or even middle of the 8th century.

As regards the place of production opinions also differ. The only certainty is that the manuscipt was at Kells in the 12th century and probably in the early 11th century. A fairly general view (Friend, Nordenfalk) is that it was written at Iona and transferred to Kells when Iona was sacked by the Vikings in 806. The Abbot of Iona, Cellach, resided at Kells for about seven years. He was buried at Iona in 815. This was held to explain the unfinished state of the decoration. Brown (1972), however, has also challenged its Irish origin and proposed mainly on paleographical grounds, but also because of similarities in layout and organization with the Book of Lindisfarne (no. 9) and for other reasons, an origin in northern England or even the Pictish kingdom.

The manuscript is the most lavish of all Insular books in its decoration, and the initial pages reach the ultimate point in the development from the humble initials of the Cathach of St. Columba (no. 4) in size, richness, and imaginative splendour. The illumination would presumably have been executed over a period and the fact that it is unfinished, given the scale of the decoration, need not necessarily be attributed to some outside catastrophe. Henry (1972) has proposed that three artists were mainly responsible for the illumination, the Goldsmith (named for the resemblance of his patterning to the intricacies of such metalwork as the Tara brooch) for ff. (?)5, 29, 33, 34, 130, 292, that is mainly the initial pages and the eight circle cross; the 'Illustrator' for the miniatures on ff. 7ᵛ, 114, and 202ᵛ, and

possibly for the last of the four-symbol pages (f. 290ᵛ), the initial page (f. 8) and some of the work on the Canon Tables; and lastly the 'Portrait Painter' for ff. 28ᵛ, 32ᵛ, 291ᵛ, and possibly the Matthew four-symbol page (f. 27ᵛ). She also sees three scribes as mainly responsible for writing the text, one or other of whom may also possibly have been one or other of the illuminators.

In addition to the great illuminated pages almost every page of text is decorated with initials, filling designs, and calligraphic flourishes. As with other Insular manuscripts script and illumination are closely interconnected, and it is highly likely, therefore, that scribes were also artists. Textual decoration, somewhat comparable though much less lavish is found in the Barberini Gospel Book (no. 36) and the Book of Cerne (no. 66). The filling designs to mark line overlaps in the text, called in Irish 'turn in the path' or 'head under the wing', are full of imaginative fantasy and humour which finds its nearest parallel in the marginal drolleries of Gothic manuscripts of five centuries later. As with the Gothic marginalia there is a problem as to whether any meaning or connection with the text is intended, a question judiciously discussed by Henry (1972). For instance, a cock and two hens are painted on f. 67 where the parable of the sower is narrated.

In addition to the sheer quality and scale of its ornament there are three particular features which have been noted as distinguishing Kells from the other Insular Gospel Books. These are the use of organic plant ornament, the miniatures inserted in the text, and the use of the so-called 'Beast Canon Tables'. These three features must indicate either that a totally new model or models had become available to the artists of Kells, or that there was an intermediary development in Insular illumination from the early and mid 8th century which is now lost to us. It is still difficult to decide between these alternatives. For example, Friend saw the organic plant ornament (e.g. f. 202) as an indication of the use of late 8th-century Carolingian sources which were dependent on newly acquired late antique models. However, the Leningrad Bede (no. 19) of *c.* 746 has plant ornament in an initial B which might have been more developed in more sumptuous or later manuscripts.

The same problem exists with the inserted miniatures. Three surviving Eastern Gospel Books (Codex Rossanensis, Rossano; Codex Sinopensis, Paris, B.N., suppl. Gr. 1286; Rabbula Gospel Book of 586, Florence, Laurenziana, I, 56), and one Western Gospel Book (Cambridge, Corpus Christi College MS 286), all four being of the 6th century, have illustrations. The miniatures are either prefatory or inserted in the lower margins. There is the possibility, however, that early Western Gospel Books not surviving had illustrations inserted in the text, if the illustrations of the Crucifixion and the Temptation (cf. Kells ff. 123ᵛ, 202ᵛ) in two later 9th-century western French Gospel Books go back, as seems likely, to early Christian rather than Insular or early Carolingian sources (cf. Wormald, Alexander, 1977). The earliest surviving Carolingian

Gospel Books of the Charlemagne Court School (Ada school) do not have full-page Gospel miniatures, though Koehler reconstructed an illustrated Evangelistary of the Ada school from a single surviving cutting showing the Annunciation to Zaccharias (*Journal of the Warburg and Courtauld Institutes*, 15, 1952).

Henry has also made an interesting comparison of the Temptation miniature with the same scene as shown in an Ottonian 11th-century Gospel Book from Echternach (Nuremberg, Germanisches Nationalmuseum), where the numerous New Testament scenes are likely to derive from Middle Byzantine sources. The Devil is similarly shown as a small black, winged mannikin and the Temple is a small gabled building with Christ standing on its tiled roof. The possibility of a pre-iconoclastic Eastern or Western Gospel Book, or even a Carolingian copy of such, having served as model for the miniatures in Kells cannot, therefore, be ruled out.

On the other hand, the earlier Durham Gospel Book (no. 10) has a miniature of the Crucifixion and may originally have had other miniatures, and both the Crucifixion and the Second Coming are shown in the St. Gall Gospel Book (no. 44). Moreover, McGurk (1955) has pointed out that Insular artists take over the practice from late antique Gospel Books of emphasizing certain passages of text and mark them with enlarged initials (*Latin Gospel Books*, Appendix V gives a list). This is done in Kells itself and it is a natural step to insert miniatures at these points.

On this view the extra miniatures in Kells would have been inserted as a result of an independent indigenous development and the iconographical sources could have been various. Thus the miniature of the Virgin and Child precedes the Matthew chapter list which begins with the word *Nativitas* which would have motivated its insertion. The type of image with the Child facing the Virgin is very rare and the closest parallel is the incised design of the same subject at one end of the Coffin of St. Cuthbert (fig. 6). Kitzinger has demonstrated that both representations are likely to be copies of the same Hellenizing (but not necessarily Eastern) model. Werner (1972) argues that the model was Coptic. The portrait of Christ is similarly inserted before the Genealogy of Christ and is probably copied from a Majesty composition in which Christ was surrounded by angels (cf. the *Codex Amiatinus*, no. 7). According to Friend and Werner the model also had zooanthropomorphic Evangelist symbols which were transferred by the Kells artist to f. 1 for lack of room (for another explanation of these symbols see below).

Friend's contention that a new model became available at Iona where he thought Kells was made in the late 8th century, and that this model was an early product of the Ada school, was based above all on a study of the iconography of the Beast Canon Tables. He compared the arrangement of the symbols in the Canon Tables of the Harley Gospels (B.L. Harley 2788, fig. 16) where they are also full

length and under the main arch. He also noted that after Canon IV the style and the arrangement of the Harley Canons changes and a different model was used, whose nature can be more easily seen from an examination of the Canon Tables of the Soissons Gospel Book (Paris, B.N., lat. 8850). In Kells too there is a break after Canon IV. From these two points Friend argued that Kells and Harley must have used the same model.

Friend further argued that the second break from arches to grid frame at Canon IX was due to the interruption of the work caused by the Viking raids and transfer of the manuscipt from Iona to Kells. The Ada school Gospel Book was lost or destroyed. McGurk (1955) has observed, however, that the same break from arches to grid frames occurs at Canon IX in the earlier fragmentary Canon Tables in B.L. Royal 7. C. XII (cf. no. 12). This can hardly be a coincidence. A model defective at this point must already have been circulating in north England, Iona, or Ireland in the early 8th century. Boeckler has also observed that there is no representation of the Cross in Kells, which he considers essential to what he calls the 'Dedikationsbild' type of Beast Canon as seen in Harley.

In spite of these objections it must be admitted that scholars have tended to reject Friend's conclusions without finding a satisfactory alternative explanation for the presence of the Beast Canons (no symbols are detectable from the offprint of the Canon Table arch in Royal 7. C. XII). Other features, in addition to the general point of their great sumptuousness, link the Ada School Gospel Books with Kells, particularly the triangular corner pieces above the main arches of the Canon Tables (an Eastern feature), and the frontal high-backed throne with a cloth on it of the John portrait (f. 291ᵛ, but note it has the rare feature of a cloth on the bolster as in the Barberini Gospel Book, no. 36). Henry has also drawn attention (cf. Micheli, 1939) to striking similarities with the initial decoration of a late 8th-century Psalter from Corbie in North France (Amiens, Bibliothèque Municipale, MS 18). This in turn has stylistic links with the earliest of the Ada School books, the Godescalc Lectionary (Paris, B.N., n.acq.lat. 1203). Are these connections due to Insular influence on early Carolingian art or are they rather the result of Carolingian influence on later Insular artists? Those who believe the latter will have to date the Book of Kells later (Nordenfalk, 1977). Those who wish to date the manuscript earlier (Brown, 1972) must argue the former.

If the model for the Canon Tables was not an Ada School Gospel Book only two other possibilities remain. The first is that the Beast Canons were copied from an independent late antique model (as Boeckler thought, though he implausibly argued that this was Eastern). The second possibility is that they are an Insular invention or at least development from a more rudimentary form, in other words the same possibility as for the plant ornament and the miniatures. The situation is even more complicated in that in the three other Insular Gospel Books with Beast Canons, there appear to be two traditions. The first is of zooanthropomorphic representations which are really a form of author portrait (cf. Boeckler) since they occur only on the first page above the relevant columns of Canon I as in the Barberini Gospel Book (no. 36), or form part of a series of Apostles as in the second Maeseyck Gospel Book (no. 23). The second is of half-length symbols placed under the subsidiary arches over the appropriate columns as in the first Maeseyck Gospel Book (no. 22). The first might possibly be an early Christian invention from which Insular artists developed the second. It certainly seems that the artists of Kells were aware of the first tradition, since this is the most probable explanation of the zooanthropomorphic symbols preceding Canon I on f. 1 (see above for the idea that they were transferred from a Majesty composition). It should also be noted that the Eagle symbol on f. 5 belongs to this type since it holds a book with human hand, and that some of the symbols in Kells are placed not below the main but below the subsidiary arches as in the Barberini and second Maeseyck Gospel Books. Again, as with the miniatures, we may therefore be dealing with an indigenous development in Insular art. The question of the iconographic sources must remain for the moment unresolved. In particular a detailed examination of the origin of the Beast Canons to establish when, where, and how the idea developed, is still needed to put the Canon Tables of Kells into context (cf. the divergent views of Boeckler and Rosenbaum). This will also have to take into account later Anglo-Saxon examples (cf. Alexander, 1966).

The problem of the stylistic origins of Kells is as difficult as that of its iconographic origins. Koehler in his comparisons of Kells with the St. Gall Gospel Book (no. 44) several times changed his mind as to whether Kells was a parallel or a later development. Many of the drapery conventions are similar in the two manuscripts, particularly the tubular sleeves. These are also found in the Book of Armagh (no. 53) which is securely dated to 807, and there the Evangelist symbols also provide close points of comparison. The stylistic relationship with the drawings in the Book of Armagh is one of the strongest arguments for a late dating of Kells. Certain features, particularly the use of profile human heads, are also found in the Macregol Gospel Book of before 822 (no. 54).

At the beginning of his article Friend wrote that 'the creators of the Book of Kells . . . have to a great degree succeeded in translating everything into the Celtic stylistic idiom thus rendering stylistic criticism nearly helpless in detecting the prototype'. The astounding creative fecundity of Kells is its outstanding quality, but it is this which makes the problem of its relationship with the other surviving Insular works so difficult to determine. If Iona had not been sacked the position might have been different (cf. Nordenfalk, 1977). But since Kells is the culmination of Insular manuscript production it is natural to place it at the end of the sequence of great Insular Gospel Books.

PROVENANCE: Iona was founded by St. Columba in 563. It was first raided by the Vikings in 795, it was burnt in 802, and in 806 sixty-eight members of the community were killed. In 804 Kells, co. Meath, was granted to the community as a place of refuge. The Columban community continued there into the 12th century. After the Norman Conquest an Augustinian house of Canons Regular, St. Mary's, was founded at Kells, and Kells also became for a short time the seat of a bishopric. The Book of Kells probably remained at what became the parish church of St. Columba, rather than at St. Mary's. See Gwynn, 1954 and A. Gwynn, R. N. Hadcock, *Medieval Religious Houses. Ireland*, 1970. The Annals of Ulster has the following entry under the year 1007: 'The great Gospel of Colum Cille, the chief treasure of the western world, on account of its secular cover was stolen by night from the western sacristy of the great stone church of Cenannus (Kells). That Gospel was found after twenty nights(?) and two months with its gold stolen from it, buried in the ground.' This very probably refers to the Book of Kells. The only certain evidence of its being at Kells, however, are the seven charters copied on ff. 5ᵛ, 6, 6ᵛ, 7, and 27 in the mid 12th century. They concern land in the neighbourhood of Kells with dates from c. 1033 to c. 1140. The account of Giraldus Cambrensis already referred to may describe the Book of Kells if his description of it as amongst the 'marvels of Kildare' is explicable as a slip or in some other way. Notes by Gerald Plunket of Dublin in 1568, f. 334ᵛ, and by Richard Whit in 1604 (f. 289ᵛ). James Ussher, Archbishop of Armagh (1580–1656), counted the folios in 1621 (f. 334ᵛ). The manuscript evidently remained at Kells until it was sent to Dublin for safety during the occupation of Kells by Cromwellian troops in 1653. It was presented after the Restoration to Trinity College by Henry Jones, Bishop of Meath (1661–82).

FOLIATION: There are two consecutive folios numbered 36, so that the last folio is numbered 339 not 340. When Ussher counted the folios in 1621 he recorded a total of 344, so there are now four folios missing. Three of these came between ff. 100 and 197 and one after f. 200 (see Henry, 1972, p. 152). For the collation see Powell (1956) and Henry (1972). The initial pages and the miniatures are now all on singletons. The manuscript is now bound in four volumes.

LITERATURE: Westwood, *Palaeographia*, nos. 16, 17; *id.*, *Facsimiles*, 25–33, pls. VIII–XI, LI. 1; J. H. Todd, 'Descriptive remarks on illuminations in certain Ancient Irish Manuscripts', *Vetusta Monumenta* (Society of Antiquaries of London), 6, 1869, 4 ff., pl. XLIV; Gilbert, *Facsimiles*, I, ix–xii, pls. VII–XVII; II, xliv, pls. LIX–LXI; *Pal. Soc.*, I, pls. 55–8, 88–9; T. K. Abbott, *Celtic ornaments from the Book of Kells*, 1892–5, pls. I–L; T. K. Abbott, *Catalogue of the manuscripts in the library of Trinity College, Dublin*, 1900, 7; E. Sullivan *The Book of Kells*, 1914, pls. I–XXIV; Zimmermann, *Vor-*

karolingische Miniaturen, 22, 27–8, 31–3, 35–6, 95–9, 118, 234–40, pls. 166–84; J. Brøndsted, *Early English Ornament*, 1924, 71, 84–5, 143, 275 n. 2, fig. 71; K. Pfister, *Irische Buchmalerei*, 1927, pls. I–IV and 1–19; Saunders, *English illumination*, 3–8, 10–11, pls. 4–7; W. R. Hovey, 'Sources of the Irish illuminative art', *Art Studies*, 6, 1928, 105–20, figs. 15, 22, 26; Kenney, *Sources*, no. 471; Kendrick, *Anglo-Saxon*, 95, 145, 147, 167; A. Schardt, *Das Initial*, 1938, 14, 17, pls. pp. 11, 13, 15–16, 18–19, 21–2; Micheli, *L'enluminure*, 10–11, 13, 17, 19, 20, 24–5, 29, 42, 50, 79, 85, 140, pls. 1, 14; A. M. Friend, 'The Canon Tables of the Book of Kells', *Studies in memory of Arthur Kingsley Porter*, II, 1939, 611–41, pls. 1–11, 20–2; H. Swarzenski, review of Friend, *Art Bulletin*, 24, 1942, 287–8; Masai, *Origines*, 29 ff., 54 ff., 111 ff., 122 ff., *passim*, pls. VI. 1, XXI–XXIX; E. H. Alton, P. Meyer, *Evangeliorum Quattuor Codex Cenannensis*, 3 vols., full facsimile, 1951; A. Gwynn, 'Some notes on the history of the Book of Kells', *Irish Historical Studies*, 9, 1954, 131–61; Duft, Meyer, *St. Gall*, figs. 7, 12, 17, 29, 42, 47, 71, 83, 88, 98–100; P. McGurk, 'Two notes on the Book of Kells and its relation to other Insular Gospel Books', *Scriptorium*, 9, 1955, 105–7; E. Rosenbaum, 'The Vine Columns of Old St. Peter's in Carolingian Canon Tables', *Journal of the Warburg and Courtauld Institutes*, 18, 1955, 8; A. Boeckler, 'Die Kanonbogen der Ada-Gruppe und ihre Vorlagen', *Münchner Jahrbuch der bildenden Kunst*, N.F. 5, 1954, 18–19; A. Boeckler, 'Formgeschichtliche Studien zur Adagruppe', *Bayerische Akademie der Wissenschaften, Abhandlungen, phil.-hist. Kl*, N.F. 42, 1956, 28 f., pls. 22d, 23d, 24b; R. Powell, 'The Book of Kells. The Book of Durrow. Comments on the vellum, the make-up and other aspects', *Scriptorium*, 10, 1956, 3–21; E. Kitzinger, 'The Coffin Reliquary', *The Relics of St. Cuthbert*, ed. C. F. Battiscombe, 1956, 223, 226, 248 ff., 264 n. 7, 304, pl. XIV. 1; Nordenfalk, *Early Medieval*, 109, 113–15, 118, 126, 135, 163, pl. p. 115; M. Schapiro, 'The decoration of the Leningrad manuscript of Bede', *Scriptorium*, 12, 1958, 201, 204–7, pls. 25 c, e; W. O'Sullivan, 'The donor of the Book of Kells', *Irish Historical Studies*, 11, 1958–9, 5–7; W. Oakeshott, *Classical Inspiration in Medieval Art*, 1959, 37–8, 125, pls. 55a, 56; *Codex Durmachensis*, figs. 3, 28, 35, 50, 52–5, 101; *Codex Lindisfarnensis*, xxiv, 105, 163, 190 ff., 257, 273–4, pls. 31b, 33e, 39a; McGurk, *Latin Gospel Books*, no. 87; O.-K. Werckmeister, 'Die Bedeutung der 'Chi' Initialseite im Book of Kells', *Das erste Jahrtausend. Textband*, II, ed V. H. Elbern, 1964, 687–710, pls. 1, 2, 7–10, 15–16, fig. 2; Henry, *Irish Art*, I, 87–8, 116, 145–6, 173, 183, 186, 202, 205, 207, fig. 9; J. J. G. Alexander, 'A little-known Gospel Book of the later eleventh century from Exeter,' *Burlington Magazine*, 108, 1966, 14–15; W. O'Sullivan, 'The Book of Kells', *Great Books of Ireland* (*Thomas Davis Lectures*), 1967, 14–25, pl. 8; Werckmeister, *Irisch-northumbrische Buchmalerei*, 101–75, pls. 26–7, 29b, 36a, 38a, 39, 40e, 41–2, 46–8; Henry, *Irish Art*, II, 58–9, 64, 66, 68–95, 97, 99, 101, 108–10, 119–20, 126, 151, 164–5, 181, 188, 195–6, 198, 205, figs. 8–10, 12–13, 41, pls. 17,

19–28, 31–3, 35, 38–9, A–H, J; C. Nordenfalk, 'An illustrated Diatessaron', *Art Bulletin*, 50, 1968, 129, 134, pl. 9; M. Werner, 'The four Evangelist Symbols page in the Book of Durrow', *Gesta*, 8, 1969, 3–17, fig. 7; *C.L.A.*, II, no. 274; M. Werner, 'The *Madonna and Child* miniature in the Book of Kells', *Art Bulletin*, 54, 1972, 1–23, 129–39, pls. 1, 14–15; Koehler, *Buchmalerei*, 5, 11–15, 17–18, 24, 41–6, 67, 73 ff., 88, 94, 99, 101–2, 187–91; T. J. Brown, 'Northumbria and the Book of Kells', *Anglo-Saxon England*, 1, 1972, 219–46, pls. IIc, III a, c, IVc, V a, c; M. Schapiro and seminar, 'The miniatures of the Florence Diatessaron', *Art Bulletin*, 55, 1973, 527, 529; Henry, *Kells, passim*, pls. 1–126; Nordenfalk, *Celtic*, 10, 16–17, 24, 26, 108–9, 112–13, 116–17, 120–4, pls. 39–47, fig. VI; F. Wormald, J. J. G. Alexander, *An early Breton Gospel Book* (Roxburghe Club), 1977, 6–7.

EXHIBITED : *Treasures from Trinity College, Dublin*, London, Burlington House, 1961, no. 85, 3 pls.

53. Dublin, Trinity College MS 52

New Testament, etc. (Book of Armagh)
c. 195 × 145 mm., ff. 217 (ff. 1, 41–4 missing but included in the foliation)
c. 807. Armagh

Ills. 221, 226, 227, 229, 230

The volume contains three distinct parts, the first (ff. 2–24) documents in Latin and Irish relating to St. Patrick, the second (ff. 25–190) the New Testament, and the third the Life of St. Martin, etc. (ff. 191–221). The decoration consists of line drawings of the symbols of the Evangelists with on f. 32^v all four symbols preceding St. Matthew, on f. 53^v the Lion of St. Mark, on f. 68^v the Calf of St. Luke, and on f. 90 the Eagle of St. John. Initials to the Gospels are: L (f. 33), 'Xp' (f. 33^v), 'In' (f. 54), Q (f. 69), and 'In p' (f. 90). There are also minor initials in part I (f. 20), and in part II for the Prefaces (ff. 25, 105), and for the Epistles and Acts: Romans (f. 108), Corinthians I (f. 115), Corinthians II (f. 122), Galatians (f. 127), Ephesians (f. 129^v), Philippians (f. 132), Thessalonians I (f. 134), Thessalonians II (f. 135^v), Colossians (f. 136^v), Laodiceans (f. 138), I Timothy (f. 138^v), II Timothy (f. 140), Titus (f. 141^v), Philemon (f. 142), Hebrews (f. 143), I James (f. 150), I Peter (f. 152), II Peter (f. 154), I John (f. 155), II John (f. 157), III John (f. 157^v), Jude (f. 158), Apocalypse (f. 159^v, 160), Acts (f. 171). There are also a number of initials in Part III (ff. 191, 191^v, 200^v, 214). The initials of the later part, the Acts, Epistles, and Life of St. Martin, are coloured in yellow, red, green, and blue. On f. 170 there is a diagrammatic representation of Jerusalem with its twelve gates each inscribed with its precious stone, its tribe, and its Apostle. The 'walls' are simple rectangles filled with interlace.

On f. 52^v is an inscription to the effect that the manuscript was written at the bidding of Torbach (Abbot of Armagh, 807, died 808) by the scribe

Ferdomnach who signs on ff. 67ᵛ, 89, 214, and 220. Lowe ascribes ff. 20–104, 212–20 to Ferdomnach, and ff. 105–211 and ff. 2–24 to two other scribes. Ferdomnach died in 845 according to the Annals of Ulster.

The manuscript is particularly important because it is dated and certainly Irish. The Evangelist symbols can be compared to those in the Book of Kells (no. 52) and they probably later served as models for the two Harley Gospel Books (nos. 76, 77). They all have four wings, but none have haloes and only the Man on f. 32ᵛ holds a book. The Eagle on the same page and on f. 90 holds a fish (? salmon) in its talons. Both the Eagle and the Calf of St. Luke have bust heads of the other three symbols on their wings, presumably again to emphasize the concordance of the Gospels (cf. the Trier Gospel Book, no. 26). The symbols give the impression of being terrestrial types (cf. the Books of Durrow, Echternach, and Trier, nos. 6, 11, 26) to which wings have been added. The initials are decorated with animal heads, birds, fish (e.g. f. 33ᵛ), interlace, and trumpet spirals. They are of fine quality and can be compared to those in the two Priscian manuscripts (nos. 63, 68). An unusual survival is the leather book satchel of probably the first half of the 11th century. It is stamped with interlace and zoomorphic patterns.

PROVENANCE: In 937 a *cumdach*, which does not survive, was provided for the manuscript by Donnchadh, son of Flan, King of Ireland. Sold or pledged by the last of its hereditary Keepers, Florence MacMoyne, *c.* 1680. Arthur Brownlow, before 1707, and Brownlow family until 1853 when bought by Bishop William Reeves. Bought from him by Lord John George Beresford, Primate of Ireland, and given to Trinity College in 1854.

LITERATURE: Westwood, *Palaeographia*, no. 19; *id.*, *Facsimiles*, 80–2, pl. LIII. fig. 10; Gilbert, *Facsimiles*, I, xiv–xvii, pls. XXV–XXIX; T. K. Abbott, *Catalogue of the manuscripts in the library of Trinity College, Dublin*, 1900, 6; W. M. Lindsay, *Early Irish Minuscule Script*, 1910, 24–30, pl. IX; J. Gwynn, *Liber Ardmachanus. The Book of Armagh*, 1913 (reproduces all the illuminations); Zimmermann, *Vorkarolingische Miniaturen*, 23, 31, 34, 103–4, 251, pls. 206–7; K. Pfister, *Irische Buchmalerei*, 1927, pl. 28; Kenney, *Sources*, no. 474; E. Gwynn, *Book of Armagh. The Patrician Documents* (Facsimiles in collotype of Irish manuscripts, III), 1937 (pls. of ff. 2–24ᵛ); Micheli, *L'enluminure*, 26, 41, 49, pl. 53; Masai, *Origines*, 43, pl. VI. 3; Duft, Meyer, *St. Gall*, figs. 2, 20; F. Henry, 'An Irish manuscript in the British Museum', *Journal of the Royal Society of Antiquaries of Ireland*, 87, 1957, 151 ff.; *Codex Durmachensis*, figs. 24, 33, 51, 67; Rickert, *Painting in Britain*, 24; Henry, *Irish Art*, II, 3, 4, 7, 20, 41, 58–9, 88, 97, 100–5, 121, pls. 18, 29, 30, 33; Werckmeister, *Irisch-northumbrische Buchmalerei*, 15 f.; L. Bieler, 'The Book of Armagh', *Great Books of Ireland* (*Thomas Davis lectures*), 1967, 51–63, pl. 5; *C.L.A.*, II, no. 270; T. J. Brown, 'Northumbria and the Book of Kells', *Anglo-Saxon England*, I, 1972,

222, 242; Koehler, *Buchmalerei*, 14; Henry, *Kells*, 151, 153, 155, 183, 198–9, 212–13, 225, figs. 6, 51, 53.

EXHIBITED: *Treasures of Trinity College, Dublin*, Burlington House, London, 1961, nos. 82–3, 2 pls.

54. Oxford, Bodleian Library MS Auct. D. 2. 19 (S.C. 3946)

Gospel Book (Macregol or Rushworth Gospels)
348 × 264 mm., ff. 169
Early 9th century. Birr, Co. Offaly, Ireland

Ills. 262–264, 266–269

The illumination consists of Evangelist portraits of St. Mark (f. 51ᵛ), St. Luke (f. 84ᵛ), and St. John (f. 126ᵛ) and *incipit* pages for each Gospel, 'Lib' (f. 1), 'Ini' (f. 52), 'Q' (f. 85), and 'In pr' (f. 127). The Evangelists are frontal seated figures, St. Mark carrying a book, St. Luke dipping his pen to the right, and St. John writing on a scroll on his lap. Their symbols are placed above their heads. The symbols do not have books and are reminiscent of the terrestrial types of Durrow (no. 6), even though they have wings. The frames are heavy and elaborately patterned with interlace, key, fret, pelta, and other designs and also animal and bird interlace. Human forms, especially heads, are also incorporated. On the Evangelist pages the figures are flanked by panels of pattern inside the main frame. On the initial pages the frames are on three sides and the continuation lettering is on coloured panels in yellow. The colours are limited to orange, yellow, green, black, and pinkish brown.

The manuscript has to be seen in the original as black and white reproduction tends to blur the decoration and make it look imprecise, which it is not. The colours are carefully worked out with the Insular principle of alternation, and their thick texture gives the impression of enamelling.

The first four and the last pages of St. Matthew's Gospel have plain coloured frames as do the first two pages of St. Mark's and St. Luke's Gospels (cf. nos. 10, 21, and 52). The last three pages of St. John's Gospel (ff. 168ᵛ, 169, 169ᵛ) are framed with broader patterned panels. On the last page (f. 169ᵛ) is Macregol's colophon: *Macregol dipinxit hoc evangelium. Quicumque legerit vel intellegerit istam narrationem orat pro macreguil scriptori.* This is particularly interesting in showing that scribe and illuminator are the same person. From it the date can also be inferred (see below).

There are some smaller initials to chapters and a four-line 'Xpi' in yellow on orange and brown for the Matthew genealogy (f. 2ᵛ). On the blank page preceding the St. Mark portrait (f. 51) a later, (?) 12th-century hand has drawn another portrait of St. Mark differing slightly from that on f. 51ᵛ (cf. no. 36). Other drawings, presumably by the same artist, of half-length figures are on ff. 30, 36 (cf. also smaller drawings in the lower margin, ff. 27ᵛ, 29, 46, 49, 122) where a syllable overlaps into the lower margin from the last word of the last line.

The manuscript is one of the latest of the *de luxe* Gospel Books. The seated Evangelists can be compared to those in the St. Gall Gospel Book (no. 44) for their thrones and the way in which the symbols are placed above their heads. Both the fact that Luke and John are shown writing as well as the scroll held by St. John suggest a mixture of sources (cf. the Book of Lindisfarne, no. 9, and the Barberini Gospel Book, no. 36).

PROVENANCE: Macregol is identifiable as the Abbot of Birr who died in 822. Owun and Farmon, a priest at Harewood, near Ross-on-Wye(?), glossed the Gospels in Old English, second half of 10th century, f. 168ᵛ. The gloss derives from the same source as that in Lindisfarne (no. 9). Owned by John Rushworth, clerk of the House of Commons, in 1650, and given by him to the Bodleian Library, perhaps in 1681.

LITERATURE: Westwood, *Palaeographia*, no. 44; *id.*, *Facsimiles*, 53–6, pl. XVI; Gilbert, *Facsimiles*, I, xiii, pls. XXII–XXIV; *Pal. Soc.*, I, pls. 90–1; S. Hemphill, 'The Gospels of Mac Regol of Birr: a study in Celtic illumination', *Proceedings of the Royal Irish Academy*, 29, Section C, no. 1, 1911–12, 1–10, pls. I–V; Zimmermann, *Vorkarolingische Miniaturen*, 31, 34, 36, 102, 106–7, 117, 247–8, pls. 199–204; K. Pfister, *Irische Buchmalerei*, 1927, pls. 26–7; Saunders, *English Illumination*, 12, pls. 10–11; Kenney, *Sources*, no. 472; Kendrick, *Anglo-Saxon*, 202; Micheli, *L'enluminure*, 20, 29; Masai, *Origines*, 48, 120, pl. XXX; Duft, Meyer, *St. Gall*, figs. 6, 23, 37, 49, 52, 63, 66, 74, 77, 93, 103, 104; Nordenfalk, *Early Medieval*, 121; Ker, *Catalogue*, 352 (no. 292); *Codex Durmachensis*, fig. 113; McGurk, *Latin Gospel Books*, no. 33; Rickert, *Painting in Britain*, 24; Henry, *Irish Art*, I, 116, 162, 198–9, pls. 110, N; T. J. Brown, 'Northumbria and the Book of Kells', *Anglo-Saxon England*, I, 1972, 221, 224, 242, 246; *C.L.A.*, II, no. 231; Koehler, *Buchmalerei*, 15, 16 24; Pächt and Alexander, III, no. 1269, pls. CXIV–CXVI; Henry, *Kells*, 152, 155, 205, 213, 225, figs. 7, 55.

55. Würzburg, Universitätsbibliothek Cod. M. p. th. f. 69
St. Paul, Epistles
286×225 mm., ff. 62
Late 8th century. Germany (Würzburg or area)
Ill. 265

The illumination consists of a miniature (f. 7ᵛ) and initials to the various Epistles. The miniature is framed by an arch decorated with rosettes in squares and circles. Above is a bearded Christ on the cross dressed in a long robe (cf. nos. 10, 44) and flanked below by the two thieves shown smaller. Above the arms of the cross are two birds facing inwards. Below, are two winged angels(?) on the left and two winged birds on the right. Underneath the cross Christ is shown in a boat with nine figures, evidently

the scene of the Calming of the Storm. The first eight leaves are misbound and the original order was 7, 8, 1–6, so that the miniature preceded the text. The extreme stylization of the figures and the colouring in orange, yellow, and black recall Irish illumination such as that in the Macregol Gospels (no. 54). It seems likely that this is a copy of an Irish model. The initials show a combination of Insular and Carolingian features. Bischoff (p. 11) notes Irish features in the script found also in the Macregol Gospels.

PROVENANCE: Number 32 in the Würzburg Cathedral Library catalogue of *c.* 800, and also in the catalogue of *c.* 1000.

LITERATURE: Zimmermann, *Vorkarolingische Miniaturen*, 109, 257–8, pls. 219e, 220; K. Pfister, *Irische Buchmalerei*, 1927, pl. 32; E. A. Lowe, 'An 8th century list of books in a Bodleian manuscript from Würzburg', *Speculum*, 3, 1928, 9; Kenney, *Sources*, no. 493; Micheli, *L'enluminure*, 11, 69, pls. 33, 91; Masai, *Origines*, 15 f., pl. XXXIV; B. Bischoff, J. Hofmann, *Libri Sancti Kyliani*, 1952, 8, 11, 102, etc.; *C.L.A.*, IX, no. 1424.

EXHIBITED: *Franconia Sacra*, Würzburg, Munich, 1960, c. 5; *Bayerns Kirche im Mittelalter*, Munich, 1960, no. 172, pl. 3; *Karl der Grosse*, 1965, no. 448, pl. 69.

56. Paris, Bibliothèque Nationale MS nouv. acq. lat. 1587
Gospel Book
295×245 mm., ff. 109
8th to 9th century. (?) Brittany
Ills. 270–273

The illumination consists of a frontispiece (f. 1ᵛ) and initials to the Gospels, L (f. 2), 'Xp' (f. 2ᵛ), I (f. 32ᵛ), Q (f. 52ᵛ), F (small, three lines, f. 53), and 'In' (f. 85ᵛ). The frontispiece has a central panel of interlace surrounded by a panel frame with zoomorphic interlace (centre sides), interlace (four corners), and paired animals with interlacing tails (centre top and bottom). The initials L and 'Xp' (ff. 2, 2ᵛ) are six to seven lines high and have continuation lettering in black with colour infilling. The lower left cross-bar of the X ends with a human head (cf. the Leiden Pliny, no. 18) which seems to have been drawn in dry-point as an animal head, however. The other initials are larger, whole page or almost whole page. They have continuation lettering in black on coloured panels with similar ornament on three sides. Initials and frames are outlined with a double row of orange dots. There are a number of (?) later dry-point sketches of interlace and one of a cock (f. 75). The colours used throughout the manuscript are confined to green, orange, and yellow. The imprints visible on f. 31ᵛ and especially ff. 50ᵛ, 51ᵛ suggest that the Mark and Luke *incipit* pages were drawn with a dry-point after the gatherings were assembled or even bound (cf. Powell on the Lichfield Gospel Book, no. 21). On f. 109 after St. John is a prayer in the same script, so by the scribe: *Ego Holcondus mihi Trinitas misereatur amen*. The script is described by Lowe as 'a crude and rather awkward specimen of Celtic majuscule', and he further comments: 'origin uncertain. A Breton centre seems likely, but Cornwall or Wales are not to be excluded.' McGurk draws attention to the similarity of the colophon of Luke to that in B.L. MS Egerton 609, another Gospel Book possibly from Brittany. Whatever its origin the manuscript is included here as it would seem to be a copy of a very sumptuous, probably Irish, Gospel Book, with a layout of the initial pages similar to that in the Macregol Gospel Book (no. 54).

PROVENANCE: On f. 1 is the name *Uuarnerius* and on f. 109 *Tinmocniam*, both 9th century. No. 8 in the catalogue (G. Joüan and V. d'Avanne, 1706) of St. Gatien, Tours. Stolen by Guglielmo Libri in 1842 (Westwood reports it is no longer there and draws attention to Lord Ashburnham's Gospel Book) and sold by him to the 4th Earl of Ashburnham from whom acquired by the Bibliothèque Nationale in 1888. The *ex libris* 'monasterii S. Zenonis maioris Veronae', f. 109, is a Libri falsification.

LITERATURE: (Tassain, Toustain), *Nouveau Traité de Diplomatique par deux Réligieux Bénédictins de la Congregation de Saint-Maur*, III, 1757, 86, 383, pls. XXXVII, LV; Westwood, *Facsimiles*, 60–1; L. Delisle, *Catalogue des manuscrits des fonds Libri et Barrois*, 1888, 7–10, pls. II. 3, VI. 1, 6; Zimmermann, *Vorkarolingische Miniaturen*, 109, 257, pls. 217–19a; K. Pfister, *Irische Buchmalerei*, 1927, pl. 31; E. K. Rand, *A Survey of the manuscripts of Tours. Studies in the script of Tours*, I, 1929, 92–3, pls. 18–19; Kenney, *Sources*, no. 494; Micheli, *L'enluminure*, 60–1, pl. 9; Masai, *Origines*, 120, pl. XXXIII; *C.L.A.*, V, no. 684; McGurk, *Latin Gospel Books*, no. 63.

57. St. Gall, Stiftsbibliothek Cod. 1395, pp. 418–19
Gospel Book (fragment)
219 × 178 mm., single leaf
8th to 9th century. Ireland

Ill. 281

The leaf contains a portrait of St. Matthew on one side (p. 418) and charms against illness in Old Irish and Latin written by two hands in the 9th century on the other (p. 419). The Evangelist who is bearded, is seated with his legs to the right but turns frontally. He holds a pen in his right hand and a knife in his left. The knife rests on a book which is without support. His symbol, the winged Man holding a book, is placed before him. Below his chair are objects to be identified as scrolls (cf. Goldschmidt). The colours are orange, slate-blue, purple, black, and yellow. The border has corner squares and a continuous fret pattern in the panels.

The relationship of the symbol to the Evangelist has been compared to that of St. Matthew and the inspiring figure in the Book of Lindisfarne (no. 9). Whether there was an early Christian precedent for placing the symbol beside the Evangelist or whether it was an Insular addition, is uncertain. Symbols beside the Evangelist can also be seen in the Trier Gospel Book portraits of St. Mark and St. Luke (no. 26), and compare also the Tassilo Chalice mentioned in connection with the Cutbercht Gospel Book (no. 37).

PROVENANCE: Bound into a composite volume put together by I. von Arx, abbey librarian, in 1822. See also no. 58.

LITERATURE: Zimmermann, *Vorkarolingische Miniaturen*, 31, 242–3, pl. 191b; G. L. Micheli, 'Recherches sur les manuscrits Irlandais décorés de Saint-Gall et de Reichenau', *Revue archéologique*, 6ᵉ sér., 7, 1936, 207–14, fig. 3; Micheli, *L'enluminure*, 41, 70, pl. 30; A. Goldschmidt, *An early manuscript of the Aesop fables of Avianus and related manuscripts*, 1947, 31, fig. 28; Duft, Meyer, *St. Gall*, 42, 76–8, 102, pls. XV, XXVI; *C.L.A.*, VII, no. 988; *Codex Lindisfarnensis*, 162–3, pl. 31a; Koehler, *Buchmalerei*, 17; Henry, *Kells*, 157 n. 37, 183, 226, figs. 11, 33.

58. St. Gall, Stiftsbibliothek Cod. 1395, pp. 422–3
Fragment
227 × 178 mm., single leaf
8th to 9th century. Ireland

Ill. 282

The leaf has a cross page on one side (p. 422) and prayers, perhaps added later, on the other (p. 423). The cross has a central square of interlace and four panels filled with interlaced human figures at top and bottom and with interlaced birds at the sides. Unlike the earlier cross-carpet pages the field is left blank. The profile human heads can be compared to those in the Macregol Gospel Book (no. 54). The leaf was formerly thought to come from the same Gospel Book as no. 57. Duft, however, conjectures that it comes from a liturgical book.

PROVENANCE: Bound into a composite volume put together by I. von Arx, abbey librarian, in 1822.

LITERATURE: Zimmermann, *Vorkarolingische Miniaturen*, 102, 243, pl. 197a.; A. Goldschmidt, *German Illumination*, I, 1928, pl. 11a; Kenney, *Sources*, no. 557 (V); G. L. Micheli, 'Recherches sur les manuscrits Irlandais décorés de Saint-Gall et de Reichenau', *Revue archéologique*, 6ᵉ sér., 7, 1936, 207–12; Micheli, *L'enluminure*, 41, pl. 8; Åberg, *Occident*, 101, fig. 76. 5; Duft, Meyer, *St. Gall*, 76–8, 104–5, pls. XVII, XXVIII, fig. 31; *C.L.A.*, VII, no. 988; Henry, *Irish Art*, I, 116; Henry, *Kells*, 205, fig. 59.

59. Dublin, Trinity College MS A. 4. 6 (56)

Gospel Book ('Garland of Howth', 'Codex Usserianus Secundus')

243 × 175 mm., ff. 86

(?) 8th to 9th century. Ireland

Ills. 274, 275

The illumination consists of initial pages for Matthew, *Xpi autem gene* (f. 1), and Mark, *Initium Eva* (f. 22). The beginnings of Luke and John are missing. On the initial page for Matthew there are two frontal, seated figures (their feet are crossed) holding books in their left hands. The figure on the left raises his right hand; the figure on the right carries a sword (?) in his right hand. In a small square compartment above each figure is an angel. It is presumably St. Matthew, with his symbol above, who is on the left. The identity of the second figure, however, is unexplained. On the second page St. Mark stands between the stems of the 'IN' monogram. Above the cross-bar is his symbol, the Lion, half length. There is a wealth of interlace and animal-head terminals. The outer panel frames contain interlaced birds (f. 1) and cable interlace (f. 22) and terminate in animal heads at the top with their hind quarters at the bottom.

Both pages are very damaged. Only the orange minium survives with some white and yellow. Blue was also used but has mostly gone. The St. Mark has the tubular folds seen earlier in the St. Gall Gospel Book (no. 44) and the Irish Pocket Gospel Books (nos. 45–8). A similar combination of figures and initial pages (these are not exactly historiated initials) is seen in the Book of Kells (no. 52), and the Lion of St. Mark can also be compared to the Lions in Kells (e.g. f. 129ᵛ). It is not clear if the greater stylization, seen especially in the Luke page, is due to a later date or because the manuscript was made in a more provincial centre.

PROVENANCE: Found on the island 'Ireland's Eye', near Howth. There is no evidence that the manuscript belonged to Archbishop James Ussher.

LITERATURE: Westwood, *Palaeographia*, no. 19; *id.*, *Facsimiles*, 46–7; J. H. Todd, 'Descriptive remarks on illuminations in certain Ancient Irish Manuscripts', *Vetusta Monumenta* (Society of Antiquaries of London), 6, 1869, 11 ff., pls. XLIV–XLV; R. Cochrane, 'The Garland of Howth', *Journal of the Royal Society of Antiquaries of Ireland*, 5th ser., 3, 1893, 404–7, figs. 21–2; T. K. Abbott, *Catalogue of the manuscripts in the library of Trinity College, Dublin*, 1900, 7; Zimmermann, *Vorkarolingische Miniaturen*, 108, 252, pl. 210; H. C. Hoskier, *New and complete edition of the Irish Latin Gospel Codex Usser. 2 or r², otherwise known as the Garland of Howth, in Trinity College Library, Dublin*, 1919; Kenney, *Sources*, no. 477; Duft, Meyer, *St. Gall*, fig. 102; McGurk, *Latin Gospel Books*, no. 85; Koehler, *Buchmalerei*, 15; *C.L.A.*, II, no. 272.

60. St. Gall, Stiftsbibliothek Cod. 60

Gospel of St. John

268 × 190 mm., ff. 34

(?) First half of 9th century. (?) Ireland

Ills. 283, 284

The illumination consists of a portrait of St. John (p. 4) and an initial page *In principio* (p. 5). The youthful unbearded St. John is seated frontally and with both hands before him holds a book inscribed 'Johannis'. The tall uprights of his throne end in bird heads (compare the St. Mark in the Book of Dimma, no. 48). Above his head is a profile Eagle (compare the St. John in the St. Gall Gospel Book, no. 44). The orange frame is filled with yellow and black interlace at top and bottom and crossed squares or circles at the sides. Figure, throne, and frame are outlined in orange dots. The figure is reduced to a stylized pattern of bands of yellow and orange. These are the only colours used.

The uprights of the 'IN' monogram end in whorl patterns. In the centre are ferocious beast heads. The bowl of the P is formed of a bird's neck and head. A partial frame on the outer side of the page is filled with the same pattern as on p. 4. A profile human head is at the end at the top.

Zimmermann and Duft incline to think the illustration a Continental imitation of an Irish model, even though the script is thought to be Irish. A similar stage of stylization has been reached in the Macregol Gospels (no. 54) but the present manuscript is considerably weaker.

PROVENANCE: Included in the list of *Libri scottice scripti* in the St. Gall catalogue of *c.* mid 9th century. St. Gall *ex libris*, 16th century, p. 5.

LITERATURE: Westwood, *Facsimiles*, 66–7; Zimmermann, *Vorkarolingische Miniaturen*, 108, 243 f., pls. 192b, 193; Kenney, *Sources*, no. 470; G. L. Micheli, 'Recherches sur les manuscrits Irlandais décorés de Saint-Gall et de Reichenau', *Revue archéologique*, 6ᵉ sér., 7, 1936, 55–8; Micheli, *L'enluminure*, 64, pl. 35; Masai, *Origines*, 122, pl. XXXII; Duft, Meyer, *St. Gall*, 42, 44, 46, 71–2, 105–6, pls. XVIII–XIX, XXXIII–XXXIV; *C.L.A.*, VII, no. 902; McGurk, *Latin Gospel Books*, no. 118; O.-K. Werckmeister, 'Three problems of tradition in pre-Carolingian figure style', *Proceedings of the Royal Irish Academy*, 63 C, no. 5, 1963, 177–8, pl. XXVIIId; Koehler, *Buchmalerei*, 15; Henry, *Kells*, 226.

61. Turin, Biblioteca Nazionale Cod. O. IV. 20

Gospel Book (fragment)

Originally 280 × 196 mm. (see Ottino), ff. 4

(?) First half of 9th century. Ireland

Ills. 277–280

The manuscript to which these four leaves belong was burnt in the Turin fire of 1904 and they only survive because they had been removed for photography. Even so they are shrunk and the pigments discoloured (f. 1, 210×137 mm.; f. 2, 193×143 mm.; f. 128, 221×143 mm.). They were restored in 1906. The manuscript was a palimpsest containing Domenico Cavalca's *Esposizione sopra il credo* written on ff. 189 in Italy in the 15th century. The re-used parchment came from various manuscripts including the Gospel Book to which the four leaves evidently belonged.

First bifolium. Folio 1ᵃ, blank. Folio 1ᵃ verso, the Ascension. Above, a three-quarter-length Christ, blessing with His right hand and with a book in His left hand, is supported by four angels in a round mandorla. Two other angels are included in the mandorla. Below, in the centre, is another angel in a roundel and in two rows the twelve Apostles. The figures are labelled and there are also extracts from the narrative of Acts I. Folio 2ᵃ, Second Coming. In the centre Christ stands holding a cross. He is surrounded by ninety-six little figures holding books and arranged in rows. The frame is filled with a fret pattern with human heads at three corners, and at the fourth, the upper right, an angel blowing the last trumpet. On folio 2ᵃ verso is the *incipit* of Cavalca.

Second bifolium. Folio 128ᵃ: *Finisce lo primo libro . . .* Folio 128ᵃ verso, a cross-carpet page. In the centre are five panels with whorls, trumpet, and pelta patterns. The spaces between them are filled with four interlace panels at the corners whilst the cross is made up of panels filled with birds. The rectangular panels of the frame are filled with interlaced human, bird, and zoomorphic forms in balancing pairs, at the two sides, at top and bottom, and, diagonally, in the corners. The colours are yellow, orange, blue, and green now discoloured black. Folio 129, a second cross-carpet page. This time a stepped cross is filled with interlace with a similarly filled frame. The four irregular corner spaces which, as usual in Insular art, can be read either as background with the cross superimposed or as imposed on a continuous interlace ground, are filled with a fret pattern. The interlace is yellow and (?) green (now discoloured black). Folio 129ᵛ: *Incomincia li cap'li della seconda parte.* The leaves were evidently used as frontispieces for the 15th-century manuscript's two parts.

One initial, the Q to St. Luke (f. 27ᵛ, formerly f. 158), is reproduced by Cipolla and from there in *C.L.A* from the manuscript before it was burnt. This and some other initials are amongst the surviving fragments. The relationship of the two bifolia to the Gospel Book seems not to be established, i.e. what, if any, text can be read on ff. 2ᵃ verso, 128ᵃ recto and 129 verso. Zimmermann, Lowe, and McGurk consider the first bifolium with the Ascension and Second Coming to be an addition of the 11th or 12th century, but this view is rightly rejected by Henry since the four leaves are certainly related stylistically and technically and must all be of the same date and from the same manuscript.

The two miniatures form a pair as is made clear by the text of Acts inscribed on the Ascension page: *Quemadmodum vidistis eum euntem, sic veniat* (sic)

ad vos Jesus qui reversus est a vobis. The Second Coming is also shown in the St. Gall Gospel Book (no. 44). Both scenes may go back to early Christian, perhaps Eastern Mediterranean, models (cf. the Ascension in the Rabbula Gospel Book, Florence, Laurenziana, Plut. I, 56, of *c.* 586 and the later, 10th century Athelstan Psalter which has both the Ascension and the Second Coming with Christ holding the cross, see Temple, *Anglo-Saxon*, no. 5, ills. 32–3). The Second Coming miniature is important as an early stage in the creation of the later western iconography of the Last Judgement (cf. Brenk).

Henry has pointed to stylistic as well as iconographical links with the St. Gall Gospel Book (no. 44), and has suggested that this could be a product of the same scriptorium some fifty years later. The profile faces of the interlaced figures are reminiscent of the Book of Kells (no. 52), the Macregol Gospel Book (no. 54) and the St. Gall cross page (no. 58). Some relationship to the figure style of the Macdurnan Gospel Book (no. 70) is also apparent.

PROVENANCE: A 15th-century *ex libris* of Bobbio was on f. 4ᵃ of the destroyed manuscript, but the manuscript cannot be identified in the 1461 inventory. Bobbio was suppressed in 1803.

LITERATURE: G. Ottino, *I codici bobbiesi della Biblioteca Nazionale di Torino*, 1890, 56; F. Carta, C. Cipolla, C. Frati, *Atlante palaeografico-artistica*, 1899, 9–10, pl. X; C. Cipolla, *Codici bobbiesi della Biblioteca nazionale universitaria di Torino*, I, 1907, (repr. 1963), I, 111–13, pls. XXXIX–XLI; Zimmermann, *Vorkarolingische Miniaturen*, 102, 108, 117, 246–7, pls. 198, 211; Micheli, *L'enluminure*, 11, 25, 42, pl. 7; *C.L.A.*, IV, no. 466; Duft, Meyer, *St. Gall*, fig. 90; McGurk, *Latin Gospel Books*, no. 107; B. Brenk, *Tradition und Neuerung in der christlichen Kunst des ersten Jahrtausends* (Wiener Byzantinische Studien, III), 1966, 69, pl. 18; Werckmeister, *Irisch-northumbrische Buchmalerei*, 118 f.; Henry, *Irish Art*, II, 58, 95–9, 124, 169, 193, pls. 37–40; Y. Christe, *La vision de Matthieu XXIV–XXV*, 1973, 54, fig. 86; Henry, *Kells*, 152, 163, 165, 173, 205, 214, 226, figs. 19, 20, 30, 61.

EXHIBITED: *Mostra storica nazionale della miniatura*, Palazzo di Venezia, Rome, 1954, no. 32, pl. XII.

62. Milan, Biblioteca Ambrosiana C. 301. inf.
Ps. Theodore of Mopsuestia, Commentary on the Psalms
330×230 mm., ff. 146 (paginated 6–298)
Early 9th century. Ireland

Ill. 316

The illumination consists of fairly simple initials in pen without colour. On f. 2 (p. 8) an initial D has a face drawn in the bowl and on f. 72 a Q (Ps. 52) has a cat's head. The style of drawing recalls the Book of Armagh (no. 53) and the St. Gall Priscian (no. 68). The scribe, Diarmait, signs his name on f. 146ᵛ (p. 298). He was probably working at Bangor, or perhaps in Leinster. Glosses are quoted as being by Maelgaimrid who is probably to be identified with an individual recorded as dying in 839.

PROVENANCE: *Ex libris* of Bobbio, f. 2 (p. 8), 15th century, and no. 89 of the 1461 inventory. 'Adelgisus', Carolingian minuscule, p. 162, 9th century.

LITERATURE: W. M. Lindsay, *Early Irish Minuscule Script*, 1910, 70 ff.; Kenney, *Sources*, nos. 47, 515; R. I. Best, *The Commentary on the Psalms with glosses in Old-Irish preserved in the Ambrosian Library*, 1936 (full facsimile); *C.L.A.*, III, no. 326; F. Henry, 'Les débuts de la miniature Irlandaise', *Gazette des Beaux-Arts*, 6e pér., 37, 1950, 5–34, fig. 13. II–IV.

63. Leiden, Universiteitsbibliotheek MS B. P. L. 67
Priscian, Periegesis Dionysii and Institutiones Grammaticae
225 × 160 mm., ff. 207
c. 838. Ireland, (?) Armagh

Ill. 317

The illumination consists of initials to the books of the *Institutiones* in black outlined in red with black spots and with terminals of interlace, spirals, and trumpet pattern and animal or human heads. On f. 23ᵛ the N has a cat perched on top. The manuscript is signed by the scribe Dubtach with the date 11 April 838, at the end of the *Periegesis* (f. 7ᵛ). Probably two other scribes worked on it. The style of script and initials links the manuscript with the Book of Armagh (no. 53).

PROVENANCE: A poem written in the margin probably by an Irishman suggests the book was taken to Soissons, 9th century (Henry). Given by Magister Baldewinus to the Abbey of Egmond under Abbot Stephen V (d. 1105), according to a catalogue of *c.* 1520–30. Remains of the Egmond pressmark survive. Lazarus Schoener in Corbach bei Cassel, 1583. Jonas Gruter, d. 1627. In the Leiden catalogue of 1716.

LITERATURE: *New Pal. Soc.*, I, pls. 32–3; W. M. Lindsay, *Early Irish Minuscule Script*, 1910, 36–40; Zimmermann, *Vorkarolingische Miniaturen*, 23 n. 2, 104, 251–2, pls. 208 c–e; Kenney, *Sources*, nos. 364(i), 366, 533; Micheli, *L'enluminure*, 41, 129; G. I. Lieftinck, *Manuscrits datés conservés dans les Pays-Bas*, I. *Les manuscrits d'origine étrangère*, 1964, 73–74, pls. 11–16; Henry, *Irish Art*, II, 58–9, 100–2; Henry, *Kells*, 225.

64. Valenciennes, Bibliothèque Municipale MS 99
Apocalypse
270 × 200 mm., ff. 40
Early 9th century

Ills. 302–309

The manuscript contains thirty-eight framed minia-tures. The text is written on the versos (ff. 3ᵛ–39ᵛ) and the miniatures are painted on the rectos opposite (ff. 3–40), except for ff. 12ᵛ–13 on which the minia-tures are half-page. The frames are of blank panels, only the first (f. 3ᵛ) being filled with interlace pat-terns. On f. 2 is a plan drawn in red ink and labelled *Sancta* [sic] *tabernaculum. Sancta sanctorum.* The scribe signs his name: *Otoldus presbiter*, f. 39ᵛ. He also wrote the Gospel Book from St. Martin, Mainz (formerly Gotha, now Munich, Bayerische Staats-bibliothek, Clm. 28561), and the Apocalypse was formerly attributed to a Middle Rhine scriptorium by Bischoff (1965) who now, however, considers an origin in the north-western part of the Carolingian Empire likely, perhaps in Liège by comparison with the Antwerp Sedulius (no. 65, cf. Klein, 1972).
A closely similar set of illustrations with similar legends is contained in a late 9th-century Apocalypse in Paris, Bibl. Nat., n. acq. lat. 1132. The format of the illustrations is different, however—they are usually a horizontal not a vertical rectangle—and there are no interlace patterns. Both manuscripts derive from a common model, according to Klein (1972) an Italian 7th-century Apocalypse.
The Valenciennes Apocalypse is included here because it seems likely that its immediate model was an Insular, probably Northumbrian, book. This is suggested by the style and the use of interlace. As is well known Bede relates that Benedict Biscop brought back from Rome pictures (*imagines*) of the Revelation of St. John for the north wall of his church at Monkwearmouth. There are signs that the Northumbrian illuminator reworked the cycle. Nordenfalk (1977) has also compared the frame on f. 3ᵛ with that on f. 172ᵛ of the Durham Cassiodorus (no. 17) which he therefore attributed to Wearmouth/Jarrow.

PROVENANCE: No. 21 of the catalogue of the Bene-dictine Abbey of St. Amand, near Valenciennes, 1150–68. Transferred to Valenciennes in 1790.

LITERATURE: M. A. Molinier, *Catalogue général des manuscrits des bibliothèques publiques de France*, XXV, 1894, 229–30; A. Boinet, *La miniature Carolingienne*, 1913, pls. 157–9; H. Omont, 'Manuscrits illustrés de l'Apocalypse aux IXe et Xe siècles', *Bulletin de la Société française de reproductions de manuscrits à peintures*, 6, 1922, 62–4, 73–84, pls. 14–28; W. Neuss, *Die Apokalypse des Hl. Johannes in der altspanischen und altchristlichen Bibel-illustration* (Spanische For-schungen der Görresgesellschaft), 1931, 247 ff., 286, pl. 277; M. R. James, *The Apocalypse in Art*, 1931, 22 (no. IV), 37–8; A. Goldschmidt, *An early manu-script of the Aesop Fables of Avianus and related manuscripts*, 1947, 5, 27 ff., 30 ff., 34; F. von Jura-schek, 'Die Apokalypse von Valenciennes', *Ver-öffentlichung der Gesellschaft für österr. Frühmittel-alterforschung*, I, 1954; Nordenfalk, *Early Medieval* 122, 140; D. H. Wright, 'The Codex Millenarius and its model', *Münchner Jahrbuch der bildenden Kunst*, 3rd ser., 15, 1964, 48; B. Bischoff, 'Panorama der Handschriftenüberlieferung aus der Zeit Karls des Grossen', *Karl der Grosse. Lebenswerk und*

Nachleben, II. Das geistige Leben, ed. B. Bischoff, 1965, 235; D. H. Wright, 'The Italian stimulus on English Art around 700', *Stil und Überlieferung in der Kunst des Abendlandes. Akten des 21. Internat. Kongress für Kunstgeschichte, Bonn, 1964,* I, 1967, 88–9, pl. 6/1, 3; J. Hubert, J. Porcher, W. F. Volbach, *Carolingian Art,* 1970, 181, pl. 168; R. Laufner, P. K. Klein, 'Trierer Apokalypse. Vollständige Faksimile-Ausgabe'. Kommentarband (*Codices Selecti,* XLVIII), 1975, 52 ff., 104 ff., figs. 28, 60, 65–6; Nordenfalk, *Celtic,* 87.

EXHIBITED: *Les manuscrits à peintures en France du VIIᵉ au XIIᵉ siècle,* Bibliothèque Nationale, Paris, 1954, no. 97; *Karl der Grosse,* 1965, no. 444.

65. Antwerp, Museum Plantin–Moretus MS M. 17. 4

Sedulius, Carmen Paschale. Prosper, Epigrammata.
250×165 mm., ff. 76
Early 9th century. Liège

Ills. 285–301

The *Carmen Paschale* by the 5th-century Christian poet Sedulius (ff. 1–41) is illustrated by a full-page frontispiece and sixteen miniatures set without frames in the text or in the upper or lower margins. Two leaves are missing after f. 19 (the missing verses, Bk. III, 9–103, are supplied by a 12th-century hand on a palimpsest leaf, f. 20), and one of these will certainly have contained a miniature. Two more leaves are missing after f. 34 (Bk. V, 145–253). The frontispiece (f. 1) shows Christ enthroned frontally carrying a book in his left hand. He sits under an arch and there is an inscription, apparently *ERICUS*.
The miniatures show four Old and twelve New Testament subjects. They are Abraham's sacrifice of Isaac (damaged, f. 8); Jonah thrown out of the Boat (f. 9ᵛ); Jonah regurgitated by the Whale (f. 10); Daniel in the Lions' Den with the Prophet Habakkuk carried by the Angel to give him Food (f. 10ᵛ); four Evangelist symbols, half-length, winged, and carrying books (the Eagle is damaged), adoring the Cross (f. 13); the Adoration of the Magi (f. 15ᵛ); the Slaughter of the Innocents (f. 16); the Healing of the Blind Man and of the Woman with a Crooked Spine (for the identification see Pächt, 1962, f. 22ᵛ); St. Peter catching a Fish in a Fish Tank (f. 25); Christ and the Woman taken in Adultery (f. 30); the Raising of Lazarus (f. 30ᵛ); the Entry into Jerusalem (f. 31ᵛ); Christ about to wash St. Peter's Feet (f. 32), the Betrayal shown symbolically with a Crowd behind and a Wolf (head defaced) and a Lamb Confronted (*lupus oscula porrigit agno,* f. 33); St. Peter's Betrayal with Christ on the left, the Cock on the Column, St. Peter standing and St. Peter seated grieving (f. 33ᵛ); Christ's Command to St. Peter to 'feed my sheep' (f. 38). The colours used are restricted to brown, yellow, orange, and green.
On f. 68ᵛ is the subscription: *Finit. Fines Cuduini.* It has been plausibly suggested that this refers to

Cuthwine, Bishop of Dunwich, who is mentioned by Bede as having brought from Rome an illustrated manuscript of the 'Passions and labours of St. Paul'. Probably, therefore, Cuthwine also brought to England a copy of the *Carmen Paschale* with a cycle of illustrations going back to an archetype prepared in connection with an edition of Sedulius' poem made after his death in 494. In style the illustrations of the archetype will have been comparable to the mosaics of Sant'Apollinare Nuovo, Ravenna, of *c.* 500 (Koehler). There, too, in the scene of Christ foretelling St. Peter's Betrayal, the cock is shown anachronistically.
The miniatures in the present manuscript must reflect an Anglo-Saxon 8th-century copy (Northumbrian, *c.* 700, according to Nordenfalk) deriving directly or indirectly from Cuthwine's volume. They thus provide valuable evidence of the availability of an Early Christian cycle, including especially New Testament scenes, to Insular artists. For another Carolingian copy of an Insular illustrated text, possibly from the same area, see the Valenciennes Apocalypse (no. 64). Pächt has also shown reason to believe that the Sedulius illustrations were known to the sculptor responsible for the reliefs of the screen of the Cathedral at Durham in the mid 12th century, since he has transformed the composition of f. 22ᵛ into the scene of Christ appearing to the Two Women after the Resurrection.

PROVENANCE: Attributed to the Liège Cathedral scriptorium after 814 by Bischoff. On f. 2 is the 13th-century *ex libris* inscription of the Benedictine abbey of St. James, Liège. Used by Theodore Poelman for his edition of Prosper in 1560. After his death in 1581, Poelman's papers and manuscripts, including the present manuscript, became the property of his friend and publisher Plantin.

LITERATURE: C. Caesar, 'Die Antwerpener Handschrift des Sedulius', *Rheinishes Museum für Philologie,* 56, 1901, 247–71; W. Koehler, 'Die Denkmäler der Karolingischen Kunst in Belgien', *Belgische Kunstdenkmäler,* ed. P. Clemen, 1923, 7 ff., pls. 8, 9, 19; J. Denucé, *Musaeum Plantin Moretus. Catalogue des manuscrits,* 1927, no. 176; W. Levinson, *England and the Continent in the eighth century,* 1946, 133–4; Nordenfalk, *Early Medieval,* 122; O. Pächt, *The rise of pictorial narrative in twelfth-century England,* 1962, 19–20, fig. 6; D. H. Wright, 'The Codex Millenarius and its models', *Münchner Jahrbuch der bildenden Kunst,* 3rd ser., 15, 1964, 46, fig. 11; B. Bischoff, 'Panorama der Handschriftenüberlieferung aus der Zeit Karls des Grossen', *Karl der Grosse. Lebenswerk und Nachleben, II. Das geistige Leben,* ed. B. Bischoff, 1965, 235; C. F. Lewine, '*Vulpes fossa habent* or the Miracle of the Bent Women in the Gospels of St. Augustine', *Art Bulletin,* 56, 1974, 497–8.

EXHIBITED: *Treasures of Belgian Libraries,* National Library of Scotland, Edinburgh, 1963, no. 5; *Karl der Grosse,* 1965, no. 442; *Rhein und Maas. Kunst und Kultur 800–1400,* Cologne, 1972, 165, A. 5, pl.

66. Cambridge, University Library MS Ll. I. 10

Passion narrative from the four Gospels. Prayers, etc. (Book of Cerne)
230 × 184 mm., ff. 98 (first leaf missing, foliated 2–99)
First half of 9th century.

Ills. 310–315

The illumination consists of four frontispieces, St. Matthew (f. 2ᵛ), St. Mark (f. 12ᵛ), St. Luke (f. 21ᵛ) and St. John (f. 31ᵛ). At the crown of an arch the Evangelists are represented half-length in roundels. They are frontal and hold books in their left hands and bless with their right hands, except for St. Luke who holds a pen. Under the arches are the four symbols represented full-length, winged, haloed, and holding books. The colours used are unusual, in particular a slate blue and a red-brown with some yellow, white, and orange.

The inscriptions make it clear that the pictures are intended to represent each Evangelist twice in different guises, Matthew in his human aspect, Matthew in his angelic aspect: *Hic Matheus in humanitate. Hic Matheus in angelica aspectu videtur. Hic Marcus in humanitate. Hic Marcus imaginem tenet leonis. Hic Lucas in humanitate. Hic Lucas formam accepit vituli. Hic Johannis* [sic] *in humanitate. Hic Johannis* [sic] *vertit frontem in aquilam.* In other words this is not a set of Evangelists identified by their symbols, and this is why the reversal of the usual arrangement in which the figures are placed below with their symbols as identification above, is possible.

The miniatures are therefore a combination of a formal arrangement found earlier in the Canon Tables of the Maeseyck and Trier Gospel Books (nos. 22, 23, 26) and in the Luke page of the Royal Gospel Book (no. 32) with the use of independent symbols as seen in the Books of Durrow and Echternach (nos. 6, 11). Two of the symbols, the Man and the Eagle, show some affinities with those in Durrow (cf. also the Book of Dimma, no. 48, for the Eagle). The others, the Lion and the Calf, are closer to those in the Stockholm *Codex Aureus* (no. 30) and the Royal Gospel Book (no. 32), with the significant addition to the late antique half-length symbol types of hind quarters, so that they are full-length.

The other decoration consists of initials and continuation lettering on panels, 'Et' (f. 3), E (f. 13), A (f. 22), H (f. 32), S (f. 43). The initials, the first four of which are in gold, are decorated with interlace, floral, and animal motifs in the panels of the letter or as appendages. Many of the smaller letters have animal-head terminals as in the Barberini Gospel Book (no. 36) and the Royal Gospel Book (no. 32). Many minor initials of this type also occur, particularly in the later part of the manuscript from f. 43. These initials seem to fall into two groups, the first ff. 1–42, 87ᵛ to the end, the second ff. 43–87, blue being the main colour in the first, green in the second group. From f. 87ᵛ small dragons are inserted into the text to divide off words which have run over from the line above.

On the capitals of the arches of the Mark and John pages are foliage and mask motifs respectively. On f. 21 the text is written in minuscule in red, plum, blue, plum and orange, a line at a time. A page before this folio is missing. On f. 51ᵛ a later drawing, (?) 16th century, of pattern is reminiscent of Tudor blackwork embroidery. It might conceivably, however, be connected with the binding (cf. Oxford, Bodleian Library, MS Junius 11, Temple, *Anglo-Saxon*, no. 58). Other scribbles of the same date copy the Evangelist symbols and the initials (f. 72).

Kendrick and others have attributed the manuscript to Mercia on the basis of the identification of the Aethelwald mentioned in the inscription with the Bishop of Lichfield of 818–30. Henry proposes an earlier date in the late 8th century and a connection with Lindisfarne of which an Aethelwald was Bishop 721–40. However, the arrangement of the capitals on panels, the form of the small initials, and the use of roundels on the arches, links the manuscript with the Canterbury group (nos. 29–33) and the Barberini Gospel Book (no. 36). Whether the Mercian provenance is accepted or not (cf. also no. 35), a model from Canterbury of the mid-century was presumably available and was combined with the different tradition of independent symbols stemming from Durrow (no. 6). This might tally with the strong Irish content noted by Edmund Bishop who considered the inscriptions copied from an exemplar and connected them with the Bishop of Lindisfarne, as does Dumville (1972, see below).

The type of decoration of the small initials is an important source for later Anglo-Saxon initials, for example in King Alfred's Gregory, *Cura Pastoralis* (Temple, *Anglo-Saxon*, no. 1, ills. 2–4, and cf. nos. 35, 41, 71 here).

PROVENANCE: Contemporary inscriptions give the name of Aedelvaldus episcopus (f. 21, acrostic poem in different coloured inks) or Oethelwald (f. 87ᵛ). Kuypers suggested this was Aethelweald, Bishop of Lichfield from 818 to 830 or less probably Aethelweald, Bishop of Lindisfarne from 721 to 740. Dumville argues the acrostic poem is a corrupt copy of an earlier inscription to be connected with the Bishop of Lindisfarne. There are a number of Anglo-Saxon notes and glosses of the 9th and 10th centuries. Twenty-six leaves at the beginning and twenty-eight at the end, 13th to 14th century, connect the manuscript with Cerne abbey, Dorset (founded 987). Belonged to John Moore, Bishop of Ely, whose library was given to Cambridge University by George I in 1715.

LITERATURE: Westwood, *Facsimiles*, 43–6, pl. XXIV; A. B. Kuypers, *The Book of Cerne*, 1902; Zimmermann, *Vorkarolingische Miniaturen*, 25, 108, 135–6, 294–6, pls. 293–6; E. Bishop, *Liturgica historica*, 1918, 165–70, 173–4, 192–7; J. Brøndsted, *Early English Ornament*, 1924, 121–2, 124, 138 n. 1, 245–7, 250, figs. 102, 174; K. Pfister, *Irische Buchmalerei*, 1927, pl. 39; K. Sisam, 'Cynewulf and his poetry', *Proceedings of the British Academy*, 18, 1932, 321, 331 n. 31; Kendrick, *Anglo-Saxon*,

147, 165–8, 174–5, 186, 199, pl. LXVIII; Micheli, *L'enluminure*, 31–3, 63, 136, pl. 28; W. Levison, *England and the Continent in the eighth century*, 1946, 295–302; S. M. Kuhn, 'From Canterbury to Lichfield', *Speculum*, 23, 1948, 619–27; F. Wormald, *The miniatures in the Gospels of St. Augustine*, 1954, 9–10, pls. XVII–XIX; K. Sisam, 'Canterbury, Lichfield and the Vespasian Psalter', *Review of English Studies*, N.S. 7, 1956, 9–10; *ib.*, N.S. 8, 1957, 372–3; S. M. Kuhn, 'Some early Mercian manuscripts', *ib.*, N.S. 8, 1957, 368–9; Ker, *Catalogue*, 39–40 (no. 27); *Codex Durmachensis*, fig. 38; Rickert, *Painting in Britain*, 25, pl. 17; D. H. Wright, *The Vespasian Psalter* (Early English Manuscripts in facsimile, XIV), 1967, 57; Henry, *Irish Art*, II, 60–64, 71, 73, pls. II, V; Koehler, *Buchmalerei*, 16–17, 24; Henry, *Kells*, 163, 172, 209, 214, 226, figs. 14, 22; D. N. Dumville, 'A re-examination of the origin and contents of the ninth-century section of the Book of Cerne', *Journal of Theological Studies*, N.S. 23, 1972, 374–406.

67. Paris, Bibliothèque Nationale MS lat. 10861

Lives of Saints
252 × 187 mm., ff. 123
First half of 9th century.

Ill. 319

The illumination consists of a 'Ph' monogram introducing the Life of St. Philip (f. 2). There are a number of smaller initials. The major initial may be compared with the Book of Cerne (no. 66).

PROVENANCE: *Ex libris* of the Cathedral, Beauvais, (?) 12th century. Acquired in 1834 at the sale of M. Gay of Lyon with other Beauvais manuscripts.

LITERATURE: L. Delisle, *Le cabinet des manuscrits de la bibliothèque nationale*, II, 1874, 293, 339; Micheli, *L'enluminure*, 51, pl. 86.

68. St. Gall, Stiftsbibliothek, Cod. 904

Priscian, Institutiones Grammaticae
398 × 280 mm., ff. 120
Mid 9th century. Ireland

Ill. 318

The illumination consists of initials in black pen with animals, birds, fish, and human figures, especially P (p. 2), 'Ly' (p. 3), 'Sy' (p. 21), D (p. 25), C (p. 39), S (p. 43), C (p. 76), 'Jh' (p. 174), P (p. 197), and Q (p. 212). In style they can be compared to those in the Book of Armagh (no. 53) and the Leiden Priscian (no. 63). The manuscript is important for its large number of Old Irish glosses and paleographically for its ogham script and since a number of the scribes sign their names, Maelpatricc (*depinxit*), Finguinne, Donngus, etc. The glosses, some of which are also in Latin, include personal comments, e.g. *Sudet qui legat, difficilis est ista pagina. Tertia*

hora. Tempus est prandii. ('This is a difficult page. Time for dinner!').

PROVENANCE: Poem on Archbishop Gunthar of Cologne (850–63) in Carolingian minuscule, p. 89. Not in the St. Gall catalogues of the 9th century. *Ex libris* of St. Gall, 16th century (?).

LITERATURE: Westwood, *Facsimiles*, 68; Gilbert, *Facsimiles*, I, xiii; W. M. Lindsay, *Early Irish Minuscule Script*, 1910, 40–7, pl. X; Zimmermann, *Vorkarolingische Miniaturen*, 23 n. 4, 104, 252, pls. 208 a, b, 209; Kenney, *Sources*, nos. 364(ii), 367, 533; L. Gougaud, 'Les scribes monastiques d'Irlande au travail', *Revue d'histoire ecclésiastique*, 27, 1931, 294 ff.; G. L. Micheli, 'Recherches sur les manuscrits Irlandais décorés de Saint-Gall et de Reichenau', *Revue archéologique*, 6ᵉ sér., 7, 1936, 214–19, fig. 4; Micheli, *L'enluminure*, 41–2, 127–8, pls. 54–5; Duft, Meyer, *St. Gall*, 72–4, 107–9, pls. XXXIX–XLI, fig. 35; F. Henry, 'An Irish manuscript in the British Museum', *Journal of the Royal Society of Antiquaries of Ireland*, 87, 1957, 152, 160, 164, pl. XXVI. 4; Henry, *Irish Art*, II, 31, 59, 100–102; Henry, *Kells*, 225.

69. Karlsruhe, Landesbibliothek Cod. CLXVII

Bede, De rerum natura, de temporum ratione, calendar, computistical tables, etc.
285 × 200 mm., ff. 49
(?) 8th and 9th century. (?) North France

Ill. 320

The manuscript is a palimpsest written in Irish minuscule, 9th century, on various fragments including one of a Sacramentary written in 8th century Irish majuscule (*C.L.A.*, VIII, no. 1085). The illumination on f. 32ᵛ consists of two panels, that to the left with two interlaced animals inset in the text, that below with two interlaced birds extending across the two columns of text. Micheli notes traces of a profile bird in the centre of the page, which seems to be the Eagle, symbol of St. John (cf. the Echternach Gospel Book, no. 11). The two panels differ in style. That on the left seems earlier. That below is later, probably contemporary with the later script. Notes relating to the Frankish Kings are added up to 848. There are also notes of events in Ireland in 819 and 823, and the date is arrived at from marks in the calendarial tables opposite the years 836 and 848.

PROVENANCE: Bannister suggests the manuscript was written at Péronne, near St. Quentin in North France, on the basis of the calendar. It was later at Reichenau (*Liber Augie majoris*, f. 2, (?) 12th century) with other manuscripts written by the same scribe, which are also palimpsest (*C.L.A.*, VIII, nos. 1083, 1088).

LITERATURE: H. M. Bannister, 'Some recently discovered fragments of Irish Sacramentaries',

Journal of Theological Studies, 5, 1903, 51–2; A. Holder, *Die Handschriften der grossherzoglich Badischen Hof- und Landesbibliothek in Karlsruhe, V. Die Reichenauer Handschriften, I, Die Pergamenthandschriften*, 1906, 393–8; *New Pal. Soc.*, I, pl. 34; G. L. Micheli, 'Recherches sur les manuscrits Irlandais décorés de Saint-Gall et de Reichenau', *Revue archéologique*, 6ᵉ sér., 7, 1936, 219–23, fig 5; Micheli, *L'enluminure*, 48–9, pl. 56.

70. London, Lambeth Palace MS 1370
Gospel Book (Macdurnan)
158×111 mm., ff. 216
(?) Second half of 9th century. Ireland (? Armagh)
Ills. 321–328, 354

The illumination consists of four Evangelist portraits, an introductory Cross page with Evangelist symbols (f. 1ᵛ) and initials for the Gospels. The Cross is outlined in green. The L-shaped outer panels are framed in yellow, top left, bottom right, and pinkish mauve, top right, bottom left. Inside are the four symbols, Man, top left; Eagle, top right; Calf, bottom left; and Lion, bottom right. Their frames also balance diagonally, pinkish red top left and bottom right, yellow top right and bottom left. The fret pattern in the outer frames and in the Cross is minute and worked in black and white (the parchment left uncoloured). There are lozenges of orange, green, and yellow in the frame and the same colours with the addition of the pinkish-mauve pigment are used in a mosaic of small patches like enamel work on the symbols. The leaf has been mutilated and is patched in the top left-hand corner. Similar colours are used for the Evangelists and the colours are also similarly counterbalanced. St. Matthew (f. 4ᵛ) holds a white crozier in his right hand across his body and a book in his left. The frame is of interlaced panels and frets. St. Mark (f. 70ᵛ) carries a book in his left hand and is flanked by two stylized rampant lions, probably a throne on which he is thought of as seated. The frame is a continuous band containing fret motifs with corner lozenges. Above the Evangelist in the centre is a winged symbol extending, as it were, behind and beyond the frame. It looks more like a Calf (cf. Durrow, no. 6) than a Lion. St. Luke (f. 115ᵛ), a squatter figure, holds his white crozier on the ground and a book in his left hand. The frame is of interlace panels at the corners and frets at the centre of each side. St. John (f. 170ᵛ) dips a pen into an inkwell to his right and carries a book and another pen in his left hand. The frame is of panels of fret and interlace.

The initials X (f. 5), 'In' (f. 72), Q (f. 117), and 'In' (f. 172) have panel frames with a rich repertoire of motifs similar to those of the frames of the Evangelist portraits. The X has a profile human head and two animal masks and there is another fine lion mask in the frame on f. 72. All the initials are in black. The 'Li' of St. Matthew (f. 2) is a smaller initial in black with colour fillings. Initial and text are outlined with orange dots. There are smaller initials to verses with blobs of colour and small orange cartouches for the numbers of the Ammonian sections. Single leaves with miniatures, probably from an English Psalter of the third quarter of the 13th century are inserted, the Crucifixion (f. 4), the Flagellation (f. 71), the Betrayal (f. 116), and the Last Unction (f. 171). James (1932, p. 845) suggests these were inserted by Archbishop Parker, since another similar 13th-century cutting showing the Entry into Jerusalem is inserted into Corpus Christi College, Cambridge, MS 419.

The illumination of the Gospels is of fine quality, which is not so apparent in black and white reproduction. The paint is very thick and has an enamel-like finish (cf. the Macregol Gospel Book, no. 54). The forms are stylized into linear patterns of great vigour and expressiveness, for example the entwined curls of the Evangelists' hair. Colour is used completely non-naturalistically to enhance the effect. The manuscript belongs to a group of Irish pocket-size Gospel Books most of whose Evangelists are shown standing in narrow frames and without symbols (nos. 45–9). Four-symbol pages are also found in the Books of Durrow (no. 6), Lichfield (no. 21), Trier (no. 26), Kells (no. 52), and Armagh (no. 53), and the symbols can be compared to those on the St. Mark page in the St. Gall Gospel Book (no. 44). If the book was made for, as well as used by, Macdurnan, its date and place of execution would be established. Bieler, however, has argued that the scribe was Ferdomnach who wrote part of the Book of Armagh (no. 53) and died in 846. However as Henry, who favours a later date, points out, the style of decoration is very different from that of the Book of Armagh.

PROVENANCE: An inscription (f. 3ᵛ) says that Maelbrigt Macdurnan *istum textum . . . dogmatizat*. He was Abbot of Armagh, probably from 888, and of Raphoe, and he died in 927. The inscription also records that the manuscript was given to Christ Church, Canterbury, by King Athelstan (d. 939). Various charters have been added there. Archbishop Matthew Parker (d. 1575) with his notes and binding. Owned in 1755 by Fr. Howel, mathematical instrument maker, in London. Probably acquired for Lambeth by Dr. A. C. Ducarel who became librarian in 1757.

LITERATURE: Westwood, *Palaeographia*, nos. 13, 14, 15; *id.*, *Facsimiles*, 68–72, pl. 22; Gilbert, *Facsimiles*, I, xvii–xviii, pls. XXX–XXXI; Zimmermann, *Vorkarolingische Miniaturen*, 31, 105, 248–50, pl. 205; E. G. Millar, 'Les principaux manuscrits à peintures du Lambeth Palace à Londres', *Bulletin de la Société française de reproductions de manuscrits à peintures*, 8, 1924, 7–15, pl. 1; Saunders, *English Illumination*, 8, 12, 71, pl. 12 a–b; Kenney, *Sources*, no. 475; M. R. James, *A descriptive catalogue of the manuscripts in the library of Lambeth Palace. The medieval manuscripts*, 1932, 843–5; Micheli, *L'enluminure*, 20, 25; L. Bieler, 'Insular paleography; Present state and problems', *Scriptorium*, 3, 1949,

276; P. McGurk, 'The Irish pocket Gospel Book', *Sacris Erudiri*, 8, 1956, 249–70; Ker, *Catalogue*, 346–7 (no. 284); F. Henry, 'An Irish manuscript in the British Museum', *Journal of the Royal Society of Antiquaries of Ireland*, 87, 1957, 151 ff.; Rickert, *Painting in Britain*, 24; Henry, *Irish Art*, II, 58–9, 100, 102–5, pls. 36, 42–4, colour pls. I, K, L; Werckmeister, *Irisch-northumbrische Buchmalerei*, 101 f., pl. 29a; J. Hubert, J. Porcher, W. F. Volbach, *Carolingian Art*, 1970, pl. 187; Koehler, *Buchmalerei*, 15; Henry, *Kells*, 183, 200, 225, fig. 33.

71. Oxford, Bodleian Library MS Auct. F. 4. 32, ff. 37–47, (S.C. 2176)

Ovid, Ars amatoria Book I
245×179 mm., ff. 11
(?) Late 9th century. Wales

Ill. 333

The leaves are bound up with three other parts of distinct origin which come from separate books. Parts I and III are grammatical texts, the latter annotated by a hand (Hunt's 'Hand D') which also added f. 47 in the present fragment (Part IV) and which may well be that of St. Dunstan himself. In this part (Part IV) there are two initials 'Si' (f. 37) and P (f. 37ᵛ) in black pen with biting beast heads. They form a connecting link between the initials of earlier books such as the Barberini Gospel Book (no. 36) and those of the 10th- and 11th-century Anglo-Saxon manuscripts (see Temple, *Anglo-Saxon*, no. 11, ill. 41), since the manuscript was then at Glastonbury.

PROVENANCE: Glosses in Old Welsh. Probably owned and annotated by St. Dunstan, Abbot of Glastonbury, Archbishop of Canterbury (d. 988). At Glastonbury *in custodia fratris H. Langley* (f. 47ᵛ), second half of the 15th century. Given to the Bodleian by Thomas Allen in 1601.

LITERATURE: R. Ellis, *XX Facsimiles from Latin MSS. in the Bodleian Library*, 1891, pl. I; *New Pal. Soc.*, I, pl. 82; W. M. Lindsay, *Early Welsh Script*, 1912, 7–10, pl. XI; F. Wormald, 'Decorated initials in English MSS. from A.D. 900–1100', *Archaeologia*, 91, 1945, 112–13, pl. IIIb (as Hatton 60); Ker, *Catalogue*, 355 (no. 297); R. W. Hunt, *St. Dunstan's Classbook from Glastonbury* (Umbrae Codicum Occidentalium, IV), 1961 (complete facsimile); Rickert, *Painting in Britain*, 220 n. 4; Pächt and Alexander, III, no. 17, pl. I.

72. Cambridge, University Library MS Ii. 6. 32

Gospel extracts (Book of Deer)
153×110 mm., ff. 86
(?) 9th or 10th century. (?) Scotland

Ills. 329–332, 334–340

The manuscript contains the whole of St. John's Gospel and parts of the other three Gospels. The illumination consists of Evangelist portraits and initial pages. On f. 1ᵛ are four standing figures (Evangelists or [?] a duplicated Matthew portrait and symbol) arranged around a cross, the two below carrying what are apparently reliquaries (cf. Jackson). St. Matthew (f. 4ᵛ) is frontal, bearded and holds a sword in front of him (cf. the 'Garland of Howth', no. 59). There are two smaller figures above flanking his head. St. Mark (f. 16ᵛ) is also frontal, has a halo, and holds a book or a (?) reliquary as before in front of him. St. Luke (f. 29ᵛ) is also frontal with a similar object in front of him. His arms are outstretched and penetrate the frame. St. John (f. 41ᵛ) again frontal, with the same object, is accompanied by six small figures. At the end of St. John's Gospel (f. 84ᵛ) are two similar smaller frontal figures. On f. 85ᵛ and 86 two more pages contain each four figures arranged around a cross. All the miniatures have square panel frames some of which are filled with various patterns, especially ff. 4ᵛ–5, or have corner pieces (f. 16ᵛ). The initial pages are similarly framed on all sides, L (f. 2), X (f. 5) 'In' (f. 17), Q (f. 30), 'In' (f. 42), though the initials which are rather small and formed of black strapwork with animal and human heads (f. 5), break out of the frames. A smaller initial introduces the Creed (f. 85). The colours used are simple: black, orange, and yellow. A number of embellishments of the text in a similar style (Stuart, pls. XXI–XXII) suggest that the scribe who signs his name, Ferchubus (f. 85), was also the artist.

The date and place of manufacture of the manuscript are uncertain. The stylization of the figures can be compared to that in the Southampton Psalter (no. 74) and, going back earlier, to the Book of Dimma (no. 48) or the 'Garland of Howth' (no. 59). The initials seem to presuppose developments seen in later 9th-century manuscripts such as the Gospel Book of Macdurnan (no. 70) or the Bodleian Ovid (no. 71), so that perhaps a 10th-century date is more likely.

PROVENANCE: Entries in Gaelic made in the 12th century concern the foundation of the Columban monastery of Deer, Aberdeenshire, and gifts of land to it. A Latin charter (no. VII) of King David I of Scotland (1124–53) was also entered, f. 40, mid 12th century. Deer was refounded as a Cistercian house by William, Earl of Buchan, in 1219. Purchased with the library of John Moore, Bishop of Ely (d. 1714), by George I and given to Cambridge University.

LITERATURE: *Facsimiles of National Manuscripts of Scotland*, I, 1867, no. 1, 4 pls.; Westwood, *Facsimiles*, 89–90, pl. LI. 2, 3; J. Stuart, *The Book of Deer* (Spalding Club), 1869 (reproduces all miniatures); *Pal. Soc.*, I, pls. 210–11; Zimmermann, *Vorkarolingische Miniaturen*, 109; Kenney, *Sources*, no. 502; Micheli, *L'enluminure*, 7; Duft, Meyer, *St. Gall*, fig. 96; O.-K. Werckmeister, 'Three problems of tradition in pre-Carolingian figure style', *Proceedings of the Royal Irish Academy*, 63 C, no. 5, 1963, 177–8, pl. XXVIIIc; K. Jackson, *The Gaelic notes in the Book of Deer*, 1972.

73. London, British Library Cotton MS Vitellius F. XI

Psalter

165 × 120 mm. (shrunken and damaged), ff. 59

First half of 10th century. Ireland

Ills. 347–349

The Psalter was badly damaged in the Cottonian fire of 1731. Its pages are shrunken and discoloured and have been guarded. On f. 1 a framed page shows David with his sling and the giant Goliath kneeling raising his right hand to his forehead. On f. 2 a second miniature shows David harping. He is seated in profile on a throne like an animal. He turns his head frontally. The frames are of panels of interlace and key pattern in orange, yellow, and brown (?). There are initials to each Psalm and larger initials with border for Psalm 51, Q (f. 15), and Psalm 101, D (f. 38). Henry has drawn attention to the striking similarities of the David killing Goliath scene with that on the great Cross of Muiredach at Monasterboise. Muiredach died in 924–5.

PROVENANCE: Seen in the Cotton Library by Archbishop Ussher who copied the Irish colophon now lost: The blessing of God on Muiredach . . . the scholar. Possibly from Monasterboise, therefore, especially in view of the similarity with the Cross of Muiredach. Sir Robert Cotton (d. 1631) whose library passed to the British Museum in 1753.

LITERATURE: J. O. Westwood, 'On the particularities exhibited by the miniatures and ornamentation of Ancient Irish Illuminated Manuscripts', *Archaeological Journal*, 7, 1850, 22–5, pl.; *id.*, *Facsimiles*, 85–6, pl. LI, figs. 5, 6; Gilbert, *Facsimiles*, II, xxiv, pl. XLVIII; *Catalogue of ancient manuscripts in the British Museum, II. Latin manuscripts*, 1884, 13; H. M. Roe, 'The "David Cycle" in Early Irish Art', *Journal of the Royal Society of Antiquaries of Ireland*, 79, 1949, 39–59, figs. 6 (24), 12 (42); F. Henry, 'Remarks on the decoration of three Irish Psalters', *Proceedings of the Royal Irish Academy*, 61 C, no. 2, 1960 27–33, pls. I, IVb, VI–VIII, X, XVI d, h, XIX b, e; A. O'Sullivan, 'The Colophon of the Cotton Psalter (Vitellius F. XI)', *Journal of the Royal Society of Antiquaries of Ireland*, 96, 1966, 179–80; Henry, *Irish Art*, II, 58–9, 106–8, 157, 174, 176, 178, pls. 41, 46, II.

74. Cambridge, St. John's College MS C. 9 (59)

Psalter (Southampton Psalter)

264 × 184 mm., ff. 98

(?) Early 11th century. Ireland

Ills. 350–353

Three full-page miniatures mark the threefold division of the Psalter. Before Psalm 1 David is shown fighting the Lion (f. 4ᵛ), before Psalm 51 is the Crucifixion (f. 38ᵛ) and before Psalm 101 David fighting Goliath (f. 71ᵛ). The miniatures are on the versos and on the rectos opposite are the initials B,

Q, and D respectively. Like the miniatures these have borders of interlacing motifs, animals and key patterns. Each Psalm has smaller initials, mostly four or five line. They are of two types, 'ribbon animal' and 'knotted wire' (cf. Henry) and these are used alternately through most of the manuscript. The verse initials are in black filled with yellow, orange, and mauve. The colours of the miniatures are yellow, brownish purple, lighter purple, and orange. On f. 58ᵛ a later, perhaps Romanesque, hand has copied an initial M in lead point in the margin. This would be an interesting example of the influence of Insular art on a later period.

Another Irish Psalter with miniatures is the Cotton Psalter (no. 73). Though the figures in the present Psalter are extremely stylized (cf. the Book of Deer, no. 72), the quality of the illumination is high.

PROVENANCE: Pressmark 'A.V' of St. Martin's Priory, Dover, on ff. 3ᵛ, 6, and no. 18 in the catalogue of 1389. R(obert) Benet, 16th century, said by James to be probably a Mayor of Romney. Bought from William Crashaw by Henry Wriothesley, 3rd Earl of Southampton, c. 1615 and given by his son, Thomas, 4th Earl, to the College in 1635.

LITERATURE: Westwood, *Palaeographia*, no. 18; *id.*, *Facsimiles*, 84–5, pl. XXX; M. R. James, *The ancient libraries of Canterbury and Dover*, 1903, 523; *id.*, *A descriptive catalogue of the manuscripts in the Library of St. John's College, Cambridge*, 1913, 76–8; Zimmermann, *Vorkarolingische Miniaturen*, 108–9, 253, pls. 212–13; H. M. Roe, 'The "David Cycle" in Early Irish Art', *Journal of the Royal Society of Antiquaries of Ireland*, 79, 1949, 45, 50, figs. 2 (11), 6 (26); K. Pfister, *Irische Buchmalerei*, 1927, pls. 29, 30a; Saunders, *English Illumination*, 13, pls. 13–14; W. R. Hovey, 'Sources of the Irish illuminative art', *Art Studies*, 6, 1928, 111, fig. 14; Kenney, *Sources*, no. 476; Micheli, *L'enluminure*, 11; Masai, *Origines*, pl. XXXV; Duft, Meyer, *St. Gall*, fig. 28; F. Henry, 'Remarks on the decoration of three Irish Psalters', *Proceedings of the Royal Irish Academy*, 61 C, no. 2, 1960, 23–40, pls. III, IV, VI–VIII, X–XIII, XIVa, XV, XVI b, g, XIX c, d; Henry, *Irish Art*, II, 58–9, 106–8, 119, 121, 174, 178, pls. 45, 48, M, N, O; III, 2, 47, 56, 120.

EXHIBITED: *Illustrated catalogue of illuminated manuscripts*, Burlington Fine Arts Club, London, 1908, no. 3, pl. 11.

75. Dublin, Trinity College MS A. 4. 20 (50)

Psalter and Martyrology (Ricemarch Psalter)

160 × 105 mm., ff. 159

Late 11th century (c. 1079). Wales

Ill. 346

The Psalter has large initials with borders for the tripartite division, Psalm 1, B (f. 35), Psalm 51, Q (f. 76), and Psalm 101, D (f. 118). There are smaller initials with interlace and animal heads to each

Psalm and in the Martyrology. The colours used are red, yellow, and green.

The manuscript was written by the scribe Ithael for Ricemarch and decorated by Ievan (John) as the verses composed by Ricemarch on f. 158 explain. Ricemarch (b. 1056–7, d. 1099) and Ievan were sons of Sulien, Bishop of St. David's, who died in 1091. The calendarial tables suggest a date before 1082, possibly 1079. Ievan also wrote and probably decorated the Augustine, *De Trinitate* in Cambridge (Corpus Christi College MS 199). Sulien had studied in Ireland and the debt to contemporary Irish art is evident in the initials.

PROVENANCE: William Bedell, Provost of Trinity College, Dublin, 1627–9, and Bishop of Kilmore, 1629. Bequeathed by him to Archbishop Ussher in 1641 and reached Trinity College with Ussher's books about 1665.

LITERATURE: Westwood, *Palaeographia*, no. 20; *id.*, *Facsimiles*, 87; J. H. Todd, 'Descriptive remarks on illuminations in certain Ancient Irish Manuscripts', *Vetusta Monumenta* (Society of Antiquaries of London), 6, 1869, 14 ff., pl. XLVI; Gilbert, *Facsimiles*, II, lv, pl. Appendix I; T. K. Abbott, *Catalogue of the manuscripts in the library of Trinity College, Dublin*, 1900, 6; W. M. Lindsay, *Early Welsh Script*, 1912, 32–40, pl. XVII; H. J. Lawlor, 'The Psalter and martyrology of Ricemarch', *Henry Bradshaw Society*, 47–8, 1914, 2 vols. (pls. I–LXXVI in vol. 2); Zimmermann, *Vorkarolingische Miniaturen*, 109, 254, pl. 214; Kenney, *Sources*, no. 508; F. Henry, 'Remarks on the decoration of three Irish Psalters', *Proceedings of the Royal Irish Academy*, 61 C, no. 2, 1960, 39–40, pl. XIVb; Henry, *Irish Art*, II, 106, 108, pls. 46–7; III, 3, 56, 121.

76. London, British Library Harley MS 1023
Gospel Book
200 × 142 mm., ff. 88
Early 12th century. Ireland (? Armagh)

Ills. 341, 344

The illumination consists of symbol pages for St. Mark, the Lion (f. 10ᵛ) and St. John, the Eagle (f. 64ᵛ). They are drawn in black ink with plain rectangular frames. Both are turned sideways to fill the space (cf. no. 77). The beginning of St. Matthew's Gospel is missing and a page is cut out before St. Luke, so originally all four symbols were probably present, and there may also have been Canon Tables. There are initials of the 'knotted wire' type (Henry) to St. Mark, 'In' (f. 11), St. Luke, Q (f. 34), and St. John, 'In' (f. 65) with colour panels of yellow, pink, red lead (which has turned grey), and purple.

This Gospel Book is generally assigned to Armagh on the grounds of textual similarities with the Book of Armagh (no. 53) and stylistic similarities of the symbol pages with no. 77 written in Armagh in 1138.

PROVENANCE: Acquired by Robert Harley, 1st Earl of Oxford (1661–1724), with the library of Edward Stillingfleet, Bishop of Worcester, in 1707. Purchased by the British Museum, 1753.

LITERATURE: Westwood, *Palaeographia*, no. 18; *id.*, *Facsimiles*, 93–4; Gilbert, *Facsimiles*, I, xxii, pl. XLV; Zimmermann, *Vorkarolingische Miniaturen*, 109, 255, pls. 215 c, d, 216c; K. Pfister, *Irische Buchmalerei*, 1927, pl. 30b; Kenney, *Sources*, no. 482; F. Henry, G. L. Marsh-Micheli, 'A century of Irish illumination (1070–1170)', *Proceedings of the Royal Irish Academy*, 62 C, no. 5, 1962, 146–8, pls. XXIV–XXV; Henry, *Irish Art*, III, 47, 53, 63–68, 121, 190, pls. 6, 7.

77. London, British Library Harley MS 1802
Gospel Book
165 × 121 mm., ff. 156
1138. Armagh

Ills. 342, 343, 345

The illumination consists of two surviving Evangelist symbol pages, the Lion of St. Mark (f. 60ᵛ) and the Calf of St. Luke (f. 86ᵛ). The four Gospels are introduced by initials of black interlace with animal heads and colour grounds (Henry's 'knotted wire' type), St. Mark, 'In' (f. 61) and St. John, 'In' (f. 128), and of 'ribbon interlace', St. Matthew, X (f. 20) and St. Luke, Q (f. 87). The 'knotted wire' interlace is also used for smaller initials to the Prefaces and for the L of the beginning of the Genealogy of St. Matthew (f. 3ᵛ) which is separated from the rest of the Gospel text by Prefaces, etc.

Presumably symbol pages for Matthew and John are missing. The artist solves the problem of fitting the Lion and Ox into the upright format of the frame (cf. the Book of Durrow, no. 6) by turning them on their side (cf. no. 76). The Calf turns its head frontally (cf. nos. 9, 21). The colours used are orange, green, yellow, and purple and the frames are yellow panels enclosing a variety of key and step patterns.

Notes at the end of each Gospel by the scribe Maelbrigte, writing in Armagh, refer to historical events which give the date of 1138. There are numerous glosses of considerable interest since they are connected with the gloss of Peter Lombard and may derive from lectures given by him in Paris.

PROVENANCE: Described among books in the Royal Library, Paris, by Père Richard Simon in his *Bibliothèque critique* published in 1708. Stolen by Jean Aymon in 1707 and taken to Holland. Bought in 1712 by Robert Harley, 1st Earl of Oxford (1661–1724). Purchased by the British Museum, 1753.

LITERATURE: Westwood, *Palaeographia*, no. 18; *id.*, *Facsimiles*, 93–4; Gilbert, *Facsimiles*, I, xx–xxi, pls. XL–XLII; *Pal. Soc.*, I, pl. 212; F. G. Kenyon, *Facsimiles of Biblical manuscripts in the British Museum*, 1900, pl. XVIII; Zimmermann, *Vorkaro-*

lingische Miniaturen, 109, 255–6, pls. 215 a, b, 216b; Kenney, *Sources*, no. 483; F. Henry, G. L. Marsh-Micheli, 'A century of Irish illumination (1070–1170)', *Proceedings of the Royal Irish Academy*, 62 C, no. 5, 1962, 148–52, pls. XXVI–XXVII, XLIII; C. Nordenfalk, 'An illustrated Diatessaron', *Art Bulletin*, 50, 1968, 134, fig. 29; Henry, *Irish Art*, III, 4, 47–8, 63–4, 68, 96, 120–1, pls. 10, D, F, G.

78. London, British Library Add. MS 36929
Psalter
175 × 132 mm., ff. 179
Late 12th century. Ireland

Ill. 276

The illumination consists of three frame pages preceding the tripartite division (ff. 1ᵛ, 59ᵛ, and 121ᵛ) with larger initials for Psalm 1, B (f. 2), Psalm 51, Q (f. 60), and Psalm 101, D (f. 122). The frames are of panels with interlace and fret patterns and contorted beasts. The first contains a text of sacramental absolution, the second and third appear to have had miniatures which have been erased (cf. the Southampton Psalter, no. 74 and the Cotton Psalter, no. 73). Only the hand of God remains on f. 59ᵛ. Each Psalm also has initials of interlace and beast forms alternating the types named by Henry 'knotted wire' and 'ribbon' interlace, and each verse has small

decorated capitals. On f. 59 the scribe signs his name: *Cormacus scripsit*.

The quality of the illumination is high, the initials are varied and imaginative and the colours very bright and vivid including purple, red, green, blue, orange, and yellow. Though there are some features which suggest contemporary English or Continental influence, such as the leaf forms, the manuscript in the main continues the decorative vocabulary initiated six centuries earlier. The Psalter is therefore included here to represent a number of other Irish manuscripts of the 11th and 12th centuries with similar decoration in this astonishingly uninterrupted tradition which was to continue even later in some cases.

PROVENANCE: Possibly some Cistercian connections in the text. Acquired by the British Museum in Munich in 1904. The manuscript has a 16th-century German binding.

LITERATURE: *Catalogue of Additions to the Manuscripts in the British Museum 1900–1905*, 1907, 259–260; Zimmermann, *Vorkarolingische Miniaturen*, 109, 256, pl. 216a; F. Henry, G. L. Marsh-Micheli, 'A century of Irish illumination (1070–1170)', *Proceedings of the Royal Irish Academy*, 62 C, no. 5, 1962, 161–4, pls. XXXVII–XLII; Henry, *Irish Art*, III, 54, 60, 72–3, 120, pls. A, B, H, 12, 14, 15.

ILLUSTRATIONS

The author and publishers are grateful to all institutions, museums, and libraries who have helped with illustrations for this publication, including the Master and Fellows of Corpus Christi College, Cambridge; His grace the Archbishop of Canterbury and the Trustees of Lambeth Palace Library, London; the Directors of the Stiftsbibliothek, St. Gall and the State Public Library, Leningrad.

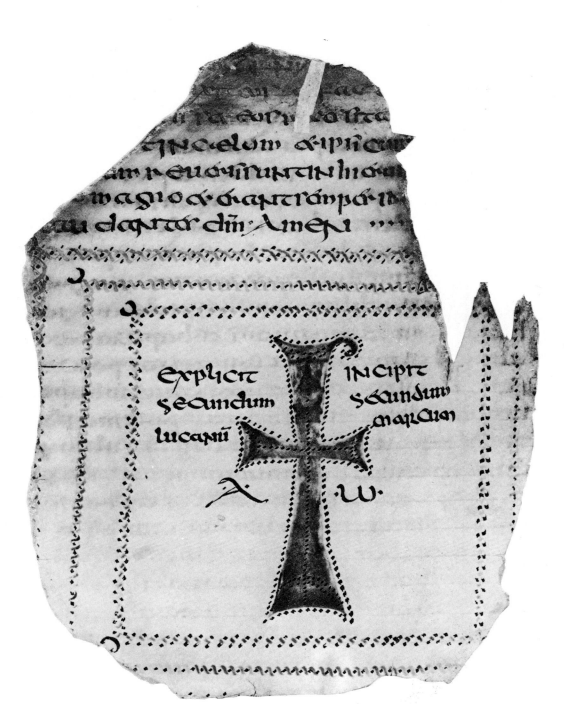

1. 'Xp' monogram. Dublin, Trinity College Lib., A. 4. 15 (55), f. 149ᵛ (cat. 1)

2–3. Initials D and Q. Dublin, Royal Irish Academy, Psalter (Cathach), f. 12ᵛ, f. 40 (cat. 4)

4–5. Initials M and Q. Dublin, Royal Irish Academy, Psalter (Cathach), f. 21, f. 48 (cat. 4)

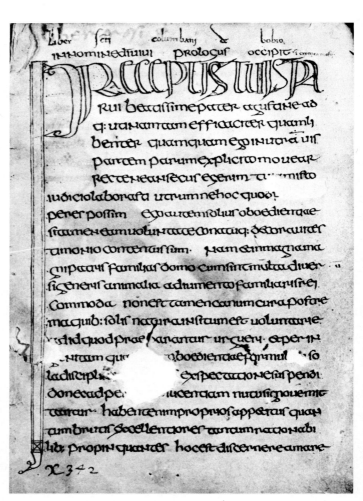

6. Frontispiece. Milan, Bibl. Ambrosiana, D. 23. sup., f. 1ᵛ (cat. 3)

7. Initial P. Milan, Bibl. Ambrosiana, D. 23. sup., f. 2 (cat. 3)

8. Initial N. Milan, Bibl. Ambrosiana, S. 45. sup., p. 2 (cat. 2)

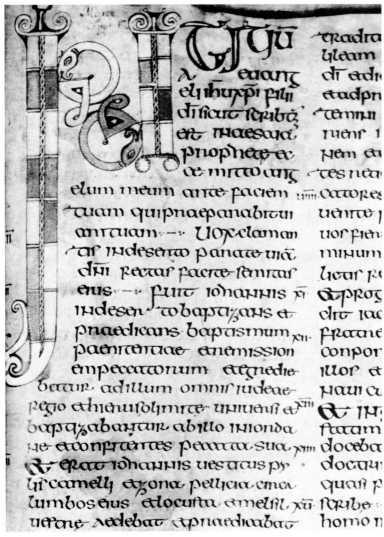

9. Opening page to St. Mark. Durham, Cathedral Lib., A. II. 10, f. 2 (cat. 5)

10. Decorative frame. Durham, Cathedral Lib., A. II. 10, f. 3ᵛ (cat. 5)

11. Cross-carpet page. Dublin, Trinity College Lib., A. 4. 5 (57), f. 1ᵛ (cat. 6)

12. Carpet page. Dublin, Trinity College Lib., A. 4. 5 (57), f. 3ᵛ (cat. 6)

13. Four-symbols page. Dublin, Trinity College Lib., A. 4. 5 (57), f. 2 (cat. 6)

14. Symbol of St. Matthew, Man. Dublin, Trinity College Lib., A. 4. 5 (57), f. 21ᵛ (cat. 6)

15. Symbol of St. Luke, Calf. Dublin, Trinity College Lib., A. 4. 5 (57), f. 124ᵛ (cat. 6)

16. Symbol of St. John, Lion. Dublin, Trinity College Lib., A. 4. 5 (57), 191ᵛ (cat. 6)

17. Symbol of St. Mark, Eagle. Dublin, Trinity College Lib., A. 4. 5. (57), f. 84ᵛ (cat. 6)

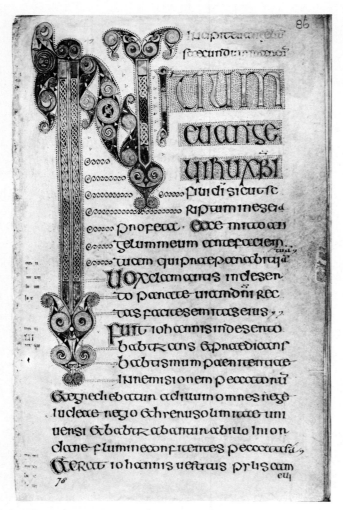

18. Opening page to St. Mark. Dublin, Trinity College Lib., A. 4. 5 (57), f. 86 (cat. 6)

19. Opening page to St. John. Dublin, Trinity College Lib., A. 4. 5 (57), f. 193 (cat. 6)

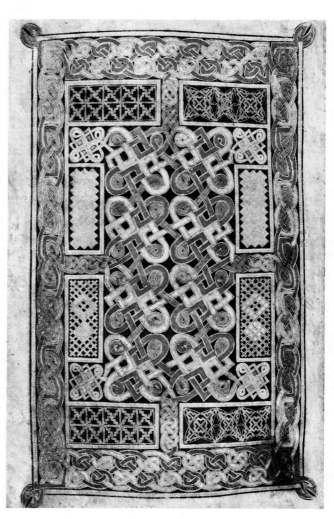

20. Carpet page. Dublin, Trinity College Lib., A. 4. 5 (57), f. 85ᵛ (cat. 6)

21. Carpet page. Dublin, Trinity College Lib., A. 4. 5 (57), f. 125ᵛ (cat. 6)

22. Carpet page. Dublin, Trinity College Lib., A. 4. 5 (57), f. 192^v (cat. 6)

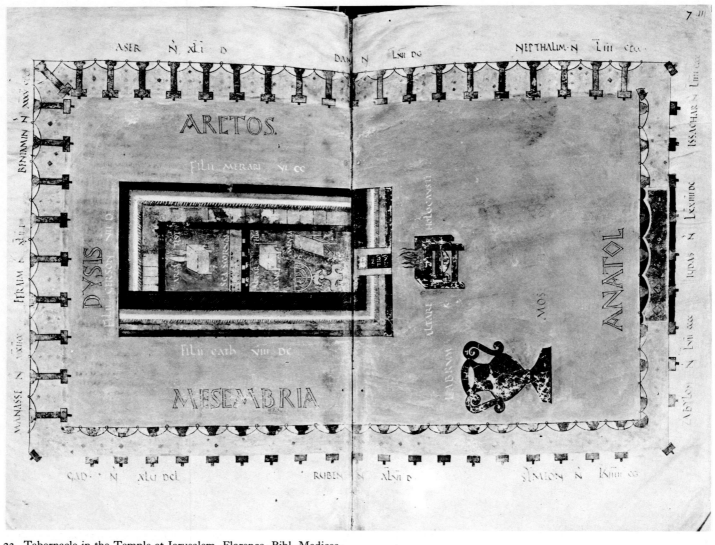

23. Tabernacle in the Temple at Jerusalem. Florence, Bibl. Medicea-Laurenziana, Amiatinus 1, f. II^v–III (cat. 7)

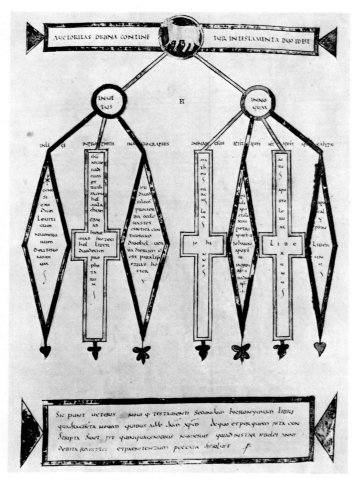

24. Books of Bible according to St. Jerome. Florence, Bibl. Medicea-Laurenziana, Amiatinus 1, f. VI (cat. 7)

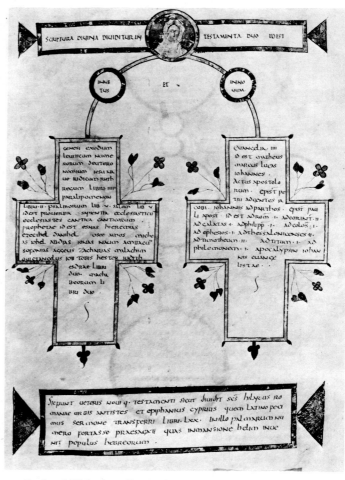

25. Books of Bible according to St. Hilary. Florence, Bibl. Medicea-Laurenziana, Amiatinus 1, f. VII (cat. 7)

26. Christ in Majesty. Florence, Bibl. Medicea-Laurenziana, Amiatinus 1, f. 796ᵛ (cat. 7)

27. Ezra. Florence, Bibl. Medicea-Laurenziana, Amiatinus 1, f. V (cat. 7)

28. St. Matthew. London, B.L., Cotton Nero D. IV, f. 25ᵛ (cat. 9)

29. St. Mark. London, B.L., Cotton Nero D. IV, f. 93ᵛ (cat. 9)

30. St. Luke. London, B.L., Cotton Nero D. IV, f. 137ᵛ (cat. 9)

31. St. John. London, B.L., Cotton Nero D. IV, f. 209ᵛ (cat. 9)

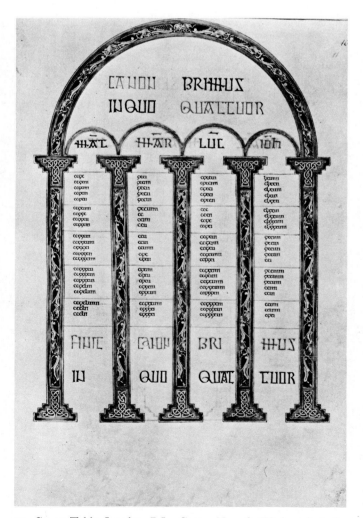

32. Canon Table. London, B.L., Cotton Nero C. IV, f. 11 (cat. 9)

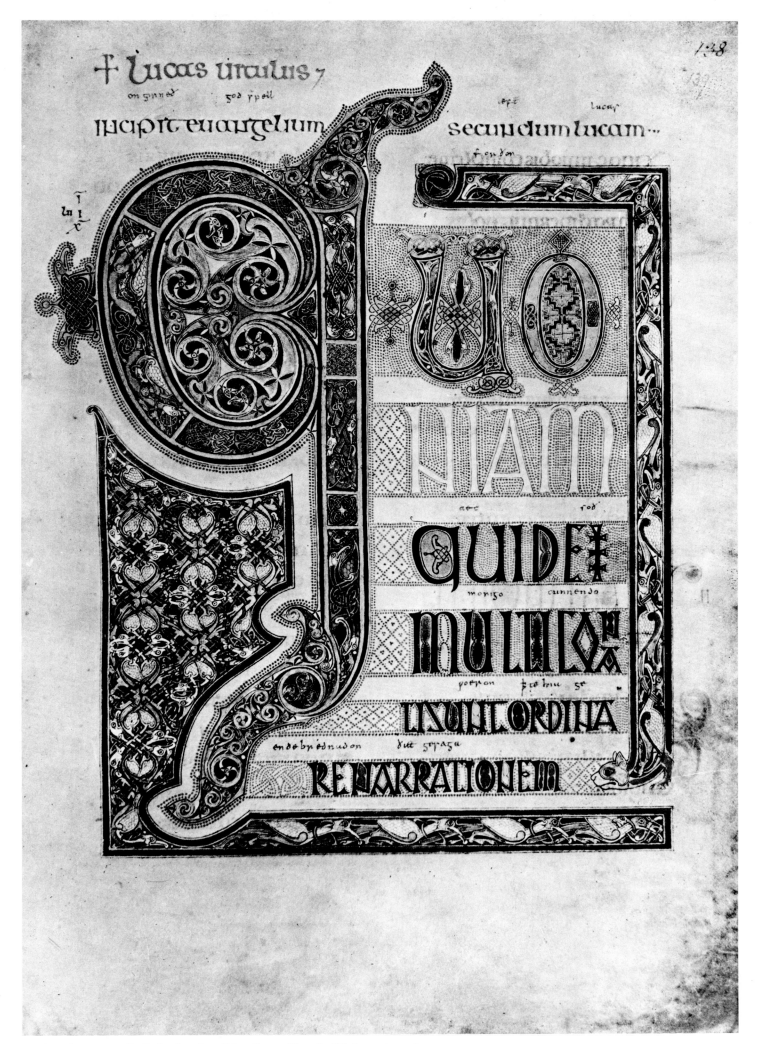

33. Opening page to St. Luke. London, B.L., Cotton Nero D. IV, f. 139 (cat. 9)

34. Cross-carpet page. London, B.L., Cotton Nero D. IV, f. 138ᵛ (cat. 9)

35. Cross-carpet page. London, B.L., Cotton Nero D. IV, f. 94ᵛ (cat. 9)

36. Cross-carpet page. London, B.L., Cotton Nero D. IV,
f. 2ᵛ (cat. 9)

37. Opening page to Jerome's preface. London, B.L., Cotton Nero D. IV,
f. 3 (cat. 9)

38. Cross-carpet page. London, B.L., Cotton Nero D. IV,
f. 26ᵛ (cat. 9)

39. Opening page to St. Matthew. London, B.L., Cotton Nero D. IV,
f. 27 (cat. 9)

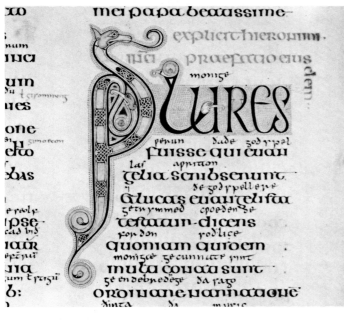

40–43. Initials P, E, M, and E. London, B.L., Cotton Nero D. IV, f. 5ᵛ, f. 8, f. 90, f. 91 (cat. 9)

44. Initial page 'Xpi' to St. Matthew. London, B.L., Cotton Nero D. IV, f. 29 (cat. 9)

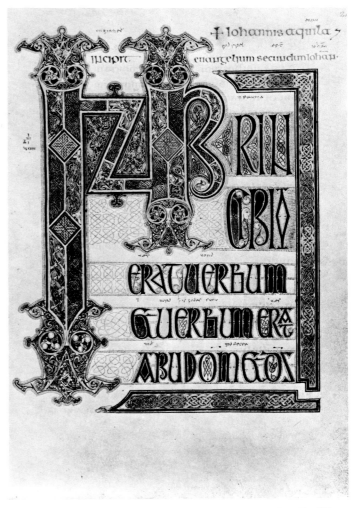

45. Opening page to St. John. London, B.L., Cotton Nero D. IV, f. 211 (cat. 9)

46. Opening page to St. Mark. London, B.L., Cotton Nero D. IV, f. 95 (cat. 9)

47. Opening page to St. John. Durham, Cathedral Lib., A. II. 17, f. 2 (cat. 10)

48. Opening page to St. John. Paris, Bibl. Nat., lat. 9389, f. 177 (cat. 11)

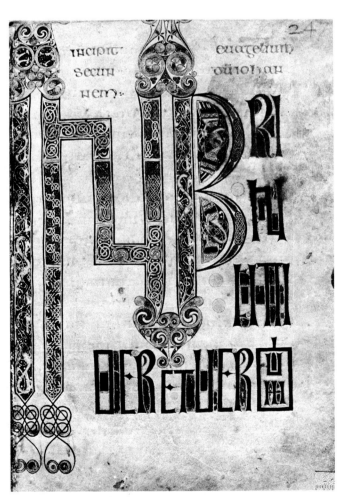

49. Opening page to St. John. Cambridge, Corpus Christi College, 197B, f. 2 (cat. 12)

50. Opening page to St. Mark. Lichfield, Cathedral Lib., Gospel book (St. Chad), p. 143 (cat. 21)

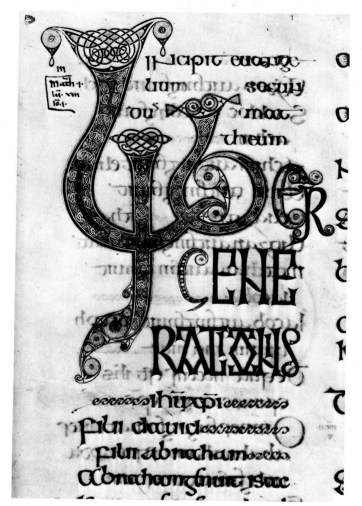

51. Initial 'Xpi'. Paris, Bibl. Nat., lat. 9389, f. 19 (cat. 11)

52. Initial 'Liber'. Paris, Bibl. Nat., lat. 9389, f. 20 (cat. 11)

53. Initial 'Quo' and F. Paris, Bibl. Nat., lat. 9389, f. 116 (cat. 11)

54. Symbol of St. Matthew, Man. Paris, Bibl. Nat., lat. 9389, f. 18ᵛ (cat. 11)

55. Symbol of St. Luke, Calf. Paris, Bibl. Nat., lat. 9389, f. 115ᵛ (cat. 11)

56. Symbol of St. Mark, Lion. Paris, Bibl. Nat., lat. 9389, f. 75ᵛ (cat. 11)

57. Symbol of St. Mark, Lion. London, B.L., Cotton Otho C. V, f. 27 (cat. 12)

58. Symbol of St. John, Eagle. Cambridge, Corpus Christi College, 197B, f. 1 (cat. 12)

IMAGO

AQUILE

59. Symbol of St. John, Eagle. Paris, Bibl. Nat., lat. 9389, f. 176ᵛ (cat. 11)

60. Frontispiece. Cologne, Dombibl., Cod. 213, f. 1 (cat. 13)

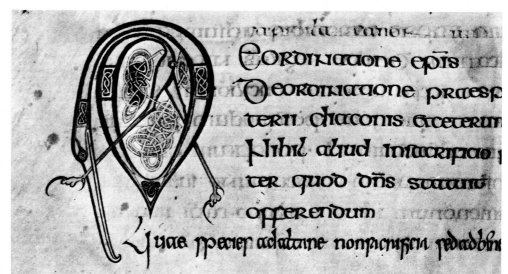

61. Initial D. Cologne, Dombibl.,
Cod. 213, f. 2ᵛ (cat. 13)

62–63. Initials D. Berlin, Deutsche Staatsbibl., Hamilton 553, f. 13, f. 48 (cat. 14)

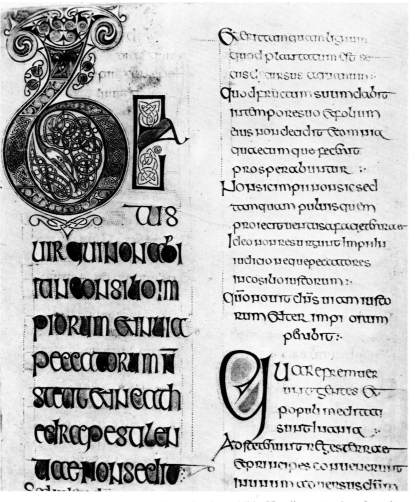

64–65. Initials B and Q. Berlin, Deutsche Staatsbibl., Hamilton 553, f. 2, f. 27 (cat. 14)

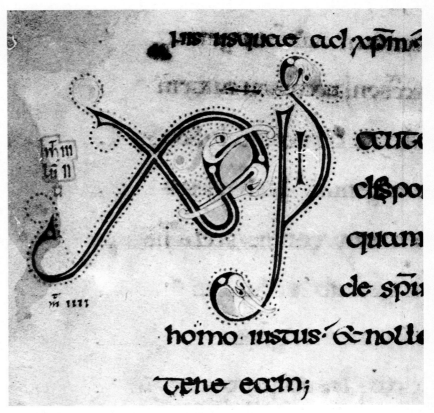

66. Initial H. Leiden, Universiteitsbibl., Voss. Lat. F. 4, f. 30 (cat. 18)

67. Initial 'Xpi'. Leipzig, Universitätsbibl., Rep. II, 35ª, f. 1ᵛ (cat. 15)

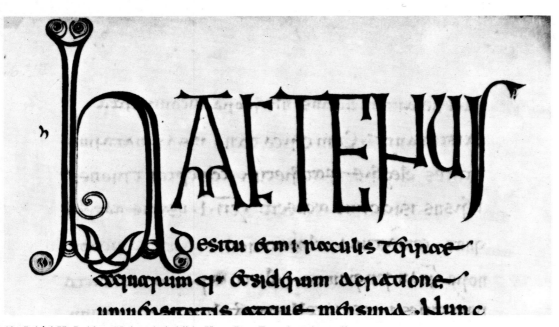

68. Initial H. Leiden, Universiteitsbibl., Voss. Lat. F. 4, f. 9ᵛ (cat. 18)

69. Initial T. Leiden, Universiteitsbibl., Voss. Lat. F. 4, f. 20ᵛ (cat. 18)

70. Initial X. London, B.L., Royal 1. B. VII, f. 15ᵛ (cat. 20)

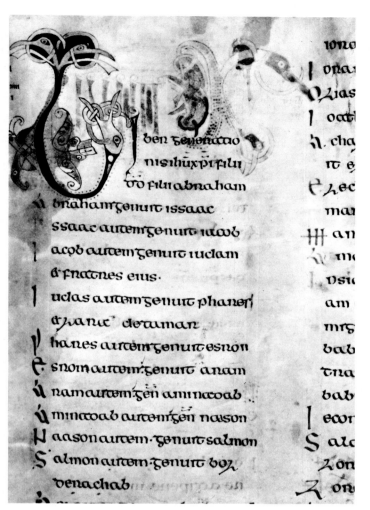

71. Initial 'Li'. London, B.L., Royal 1. B. VII, f. 15 (cat. 20)

72. Canon Table. London, B.L., Royal 1. B. VII, f. 10ᵛ (cat. 20)

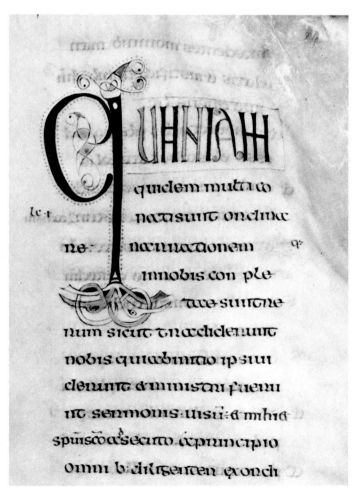

73. Initial Q. London, B.L., Royal 1. B. VII, f. 84 (cat. 20)

74. David enthroned. Durham, Cathedral Lib., B. II. 30, f. 81ᵛ (cat. 17)

75. David. Durham, Cathedral Lib., B. II. 30, f. 172ᵛ (cat. 17)

76. Initial page 'Xpi' to St. Matthew. Lichfield, Cathedral Lib., Gospel Book (St. Chad), p. 5 (cat. 21)

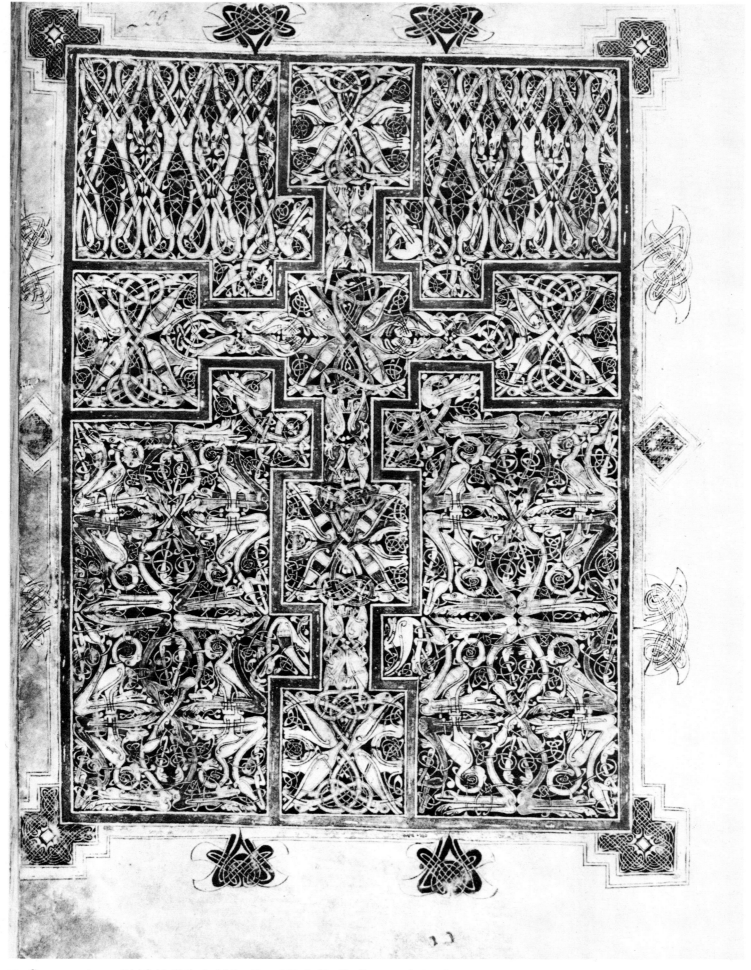

77. Cross-carpet page. Lichfield, Cathedral Lib., Gospel Book (St. Chad), p. 220 (cat. 21)

78. Initial page to St. Luke. Lichfield, Cathedral Lib.,
Gospel Book (St. Chad), p. 221 (cat. 21)

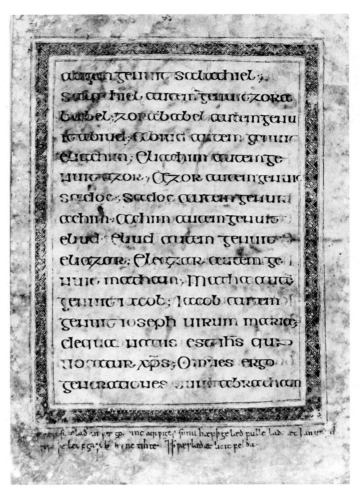

79. Genealogy of Christ. Lichfield, Cathedral Lib.,
Gospel Book (St. Chad), p. 4 (cat. 21)

80. St. Mark. Lichfield, Cathedral Lib., Gospel Book (St. Chad),
p. 142 (cat. 21)

81. Four-symbols page. Lichfield, Cathedral Lib.,
Gospel Book (St. Chad), p. 219 (cat. 21)

82. St. Luke. Lichfield, Cathedral Lib., Gospel Book (St. Chad), p. 218 (cat. 21)

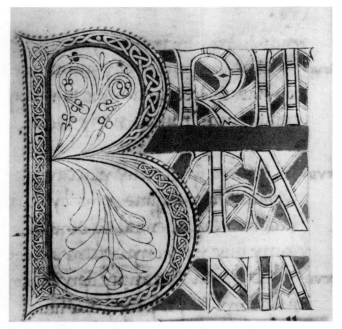

83. Initial B. Leningrad, State Public Lib., Q. v. I. 18, f. 3ᵛ (cat. 19)

84. Initial H. Leningrad, State Public Lib., Q. v. I. 18, f. 26ᵛ (cat. 19)

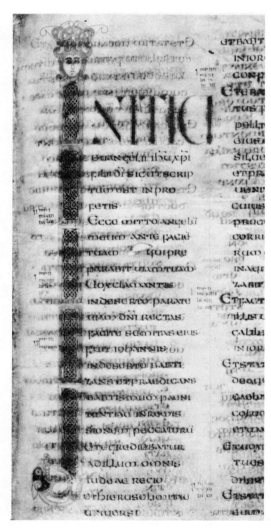

85. Initial I. Durham, Cathedral Lib., A. II. 16, f. 37 (cat. 16)

86. Canon Table. Leipzig, Universitätsbibl., Rep. I, 58ª (cat. 15)

87. Evangelist. Maeseyck, Church of St. Catherine, Trésor, s.n., f. 1 (cat. 22)

88–89. Canon Tables. Maeseyck, Church of St. Catherine, Trésor, s.n., f. 3, f. 3ᵛ (cat. 22)

90–91. Canon Tables. Maeseyck, Church of St. Catherine, Trésor, s.n., f. 5ᵛ, f. 5 (cat. 22)

92–93. Canon Tables. Maeseyck, Church of St. Catherine, Trésor, s.n., f. 2, f. 2ᵛ (cat. 22)

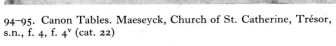

94–95. Canon Tables. Maeseyck, Church of St. Catherine, Trésor, s.n., f. 4, f. 4ᵛ (cat. 22)

96–97. Canon Tables. Maeseyck, Church of St. Catherine, Trésor, s.n., f. 6ᵛ, f. 6 (cat. 23)

98–99. Canon Tables. Maeseyck, Church of St. Catherine, Trésor, s.n., f. 7, f. 7ᵛ (cat. 23)

100–101. Canon Tables. Maeseyck, Church of St. Catherine, Trésor, s.n., f. 8, f. 8ᵛ (cat. 23)

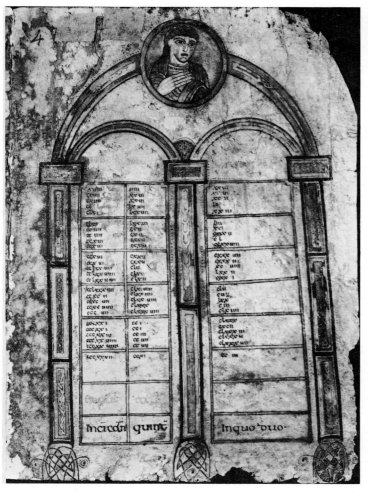

102–103. Canon Tables. Maeseyck, Church of St. Catherine, Trésor, s.n., f. 9, f. 9ᵛ (cat. 23)

104–105. Canon Tables. Maeseyck, Church of St. Catherine, Trésor, s.n., f. 10, f. 10ᵛ (cat. 23)

106–107. Canon Tables. Maeseyck, Church of St. Catherine, Trésor, s.n., f. 11, f. 11ᵛ (cat. 23)

108. Canon Table. Trier, Domschatz, Cod. 61, f. 10 (cat. 26)

109. SS. Michael and Gabriel with *Incipit* of St. Matthew. Trier, Domschatz, Cod. 61, f. 9 (cat. 26)

110. Tetramorph page. Trier, Domschatz, Cod. 61, f. 5ᵛ (cat. 26)

111. St. Matthew. Trier, Domschatz, Cod. 61, f. 18ᵛ (cat. 26)

112. St. Mark. Trier, Domschatz, Cod. 61, f. 80ᵛ (cat. 26)

113. St. Luke. Trier, Domschatz, Cod. 61, f. 125ᵛ (cat. 26)

114. Four-symbols page. Trier, Domschatz, Cod. 61, f. 1ᵛ (cat. 26)

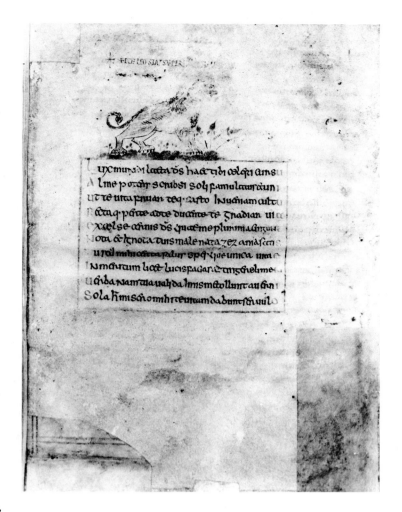

115–116. *Evangelia veritatis* page; Lion and acrostic poem. Schloss Harburg, Cod. I. 2. 4°. 2, f. 2, f. 157ᵛ (cat. 24)

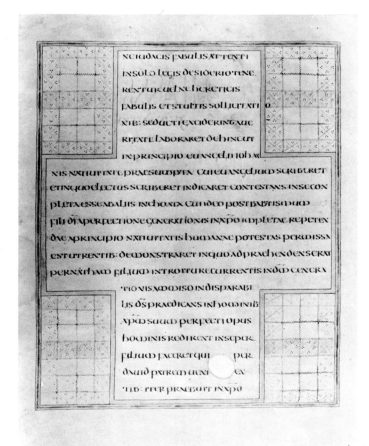

117–118. Preface to St. Luke.
Freiburg-im-Breisgau, Universitätsbibl., Cod. 702, f. 1, f. 1ᵛ (cat. 25)

119–120. Cross-carpet page; initial 'In'. Schloss Harburg,
Cod. I. 2. 4⁰. 2, f. 126ᵛ, f. 127 (cat. 24)

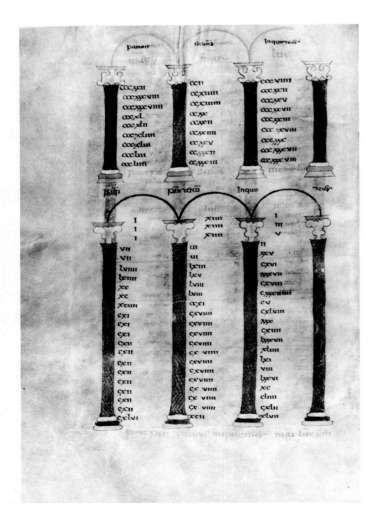

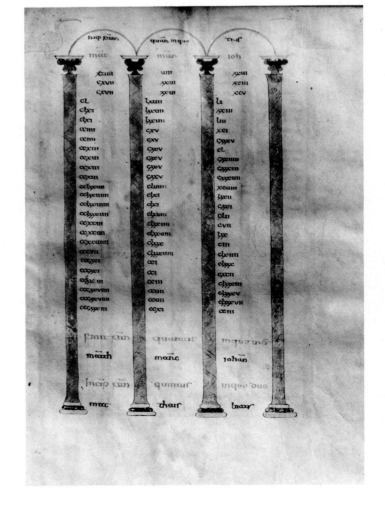

121–122. Canon Tables. Schloss Harburg,
Cod. I. 2. 4⁰. 2, f. 9ᵛ, f. 10 (cat. 24)

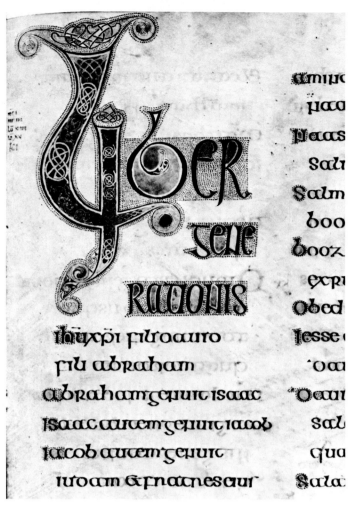

123–124. Initials L and 'Xpi'. Schloss Harburg,
Cod. I. 2. 4°. 2, f. 16, f. 16ᵛ (cat. 24)

125. Initial L. Trier, Domschatz, Cod. 61, f. 19 (cat. 26)

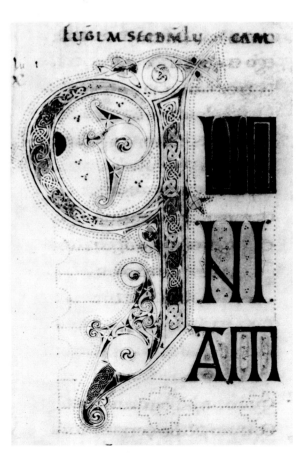

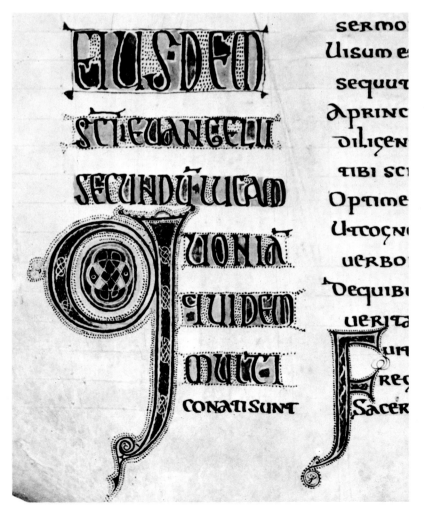

126. Initial Q. Schloss Harburg, Cod.I. 2. 4°. 2, f. 83 (cat. 24)

127. Initials Q and F. Trier, Domschatz, Cod. 61, f. 126ᵛ (cat. 26)

128. Initial 'Quo'. Gotha, Forschungsbibl., Cod. Memb. I. 18, f. 126 (cat. 27)

129. Initial 'In'. Gotha, Forschungsbibl., Cod. Memb. I. 18, f. 78 (cat. 27)

130. Initial P. Gotha, Forschungsbibl., Cod. Memb. I. 18, f. 118ᵛ (cat. 27)

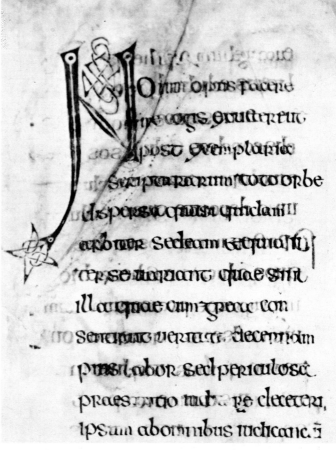

132. Initial N. Gotha, Forschungsbibl., Cod. Memb. I. 18, f. 1 (cat. 27)

131. Initial M. Gotha, Forschungsbibl., Cod. Memb. I. 18, f. 74 (cat. 27)

134. Initial A. London, B.L., Cotton Tiberius
C. II, f. 60ᵛ (cat. 33)

135. Initial A. London, B.L., Harley 2965,
f. 4ᵛ (cat. 41)

133. Initial 'In'. London, B.L.,
Royal 2. A. XX, f. 17 (cat. 35)

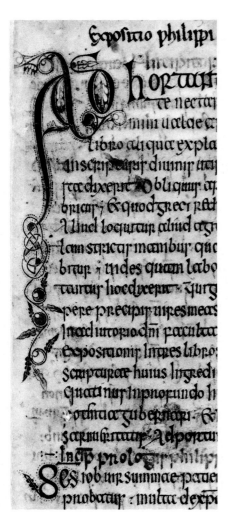

136. Initial A. Oxford, Bodl. Lib.,
Ms. Bodley 426, f. 1 (cat. 40)

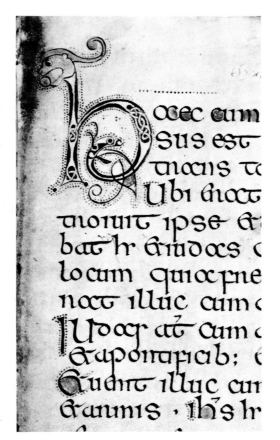

137. Initial H. London, B.L., Harley 2965,
f. 11 (cat. 41)

139. Initial D. London, B.L., Harley 2965,
f. 16ᵛ (cat. 41)

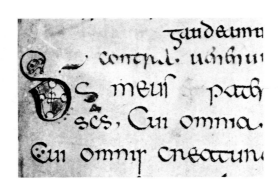

138. Initial D. London, B.L., Harley 2965,
f. 37 (cat. 41)

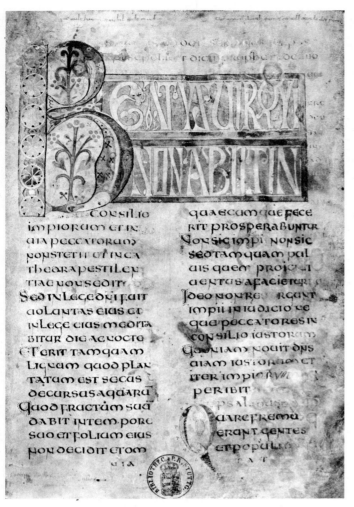

140. Initial B. Stuttgart, Württembergische Landesbibl.,
Cod. Bibl. 2° 12, f. 1 (cat. 28)

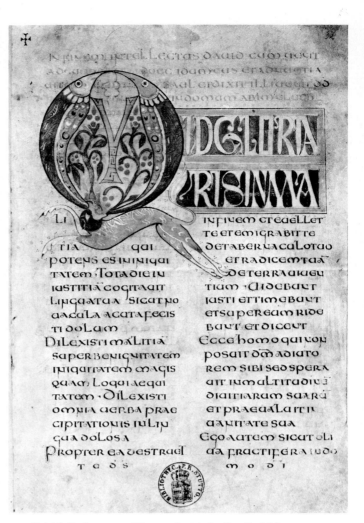

141. Initial Q. Stuttgart, Württembergische Landesbibl.,
Cod. Bibl. 2° 12, f. 32 (cat. 28)

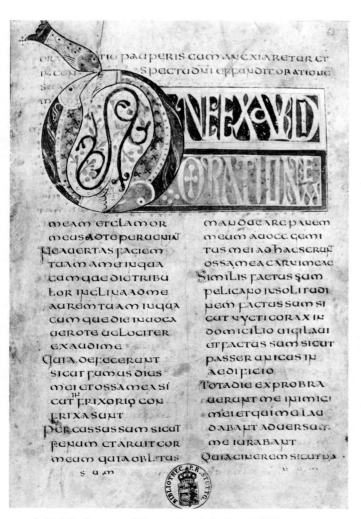

142. Initial D. Stuttgart, Württembergische Landesbibl.,
Cod. Bibl. 2° 12, f. 63 (cat. 28)

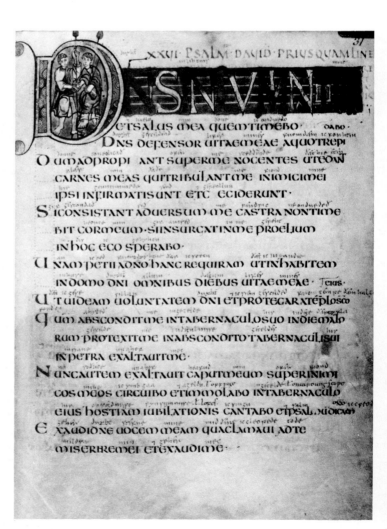

143. Initial D, David and Jonathan. London, B.L., Cotton Vespasian A. 1,
f. 31 (cat. 29)

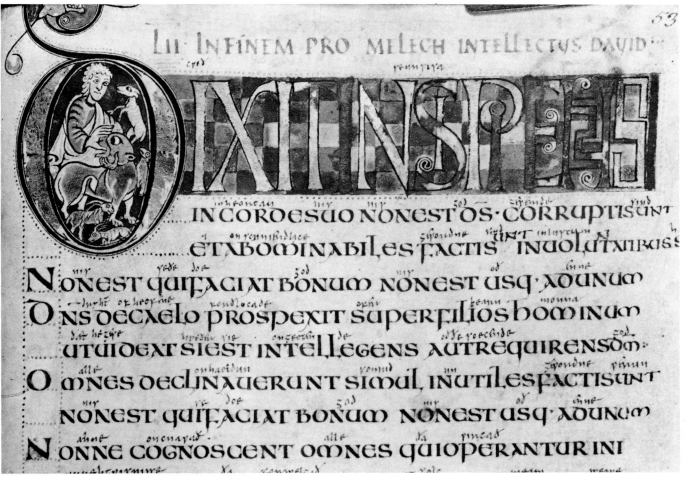

LII INFINEM PRO MELECH INTELLECTUS DAVID

DIXIT INSIPIES

IN CORDESUO NONEST OS · CORRUPTISUNT

ET ABOMINABILES FACTIS INIQUITATIBUS

NONEST QUIFACIAT BONUM NONEST USQ · ADUNUM

DNS DECAELO PROSPEXIT SUPER FILIOS HOMINUM

UTUIDEAT SIEST INTELLEGENS AUTREQUIRENS DM

OMNES DECLINAUERUNT SIMUL INUTILES FACTISUNT

NONEST QUIFACIAT BONUM NONEST USQ · ADUNUM

NONNE COGNOSCENT OMNES QUIOPERANTUR INI

144. Initial D, David and the Lion. London, B.L.,
Cotton Vespasian A. 1, f. 53 (cat. 29)

XCVII

PSALMUS IPSI DAVID

CANTATE

DNO CANTICUM NOUUM

QUIA MIRABILIA FECIT DNS

SALUAUIT EUM DEXTERA EIUS

ETBRA CHIUM SCM EIUS

NOTUM FECIT DNS SALUTARE SUUM

ANTE CONSPECTU GENTIUM REUELAUIT IUS

TITIAM SUAM

MEMOR FUIT MISERICORDIAE SUAE IACOB

ETUERITATIS SUAE DOMUS ISRAEL

145. Initial C. London, B.L., Cotton Vespasian A. 1,
f. 93ᵛ (cat. 29)

146. King David and Musicians. London, B.L., Cotton Vespasian A. 1, f. 30ᵛ (cat. 29)

147. St. John. Stockholm, Royal Lib., A. 135, f. 150ᵛ (cat. 30)

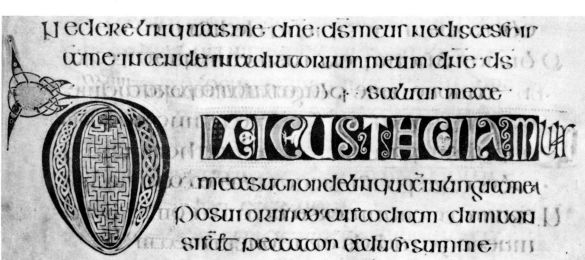

148–151. Initials S, D, E and B. New York, Pierpont Morgan Lib., M. 776, f. 27, f. 7, f. 40, f. 66 (cat. 31)

152. Initial page 'Xpi' to St. Matthew. Stockholm, Royal Lib., A. 135, f. 11 (cat. 30)

153. St. Matthew. Stockholm, Royal Lib., A. 135, f. 9ᵛ (cat. 30)

154. Canon Table. Stockholm, Royal Lib., A. 135, f. 5 (cat. 30)

155. Canon Table. Stockholm, Royal Lib., A. 135, f. 6ᵛ (cat. 30)

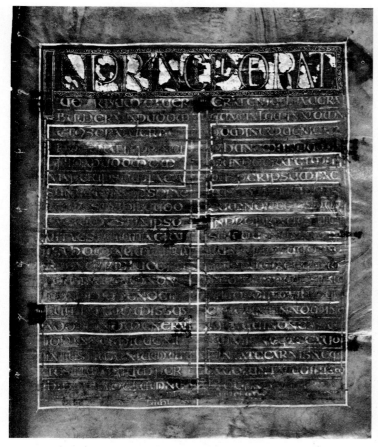

156. Opening page to St. John. Stockholm, Royal Lib., A. 135, f. 151 (cat. 30)

157. Opening page to St. Luke. Stockholm, Royal Lib., A. 135, f. 97 (cat. 30)

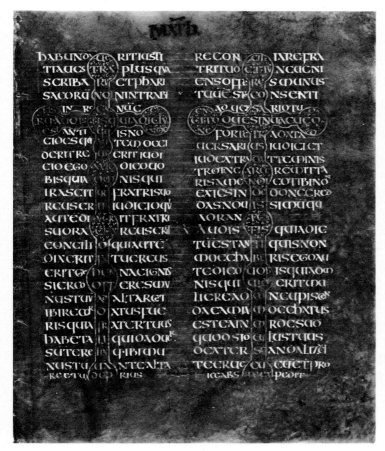

158. Purple page with inlaid crosses. Stockholm, Royal Lib., A. 135, f. 16 (cat. 30)

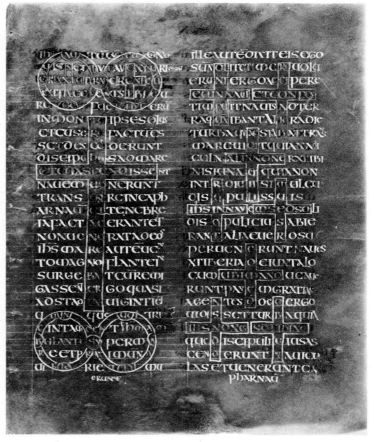

159. Purple page with inlaid crosses. Stockholm, Royal Lib., A. 135, f. 161 (cat. 30)

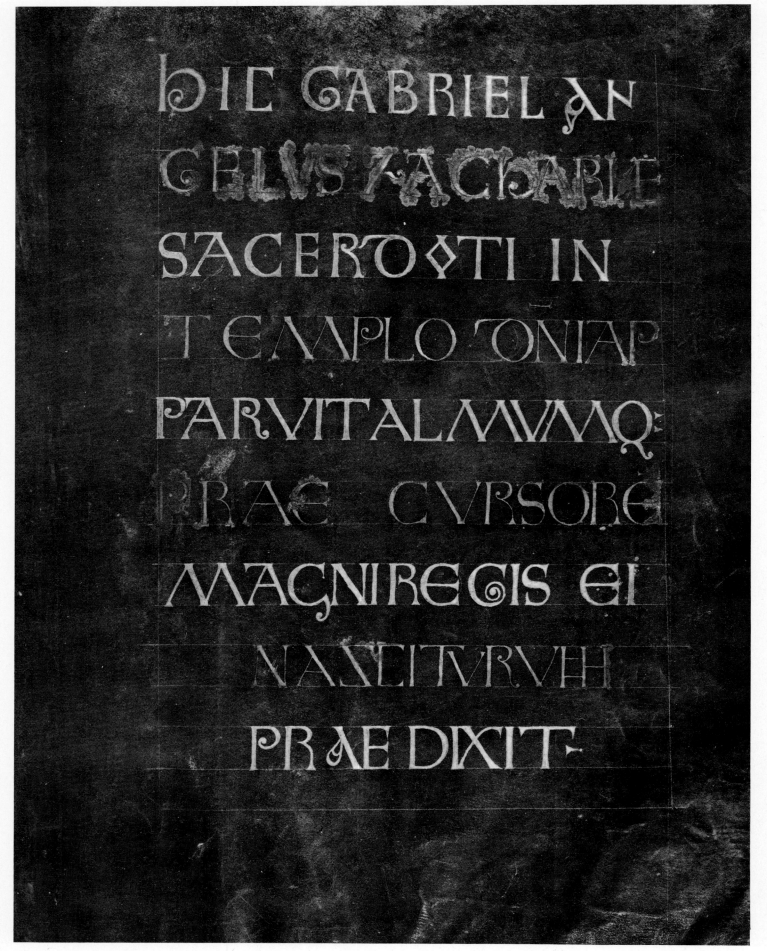

160. Display script preceding St. Luke. London, B.L., Royal 1. E. VI, f. 44 (cat. 32)

161. Opening page to St. Luke. London, B.L., Royal 1. E. VI, f. 43 (cat. 32)

162. Canon Table. London, B.L., Royal 1. E. VI, f. 4 (cat. 32)

163. Canon Table. London, B.L., Royal 1. E. VI, f. 4ᵛ (cat. 32)

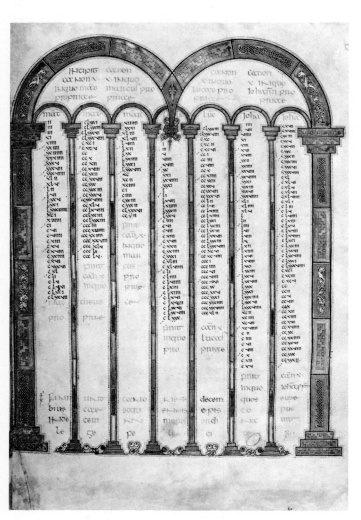

164. Canon Table. London, B.L., Royal 1. E. VI, f. 6 (cat. 32)

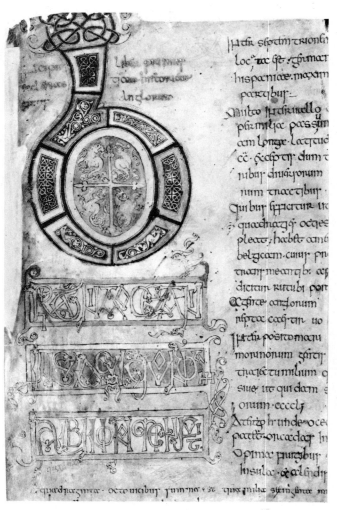

165. Initial B. London, B.L., Cotton Tiberius C. II, f. 5ᵛ, (cat. 33)

CONATISUNTORDINARE
NARRATIONEM QUAE IN
NOBIS CONPLETAE SUNT RERU
SICUT TRADIDERUNTNOBIS
QUI ABINITIO IPSI DIDERUNT
ET MINISTRI FUERUNT SERMONIS
CISUM EST ET MIHI ETSPU SCO
A OSECUTO A PRINCIPIO

166. Initial Q. Paris, Bibl. Nat., lat. 281, f. 137 (cat. 34)

NITIUM
DI SICUT
prophe
meam x
praep
uox cla
rate uix
sem
fuit ioh
zans etpr

167. Initial I. Paris, Bibl. Nat., lat. 281, f. 86 (cat. 34)

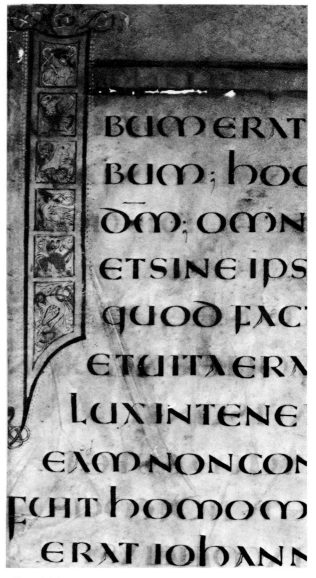

BUM ERAT
BUM; hoc
DM; OMN
ETSINE IPS
QUOD FAC
ET UITA ERA
LUX INTENE
EXA NON CON
FCIT homo
ERAT IOHANN

168. Initial I. Paris, Bibl. Nat., lat. 298, f. 2 (cat. 34)

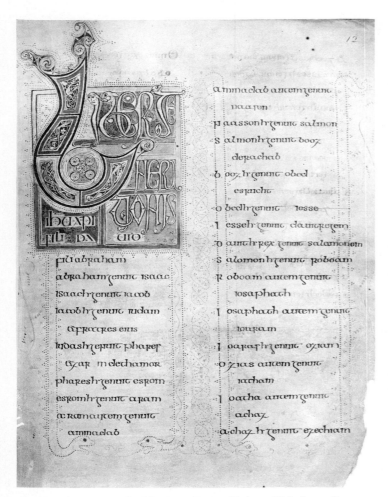

169. Opening page to St. Matthew. Rome, Vatican, Bibl. Apostolica, Barberini Lat. 570, f. 12 (cat. 36)

170. Initial page 'Xpi' to St. Mathew. Rome, Vatican, Bibl. Apostolica, Barberini Lat. 570, f. 18 (cat. 36)

171. Opening page to St. Luke. Rome, Vatican, Bibl. Apostolica, Barberini Lat. 570, f. 80 (cat. 36)

172. Opening page to St. John. Rome, Vatican, Bibl. Apostolica, Barberini Lat. 570, f. 125 (cat. 36)

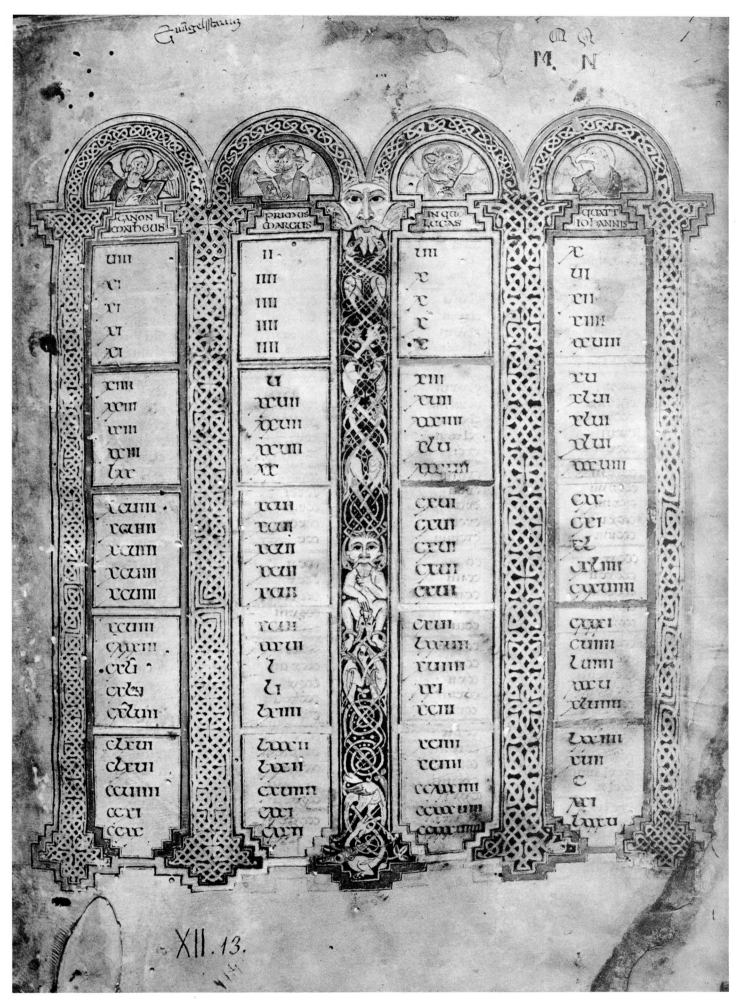

173. Canon Table. Rome, Vatican, Bibl. Apostolica,
Barberini Lat. 570, f. 1 (cat. 36)

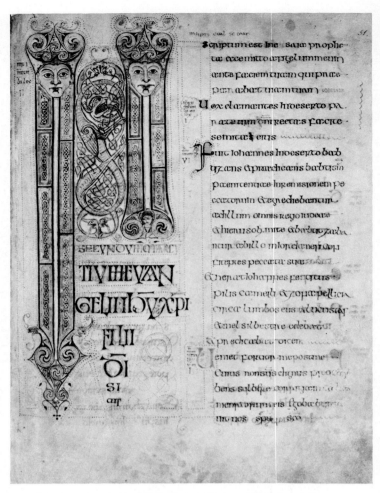

174. St. Mark. Rome, Vatican, Bibl. Apostolica,
Barberini Lat. 570, f. 50ᵛ (cat. 36)

175. Opening page to St. Mark. Rome, Vatican, Bibl. Apostolica,
Barberini Lat. 570, f. 51 (cat. 36)

176. St. Luke. Rome, Vatican, Bibl. Apostolica,
Barberini Lat. 570, f. 79ᵛ (cat. 36)

177. St. John. Rome, Vatican, Bibl. Apostolica,
Barberini Lat. 570, f. 124ᵛ (cat. 36)

Within the illustration: SCS MATHE EVANGE ... US LISTA

178. St. Matthew. Rome, Vatican, Bibl. Apostolica,
Barberini Lat. 570, f. 11ᵛ (cat. 36)

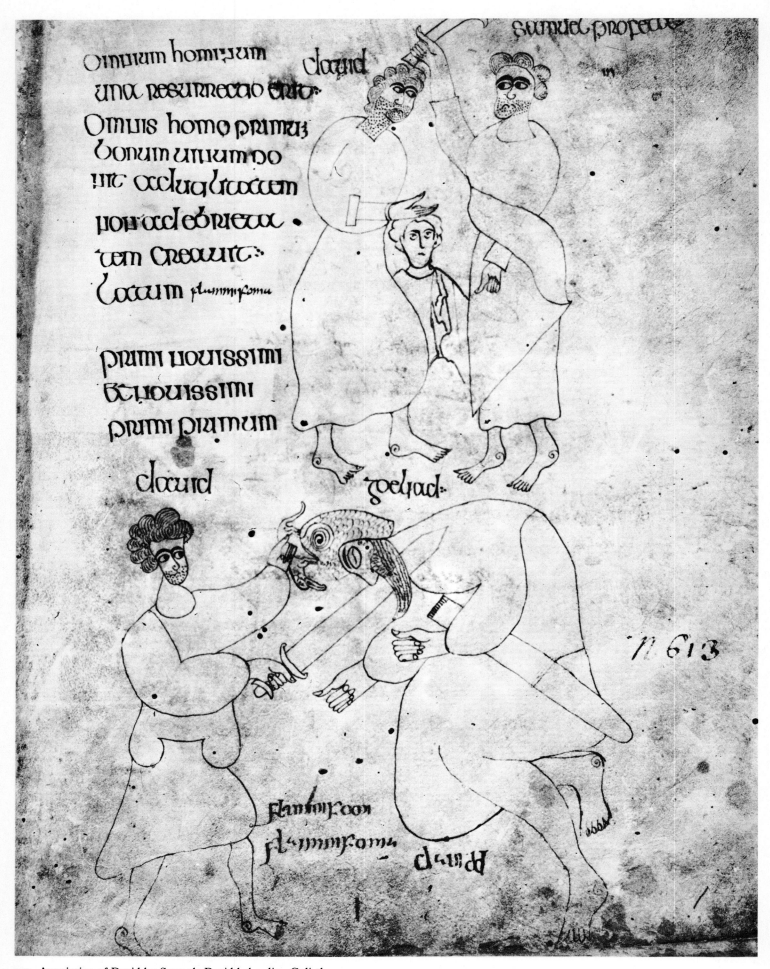

Omnium hominum
una resurrectio erit.
Omnis homo primus
bonum uinum po
nit occlug uraccum
non ad ebrieta
tem creaturt.
Locaum *flammiſomu*

primi nouissimi
et nouissimi
primi primum

179. Annointing of David by Samuel; David beheading Goliath.
Leningrad, State Public Lib., Cod. Q. v. XIV. 1, f. 1 (cat. 42)

180. St. Luke. Vienna, Nationalbibl., Cod. 1224, f. 110ᵛ (cat. 37)

181. St. Matthew. Vienna, Nationalbibl., Cod. 1224, f. 17ᵛ (cat. 37)

182. Canon Table. Vienna, Nationalbibl., Cod. 1224, f. 18 (cat. 37)

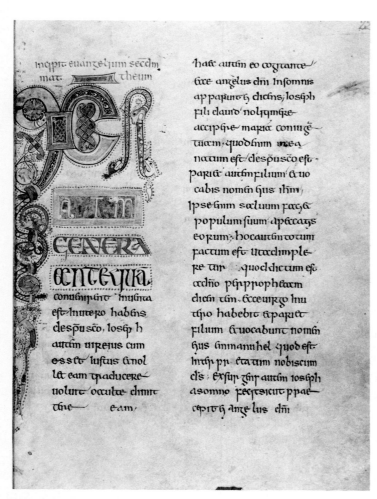

183. Opening to St. Matthew. Vienna, Nationalbibl., Cod. 1224, f. 22. (cat. 37)

184. St. Mark. Vienna, Nationalbibl., Cod. 1224, f. 71ᵛ (cat. 37)

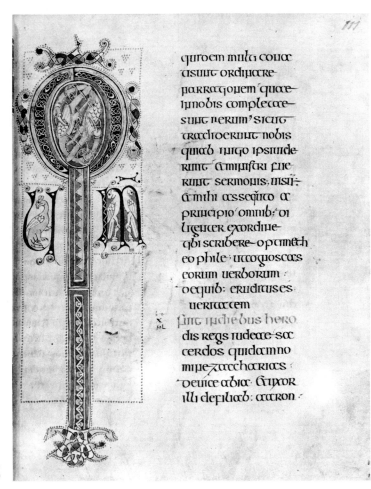

185. Opening page to St. Luke. Vienna, Nationalbibl., Cod. 1224, f. 111 (cat. 37)

186. St. John. Vienna, Nationalbibl., Cod. 1224, f. 165ᵛ (cat. 37)

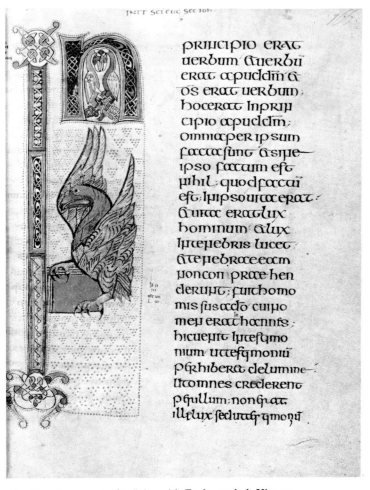

187. Opening page to St. John with Eagle symbol. Vienna, Nationalbibl., Cod. 1224, f. 166 (cat. 37)

188. Canon Table. Leningrad, State Public Lib., Cod. F. v. I. 8, f. 12ᵛ (cat. 39)

189. Canon Table. Leningrad, State Public Lib., Cod. F. v. I. 8, f. 13 (cat. 39)

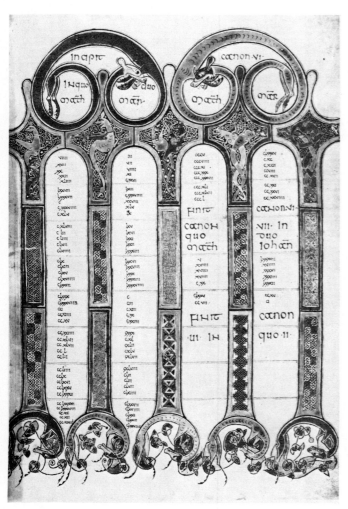

190. Canon Table. Leningrad, State Public Lib., Cod. F. v. I. 8, f. 16 (cat. 39)

191. Canon Table. Leningrad, State Public Lib., Cod. F. v. I. 8, f. 17 (cat. 39)

192. Opening page to St. Matthew. Leningrad, State Public Lib., Cod. F. v. I. 8, f. 18 (cat. 39)

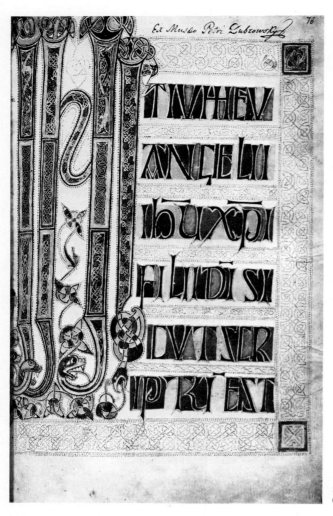

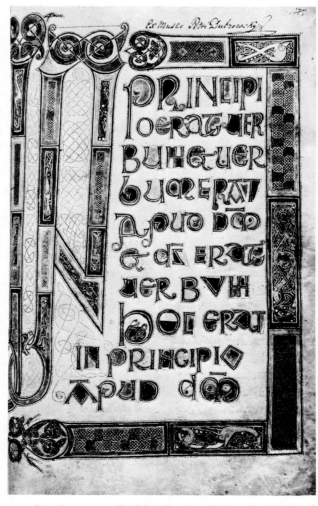

193. Opening page to St. Mark. Leningrad, State Public Lib.,
Cod. F. v. I. 8, f. 78 (cat. 39)

194. Opening page to St. Luke. Leningrad, State Public Lib.,
Cod. F. v. I. 8, f. 119 (cat. 39)

195. Opening page to St. John. Leningrad, State Public Lib.,
Cod. F. v. I. 8, f. 177 (cat. 39)

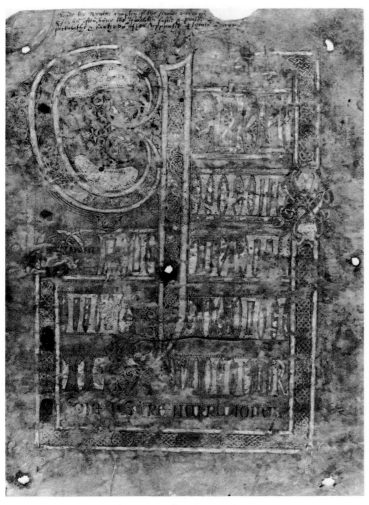

196. Opening page to St. Luke. Oxford, Bodl. Lib., MS. Rawl. G. 167, f. 1 (cat. 43)

197. Opening page to St. Matthew. Hereford, Cathedral Lib., P. I. 2, f. 1 (cat. 38)

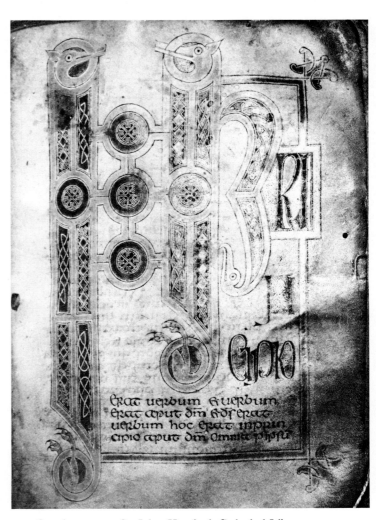

198. Opening page to St. Mark. Hereford, Cathedral Lib., P. I. 2, f. 36 (cat. 38)

199. Opening page to St. John. Hereford, Cathedral Lib., P. I. 2, f. 102 (cat. 38)

200. Carpet page. St. Gall, Stiftsbibl., Cod. 51, p. 6 (cat. 44)

201. Initial page 'Xpi'. St. Gall, Stiftsbibl., Cod. 51, p. 7 (cat. 44)

202. Crucifixion. Durham, Cathedral Lib., A. II. 17, f. 383ᵛ (cat. 10)

203. Crucifixion. St. Gall, Stiftsbibl., Cod. 51, p. 266 (cat. 44)

204. St. Matthew. St. Gall, Stiftsbibl., Cod. 51, p. 2 (cat. 44)

205. St. Luke. St. Gall, Stiftsbibl., Cod. 51, p. 128 (cat. 44)

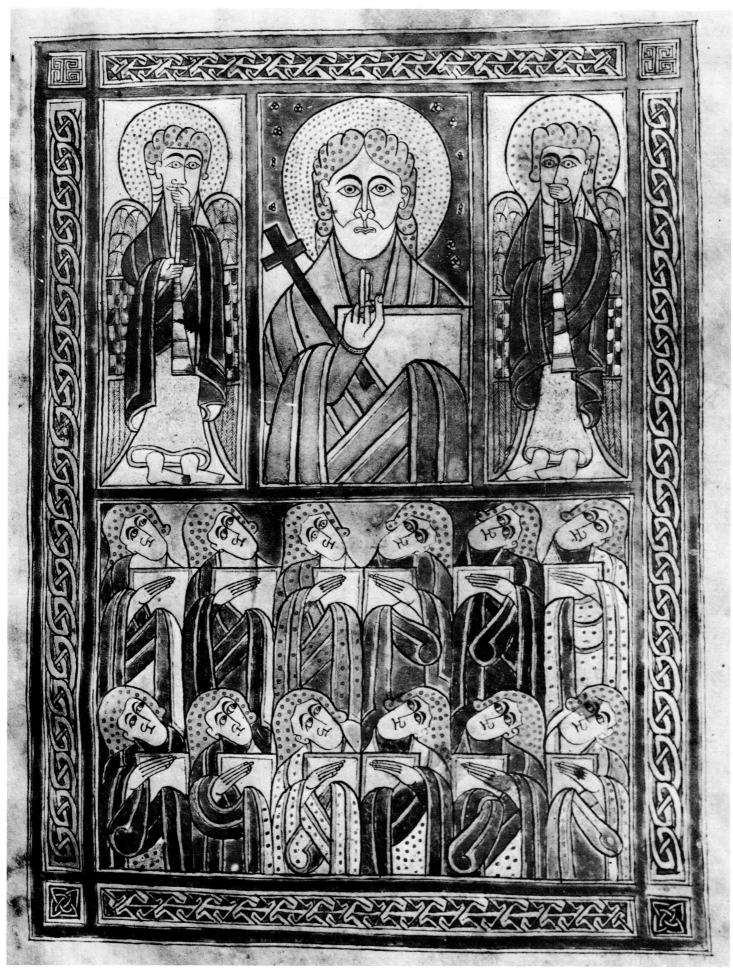

206. The Last Judgement. St. Gall, Stiftsbibl., Cod. 51, p. 267 (cat. 44)

207. St. Mark. St. Gall, Stiftsbibl., Cod. 51, p. 78 (cat. 44)

208. St. John. St. Gall, Stiftsbibl., Cod. 51, p. 208 (cat. 44)

209. St. John. Dublin, Royal Irish Academy, D. II. 3, f. 11ᵛ (cat. 47)

210. St. Matthew. Dublin, Trinity College Lib., A. 1. 15 (60), f. 12ᵛ (cat. 45)

211. St. Mark. Dublin, Trinity College Lib., A. 1. 15 (60), f. 35ᵛ (cat. 45)

212. St. John. Dublin, Trinity College Lib., A. 1. 15 (60), f. 81ᵛ (cat. 45)

213. St. Luke. London, B.L., Add. 40618, f. 21ᵛ (cat. 46)

214. Initial 'Xpi' to St. Matthew.
Dublin, Trinity College Lib., A. 1. 15 (60), f. 13ᵛ (cat. 45)

215. Initial 'Lib' to St. Matthew. Dublin, Trinity College Lib.,
A. 1. 15 (60), f. 13 (cat. 45)

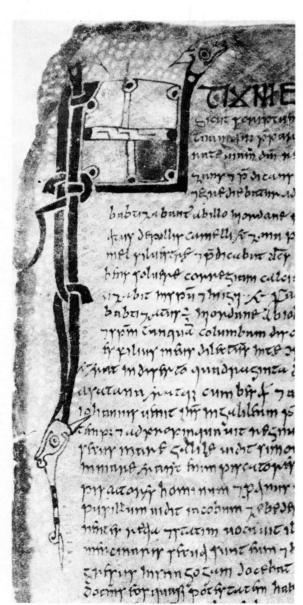

216. Initial 'Ini' to St. Mark. Dublin, Trinity College Lib.,
A. 1. 15 (60), f. 36 (cat. 45)

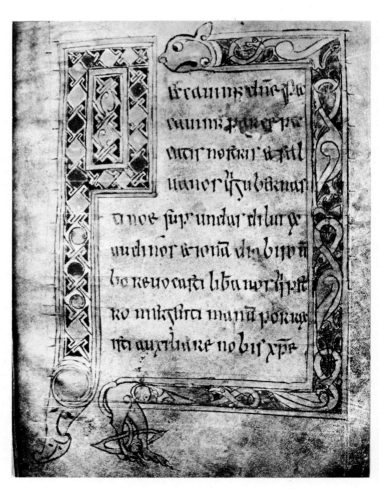

217. Initial page P. Dublin, Royal Irish Academy, D. II. 3,
f. 12 (cat. 51)

218. Opening page to St. John. Dublin, Trinity College Lib.,
A. 1. 15 (60), f. 82 (cat. 45)

219. Opening page to St. John. Dublin, Trinity College Lib.,
A. 4. 23 (59), p. 105 (cat. 48)

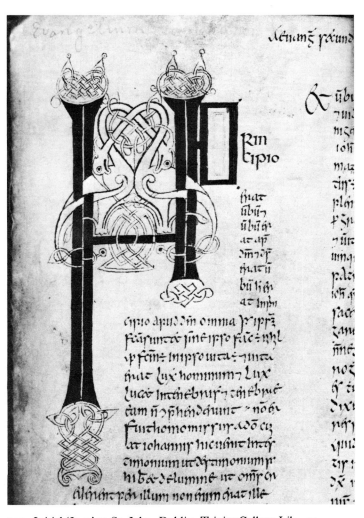

220. Opening page to St. John. Dublin, Royal Irish Academy,
D. II. 3, f. 1 (cat. 47)

221. Initial 'In p' to St. John. Dublin, Trinity College Lib., 52,
f. 90 (cat. 53)

222. St. Matthew. Dublin, Trinity College Lib., A. 4. 23 (59),
p. 2 (cat. 48)

223. St. Mark. Dublin, Trinity College Lib., A. 4. 23 (59),
p. 30 (cat. 48)

224. St. Luke. Dublin, Trinity College Lib., A. 4. 23 (59),
p. 54 (cat. 48)

225. Symbol of St. John, Eagle. Dublin, Trinity College Lib.,
A. 4. 23 (59), p. 104 (cat. 48)

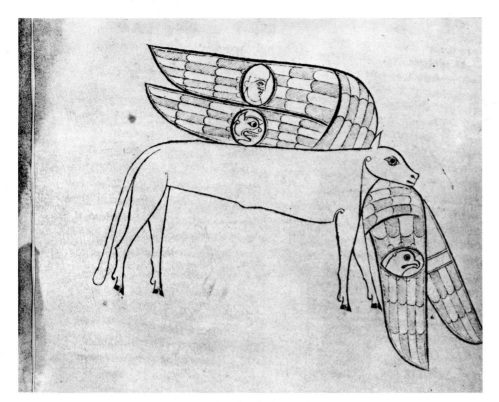

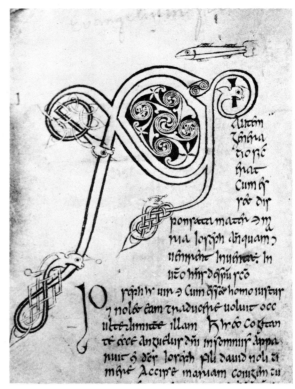

226. Symbol of St. Luke, Calf. Dublin, Trinity College Lib., 52, f. 68ᵛ (cat. 53)

227. Initial 'Xp'. Dublin, Trinity College Lib., 52, f. 33ᵛ (cat. 53)

228. St. Luke. Fulda Landesbibl., Cod. Bonifatianus 3, f. 33ᵛ (cat. 49)

229. Symbol of St. Mark, Lion. Dublin, Trinity College Lib., 52, f. 53ᵛ (cat. 53)

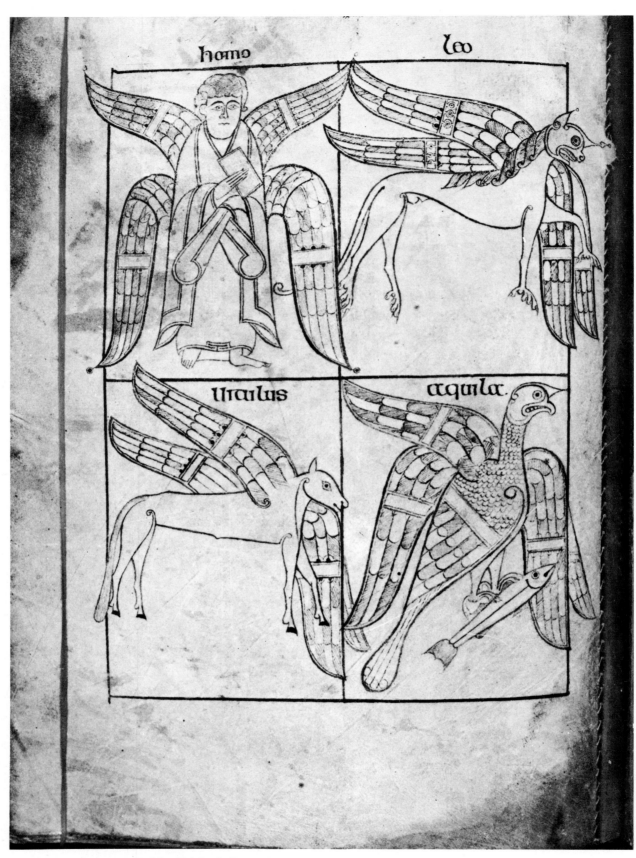

230. Four-symbols page. Dublin, Trinity College Lib., 52, f. 32ᵛ
(cat. 53)

231. Four-symbols page. Dublin, Trinity College Lib., A. 1. 6 (58),
f. 27ᵛ (cat. 52)

232. Canon Table. Dublin, Trinity College Lib., A. 1. 6 (58), f. 5
(cat. 52)

233. Virgin and Child. Dublin, Trinity College Lib., A. 1. 6 (58),
f. 7ᵛ (cat. 52)

234. Canon Table. Dublin, Trinity College Lib., A. 1. 6 (58), f. 1ᵛ (cat. 52)

235. Canon Table. Dublin, Trinity College Lib., A. 1. 6 (58), f. 2 (cat. 52)

236. Canon Table. Dublin, Trinity College Lib., A. 1. 6 (58), f. 2ᵛ (cat. 52)

237. Canon Table. Dublin, Trinity College Lib., A. 1. 6 (58), f. 3 (cat. 52)

238. Canon Table. Dublin, Trinity College Lib., A. 1. 6 (58), f. 3ᵛ (cat. 52)

239. Canon Table. Dublin, Trinity College Lib., A. 1. 6 (58), f. 4 (cat. 52)

240. Canon Table. Dublin, Trinity College Lib., A. 1. 6 (58), f. 4ᵛ (cat. 52)

241. Symbol of St. Matthew, Man. Dublin, Trinity College
Lib., A. 1. 6 (58), f. 28ᵛ (cat. 52)

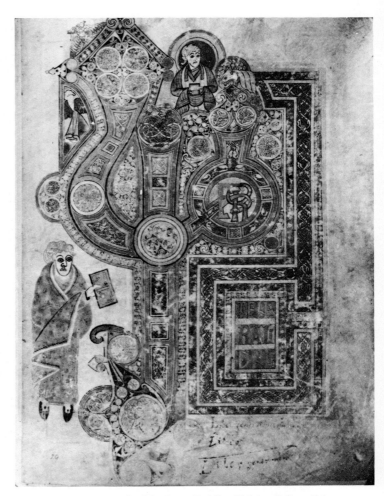

242. Opening page to St. Matthew. Dublin, Trinity College Lib.,
A. 1. 6 (58), f. 29 (cat. 52)

243. Christ enthroned, with Angels. Dublin, Trinity College Lib.,
A. 1. 6 (58), f. 32ᵛ (cat. 52)

244. Initial page 'Xp' to St. Matthew. Dublin, Trinity College Lib.,
A. 1. 6 (58), f. 34 (cat. 52)

245. Cross-carpet page. Dublin, Trinity College Lib., A. 1. 6 (58),
f. 33 (cat. 52)

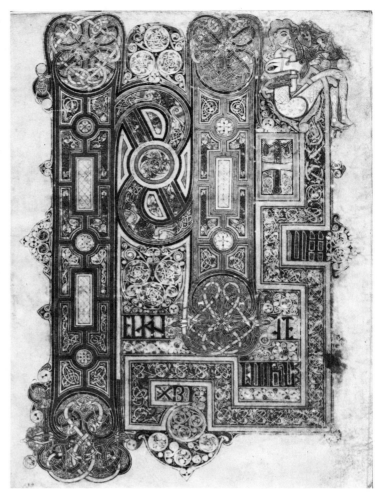

246. Four-symbols page. Dublin, Trinity College Lib., A. 1. 6 (58), f. 129ᵛ (cat. 52)

247. Opening page to St. Mark. Dublin, Trinity College Lib., A. 1. 6 (58), f. 130 (cat. 52)

248. Evangelist symbols preceding St. Luke. Dublin, Trinity College Lib., A. 1. 6 (58), f. 187ᵛ (cat. 52)

249. Opening page to St. Luke. Dublin, Trinity College Lib., A. 1. 6 (58), f. 188 (cat. 52)

250. Four-symbols page preceding St. John. Dublin, Trinity College Lib., A. 1. 6 (58), f. 290ᵛ (cat. 52)

251. St. John. Dublin, Trinity College Lib., A. 1. 6 (58), f. 291ᵛ (cat. 52)

252. Opening page to St. John. Dublin, Trinity College Lib., A. 1. 6 (58), f. 292 (cat. 52)

253. Initial page, St. Matthew XXVII, 38. Dublin, Trinity College Lib., A. 1. 6 (58), f. 124 (cat. 52)

254. Initial page, St. Luke XXIII, 56. Dublin, Trinity College Lib., A. 1. 6 (58), f. 285 (cat. 52)

255. The Temptation of Christ. Dublin, Trinity College Lib., A. 1. 6 (58), f. 202ᵛ (cat. 52)

256. Initial page, St. Luke IV, 1. Dublin, Trinity College Lib., A. 1. 6 (58), f. 203 (cat. 52)

257. Text page. Dublin, Trinity College Lib., A. 1. 6 (58),
f. 309ᵛ (cat. 52)

258–259. Text pages. Dublin, Trinity College Lib., A. 1. 6 (58),
f. 67, f. 89 (cat. 52)

260. Genealogy of Christ. Dublin, Trinity College Lib., A. 1. 6 (58),
f. 200 (cat. 52)

261. Initial page P. St. Gall, Stiftsbibl., Cod. 1395,
p. 426 (cat. 50)

262. St. Mark. Oxford, Bodl. Lib., MS. Auct. D. 2. 19, f. 51ᵛ (cat. 54)

263. St. Luke. Oxford, Bodl. Lib., MS. Auct. D. 2. 19, f. 84ᵛ (cat. 54)

264. St. John. Oxford, Bodl. Lib., MS. Auct. D. 2. 19, f. 126ᵛ (cat. 54)

265. Christ on the Cross. Würzburg, Universitätsbibl., Cod. M. p. th., f. 69, f. 7ᵛ (cat. 55)

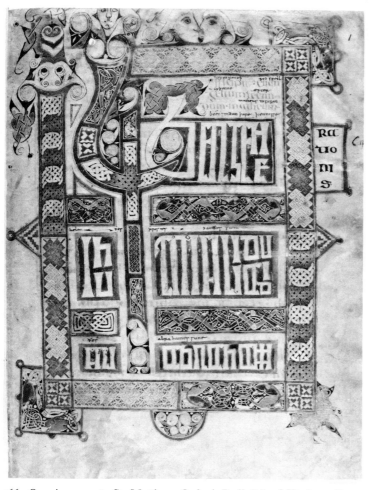

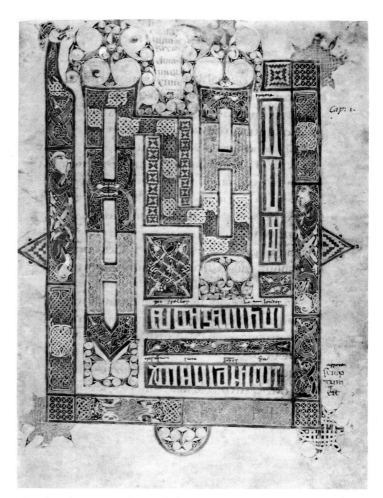

266. Opening page to St. Matthew. Oxford, Bodl. Lib., MS. Auct. D. 2. 19, f. 1 (cat. 54)

267. Opening page to St. Mark. Oxford, Bodl. Lib., MS. Auct. D. 2. 19, f. 52 (cat. 54)

268. Opening page to St. Luke. Oxford, Bodl. Lib., MS. Auct. D. 2. 19, f. 85 (cat. 54)

269. Opening page to St. John. Oxford, Bodl. Lib., MS. Auct. D. 2. 19, f. 127 (cat. 54)

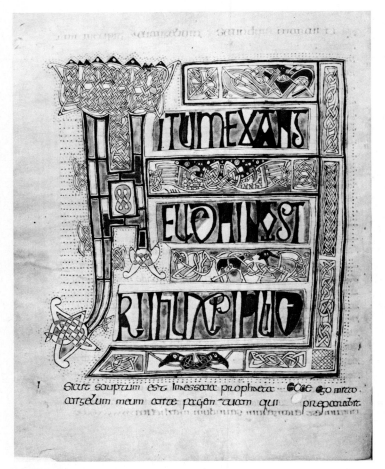

270. Opening page to St. Mark. Paris, Bibl. Nat., nouv. acq. lat. 1587, f. 32ᵛ (cat. 56)

271. Opening page to St. Luke. Paris, Bibl. Nat., nouv. acq. lat. 1587, f. 52ᵛ (cat. 56)

272. Opening page to St. John. Paris, Bibl. Nat., nouv. acq. lat. 1587, f. 85ᵛ (cat 56)

273. Frontispiece (carpet page). Paris, Bibl. Nat., nouv. acq. lat. 1587, f. 1ᵛ (cat. 56)

274. Opening page to St. Matthew. Dublin, Trinity College Lib., A. 4. 6 (56), f. 1 (cat. 59)

275. Opening page to St. Mark. Dublin, Trinity College Lib., A. 4. 6 (56) f. 22 (cat. 59)

276. Initial B to Psalm 1. London, B.L., Add. 36929, f. 2 (cat. 78)

277. Cross-carpet page. Turin, Bibl. Nazionale, Cod. O. IV. 20, f. 128ª verso (cat. 61)

278. Cross-carpet page. Turin, Bibl. Nazionale, Cod. O. IV. 20, f. 129 (cat. 61)

279. The Ascension. Turin, Bibl. Nazionale, Cod. O. IV. 20, f. 1ª verso (cat. 61)

280. The Second Coming. Turin, Bibl. Nazionale, Cod. O. IV. 20, f. 2ª (cat. 61)

281. St. Matthew. St. Gall, Stiftsbibl., Cod. 1395, p. 418 (cat. 57)

282. Cross page. St. Gall, Stiftsbibl., Cod. 1395, p. 422 (cat. 58).

283. Opening page to St. John. St. Gall, Stiftsbibl., Cod. 60, p. 5 (cat. 60)

284. St. John. St. Gall, Stiftsbibl., Cod. 60, p. 4 (cat. 60)

285. Christ enthroned. Antwerp, Museum Plantin-Moretus, M. 17. 4, f. 1 (cat. 65)

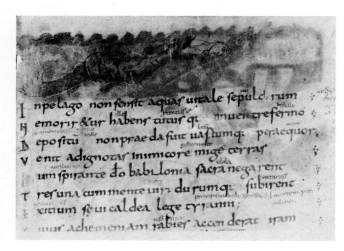

286–293. Carmen Paschale. Antwerp, Museum Plantin-Moretus, M. 17. 4 (Cat. 65)

286. Abraham's Sacrifice of Isaac, f. 8; 287. Jonah thrown out of the Boat, f. 9ᵛ; 288. Jonah regurgitated by the Whale, f. 10; 289. Daniel in the Lion's Den, f. 10ᵛ; 290. Four Evangelist Symbols adoring the Cross, f. 13; 291. Adoration of the Magi, f. 15ᵛ; 292. Slaughter of the Innocents, f. 16; 293. Healing of the Blind Man and the Woman with the Crooked Spine, f. 22ᵛ

294–301. Carmen Paschale. Antwerp, Museum Plantin-Moretus, M. 17. 4 (cat. 65)

294. St. Peter catching a Fish in a Fish-Tank, f. 25; 295. Christ and the Woman taken in Adultery, f. 30; 296. Raising of Lazarus, f. 30ᵛ; 297. Entry into Jerusalem, f. 31ᵛ; 298. Christ about to wash St. Peter's Feet, f. 32; 299. Betrayal shown symbolically, f. 33; 300. St. Peter's Betrayal and St. Peter Grieving, f. 33ᵛ; 301. Christ's Command to St. Peter—Feed my Sheep, f. 38

302. St. John receives the Scroll with the Seven Seals (Rev. I. 1). Valenciennes, Bibl. Mun., 99, f. 3 (cat. 64)

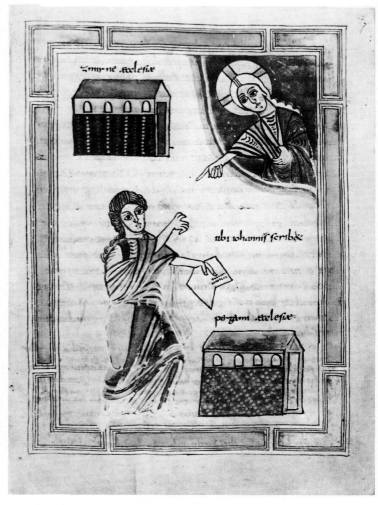

303. St. John writing to the Churches of Smyrna and Pergamon (Rev. II, 8, 12). Valenciennes, Bibl. Mun., 99, f. 7 (cat. 64)

304. Christ in Majesty (Rev. IV, 6). Valenciennes, Bibl. Mun., 99, f. 10 (cat. 64)

305. The Vision of the Lamb (Rev. V. 6). Valenciennes, Bibl. Mun., 99, f. 12 (cat. 64)

306. The Sixth Angel blowing the Trumpet (Rev. IX. 13). Valenciennes, Bibl. Mun., 99, f. 19 (cat. 64)

307. The Woman and the Dragon (Rev. XII. 1–3). Valenciennes, Bibl., Mun., 99, f. 23 (cat. 64)

308. The Harlot and the Beast (Rev. XVII. 1–5). Valenciennes, Bibl. Mun., 99, f. 31 (cat. 64)

309. Christ enthroned and the Second Death. (Rev. XX. 11, 14). Valenciennes, Bibl. Mun. 99 f. 37 (cat. 64)

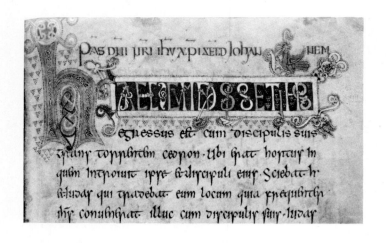

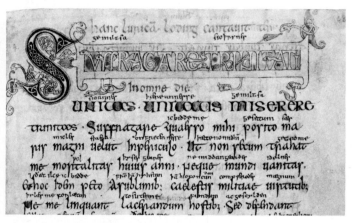

310–11. Initials H and S. Cambridge, University Lib., Ll. 1. 10, f. 32;
f. 43 (cat. 66)

312. St. Matthew. Cambridge, Univ. Lib., Ll. 1. 10,
f. 2ᵛ (cat. 66)

313. St. Luke. Cambridge, Univ. Lib., Ll. 1. 10, f. 21ᵛ (cat. 66)

314. St. John. Cambridge, Univ. Lib., Ll. 1. 10, f. 31ᵛ (cat. 66)

315. St. Mark. Cambridge, Univ. Lib., Ll. 1. 10, f. 12ᵛ (cat. 66)

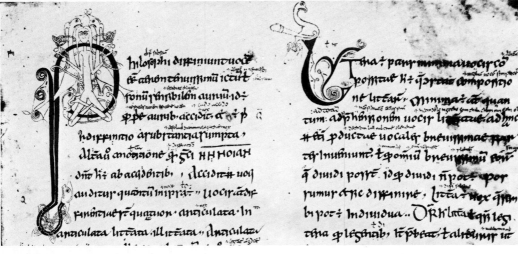

316. Initials P and D. Milan, Bibl. Ambrosiana, C. 301. inf., f. 2 (p. 8) (cat. 62)

317. Initial N. Leiden, Universiteitsbibl., B.P.L. 67, f. 23ᵛ (cat. 63)

318. Initials P and U. St. Gall, Stiftsbibl., Cod. 904, p. 2 (cat. 68)

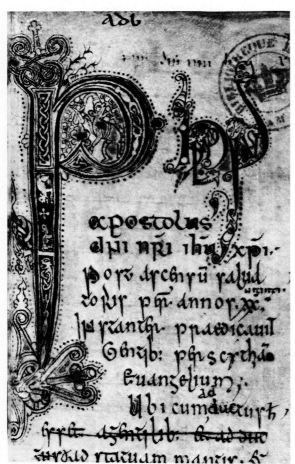

319. 'Ph' monogram. Paris, Bibl. Nat., lat. 10861, f. 2 (cat. 67)

320. Text page. Karlsruhe, Landesbibl., Cod. CLXVII, f. 32ᵛ (cat. 69)

321. Opening page to St. Matthew. London, Lambeth Palace Lib., 1370, f. 2 (cat. 70)

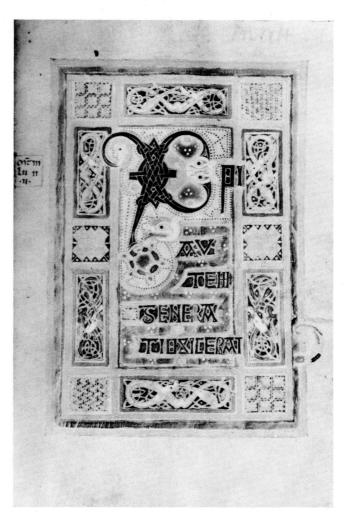

322. Initial 'Xpi' to St. Matthew. London, Lambeth Palace Lib., 1370, f. 5 (cat. 70)

323. Opening page to St. Luke. London, Lambeth Palace Lib., 1370, f. 117 (cat. 70)

324. Opening page to St. John. London, Lambeth Palace Lib., 1370, f. 172 (cat. 70)

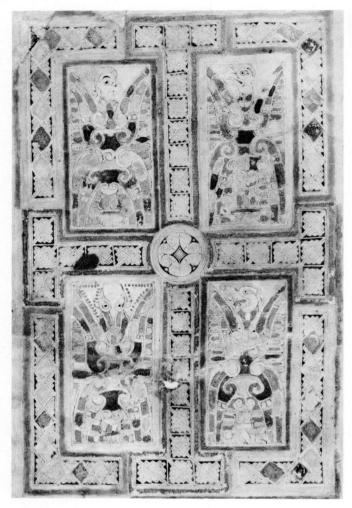

325. Four-symbols page. London, Lambeth Palace Lib., 1370,
f. 1ᵛ (cat. 70)

326. St. Matthew. London, Lambeth Palace Lib., 1370,
f. 4ᵛ (cat. 70)

327. St. Luke. London, Lambeth Palace Lib., 1370,
f. 115ᵛ (cat. 70)

328. St. John. London, Lambeth Palace Lib., 1370, f. 170ᵛ (cat. 70)

329. Two Evangelists and Angels (?) arranged round a Cross. Cambridge, Univ. Lib., Ii. 6. 32, f. 1ᵛ (cat. 72)

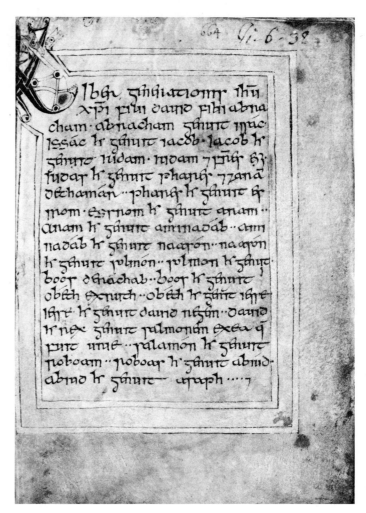

330. Opening page to St. Matthew. Cambridge, Univ. Lib., Ii. 6. 32, f. 2 (cat. 72)

331. Four figures round a Cross. Cambridge, Univ. Lib., Ii. 6. 32, f. 85ᵛ (cat. 72)

332. Four figures round a Cross. Cambridge, Univ. Lib., Ii. 6. 32, f. 86 (cat. 72)

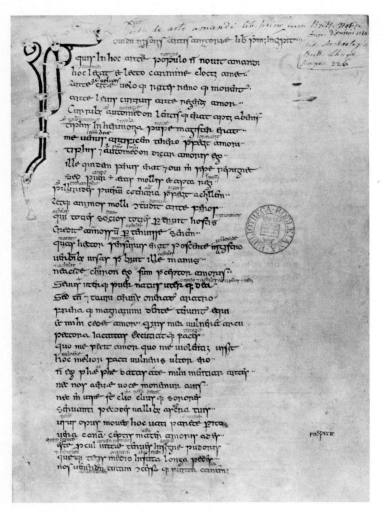

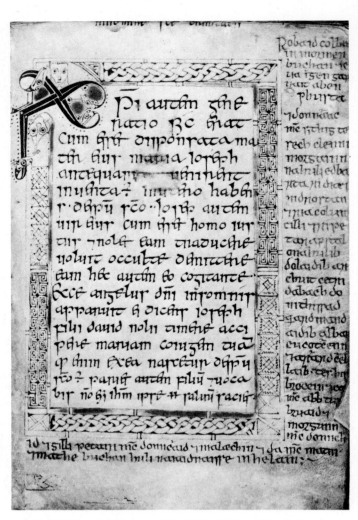

333. Initial 'Si'. Oxford, Bodl. Lib., MS. Auct. F. 4. 32,
f. 37 (cat. 71)

334. Initial X to St. Matthew. Cambridge, Univ. Lib., Ii. 6. 32,
f. 5 (cat. 72)

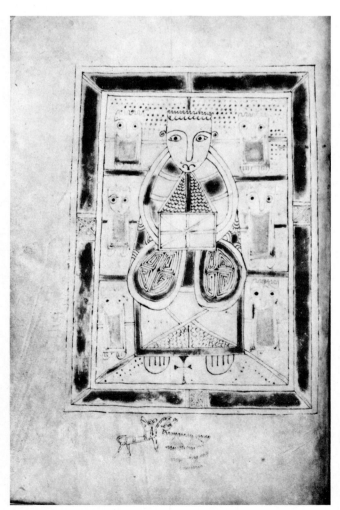

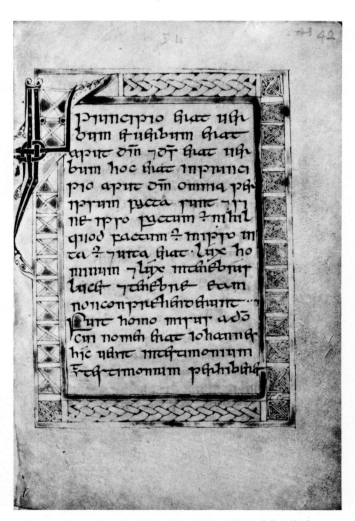

335. St. John. Cambridge, Univ. Lib., Ii. 6. 32,
f. 41ᵛ (cat. 72)

336. Opening page to St. John. Cambridge, Univ. Lib., Ii. 6. 32,
f. 42 (cat. 72)

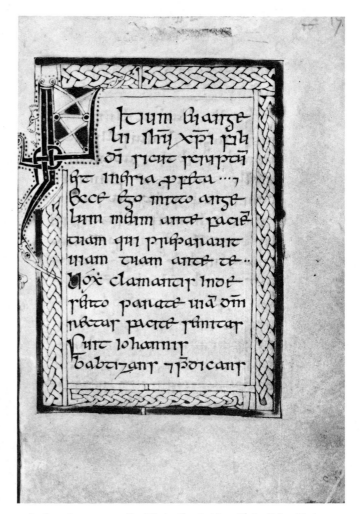

337. St. Mark. Cambridge, Univ. Lib., Ii. 6. 32, f. 16ᵛ (cat. 72)

338. Opening page to St. Mark. Cambridge, Univ. Lib., Ii. 6. 32, f. 17 (cat. 72)

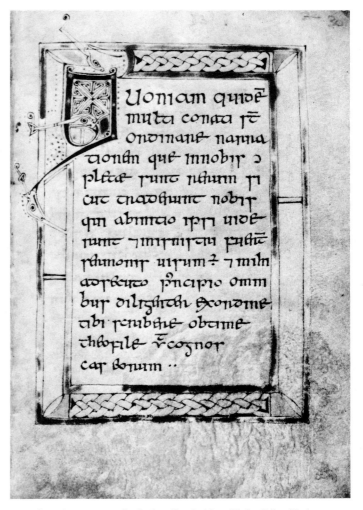

339. St. Luke. Cambridge, Univ. Lib., Ii. 6. 32, f. 29ᵛ (cat. 72)

340. Opening page to St. Luke. Cambridge, Univ. Lib., Ii. 6. 32, f. 30 (cat. 72)

Si uingm debebat. qi m uel scpton mcbnspo
ne ossporgo f libnos ondine nago solo prigi
la ano t non exponte. ut rebidi oskydhuo collo
ecco 7 auhsbiclb prueto labonit 7 do magroi
docunna rshuanktin.. pmt anguittu iohannit.,

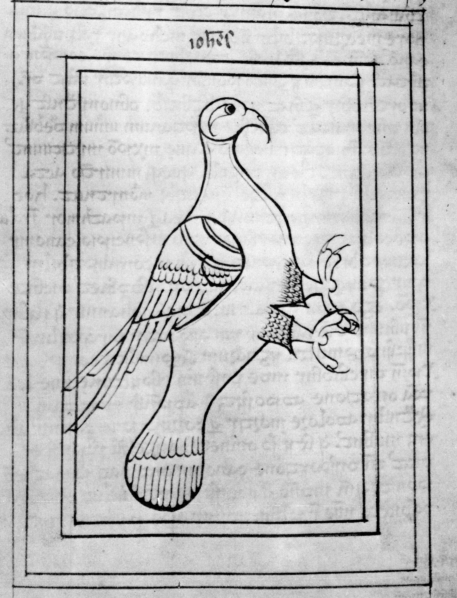

341. Symbol of St. John, Eagle. London, B.L., Harley 1023, f. 64ᵛ (cat. 76)

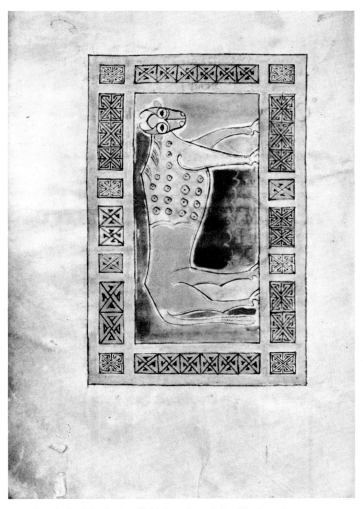

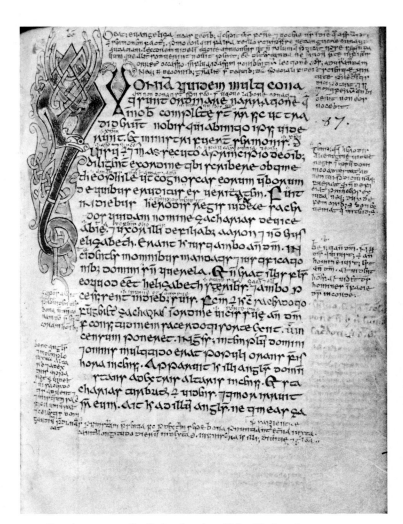

342. Symbol of St. Luke, Calf. London, B.L., Harley 1802, f. 86ᵛ (cat. 77)

343. Opening page to St. Luke. London, B.L., Harley 1802, f. 87 (cat. 77)

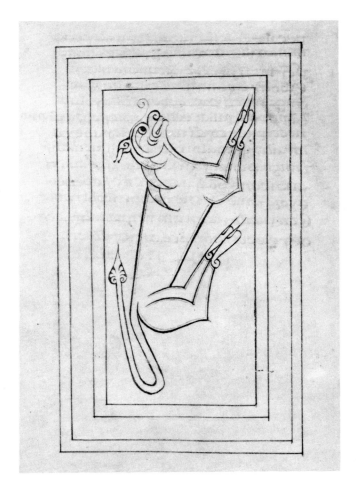

344. Symbol of St. Mark, Lion. London, B.L., Harley 1023, f. 10ᵛ (cat. 76)

345. Symbol of St. Mark, Lion. London, B.L., Harley 1802, f. 60ᵛ (cat. 77)

346. Initial B. Dublin, Trinity College Lib., A. 4.20. (50),
f. 35 (cat. 75)

347. Initial Q. London, B.L., Cotton Vitellius F. XI,
f. 15 (cat. 73)

348. David harping. London, B.L., Cotton Vitellius F. XI,
f. 2 (cat. 73)

349. David and Goliath. London, B.L., Cotton Vitellius F. XI,
f. 1 (cat. 73)

350. David fighting the Lion. Cambridge, St. John's College,
C. 9 (59), f. 4ᵛ (cat. 74)

351. Crucifixion. Cambridge, St. John's College, C. 9 (59),
f. 38ᵛ (cat. 74)

352. David and Goliath. Cambridge. St. John's College, C. 9 (59),
f. 71ᵛ (cat. 74)

353. Initial D. Cambridge, St. John's College C. 9 (59),
f. 72 (cat. 74)

354. St. Mark. London, Lambeth Palace Lib., 1370, f. 70ᵛ (cat. 70)

INDEX OF MANUSCRIPTS

References are to page numbers; figures in italics refer to illustrations and figures preceded by 'no.'
refer to the numbered entry in the Catalogue of Manuscripts

ANALYSIS OF MANUSCRIPTS IN THE CATALOGUE

I. TYPES OF BOOK

Apocalypse: no. 64
Bede, *De rerum natura*: no. 69
   Historia ecclesiastica: nos. 19, 33
Bible: no. 7
Canons: no. 13
Cassiodorus, Commentary on Psalter: no. 17
Gospel Books: nos. 1, 5, 6, 8–12, 15, 16, 20–7, 30, 32, 34, 36–9, 43–9, 52, 54, 56, 57, 59–61, 70, 72, 76, 77
Jerome, St., Commentary on Isaiah: no. 2
Lives of Saints: no. 67
New Testament: no. 53
Orosius, *Chronicon*: no. 3

Ovid, *Ars amatoria*: no. 71
Paul, St., Epistles: no. 55
Paulinus of Nola, *Carmina*: no. 42
Philippus Presbiter, Commentary on Job: no. 40
Pliny the elder, Natural History: no. 18
Prayers: nos. 35, 41, 66
Priscian, *Institutiones Grammaticae*: nos. 63, 68
Psalters: nos. 4, 14, 28, 29, 31, 73–5, 78
Sacramentaries: nos. (?) 50, 51
Sedulius, *Carmen Paschale*: no. 65
Theodore of Mopsuestia, Pseudo-, Commentary on Psalter: no. 62

II. PLACES OF ORIGIN

Armagh: nos. 53, (?)63, (?)70, (?)76, 77
Birr, Co. Offaly: no. 53
Bobbio: nos. 2, (?)3
Canterbury: nos. 29, 30, 32
Echternach: nos. 24, (?)25, (?)26, (?)28
Iona: (?) no. 52
Liège: no. 65

Lindisfarne: nos. 9, (?)10
Monkwearmouth/Jarrow: nos. 7, 8, 19
Roscrea, Co. Tipperary: no. 48
Salzburg: (?) no. 37
Tech-Moling, C. Carlow: no. 45
Würzburg: (?) no. 55
York: (?) no. 22

GENERAL INDEX